What's in a Word?

OTHER BOOKS BY MARIO PEI

All About Language
The Book of Place Names (with E. Lambert)
The Families of Words
First-Year French (with E. Méras)
Getting Along in French (with J. Fisher)
Getting Along in German (with R. Politzer)
Getting Along in Italian
Getting Along in Russian (with F. Nikanov)
Getting Along in Spanish (with E. Vaquero)
Glossary of Linguistic Terminology
How to Learn Languages and What Languages to Learn
Invitation to Linguistics
The Italian Language
The Language of the Eighth-Century Texts in Northern France
Language for Everybody
Language Today (with others)
The Many Hues of English
One Language for the World
Our Names (with E. Lambert)
Our National Heritage
The Story of the English Language
The Story of Language
Swords of Anjou
Talking Your Way Around the World
Voices of Man
The World's Chief Languages

MARIO PEI

What's in a Word?

Language—
Yesterday, Today, and Tomorrow

Hawthorn Books, Inc.
Publishers—New York

ACKNOWLEDGMENTS

The author wishes to thank the following publications for permission to reprint, either in whole or in part, previously published material:

Boys' Life (published by Boy Scouts of America, December 1961) for "Language and You."

Saturday Review for "Animal Voices" (originally published as "How Did Language Begin?"), "Curious Couples," "The Big Mystery in Small Words," "Parallel Proverbs," "The Challenge of Linguistic Realism," and "Ending the Language Traffic Jam."

Hablemos for "Contributions from Spanish."

Town and Country (The Hearst Corp.) for "How To Be Impolite in Twenty-seven Languages" and "A Universal Language Can Be Achieved."

The New York Times Magazine for "Betraying Words" (originally published as "The Mark of the Native") and "Man Talks in 3000 Tongues," copyright © 1960, 1946 by The New York Times Company. Reprinted by permission.

Mary Today for "What's in a Name?"

The World Telegram & Sun for "The Language of Holidays" (originally published as "The Language of Christmas Is Rich in Every Tongue," copyright 1956).

Holiday Magazine (The Curtis Publishing Co.) for "The Language of Colors Is Not International" (originally published as "A Babel of Colors").

Le Lingue del Mondo (Florence, August–September 1948) for "So Spanish Is All You Need in Latin America?"

J. B. Lippincott Co. for "Books and Language."

Publishers' Weekly (September 30, 1963) for "Languages in Paperbacks."

Saturday Evening Post (© 1959 The Curtis Publishing Co.) for "Languages for Scientists" (originally published as "Science Students Should Know One Foreign Language").

The French Review (December 1944) for "An Experiment in Conversation."

The Modern Language Journal (May 1948) for "Languages for the Very Young."

German Quarterly (November 1951) for "Fashions in Language."

UNESCO Courier (November 1963) for "One Language for the World."

The International Language Review (July–September 1963) for "The Case for Esperanto" (originally published as "Remarks on the Esperanto Symposium").

Contents

Introduction

This book is meant both to entertain and to instruct. The material has been selected with a view to bringing into prominence certain areas of language, or areas connected with language, that are not ordinarily dealt with in linguistic manuals but interest the general reader because they link language with other aspects of life.

It is only in recent times that linguistic science has begun to branch out from its traditional disciplines of historical and descriptive linguistics and has started to explore some of these fascinating realms. Today we have a science of paralinguistics which deals with gestures, facial and bodily expressions, postures and attitudes, voice inflections, all of which subtly modify the meanings conveyed by the spoken message. Sociolinguistics places language in juxtaposition with numerous intricate social and cultural phenomena. Psycholinguistics explores the ways in which language affects, or is affected by, the mental and spiritual processes of the individual or group. Geolinguistics deals with the distribution of languages throughout the world, the numbers, characteristics, and cultural backgrounds of their speakers, the significance of both languages and speakers to people engaged in various activities of a governmental, military, or commercial nature.

Some of the chapters in this collection may be described as early attempts to investigate these subsidiary fields, made before the fields themselves were recognized. Others go beyond. In form, they are all composed in such a way as to be perfectly clear to the intelligent reader. It could not be otherwise, for some of the material first appeared in the pages of widely read magazines and newspapers.

The reader will find a discussion of such topics as animal voices

7

and how they are heard and reproduced by speakers of various tongues; English words which seem altogether unrelated, like *bull* and *fool*, yet go back to the identical root form; the mystery that surrounds the origin of some of our shortest and most common words; proverbs which, in various languages, say the same thing through an altogether different imagery; expressions of politeness and insult, and the ease with which they can be confused; the "shibboleth" words that may spell life or death to the one who utters them; the strange symbolism of colors and color words throughout the world; the astounding lack of linguistic realism in literature and on TV.

More serious in purpose and scope are the discussions of the role of books and the printed word generally in modern life; the significance of language, both native and foreign, to the education of the individual; the way in which foreign languages are viewed and imparted on the American scene.

Last in the book is an extended discussion of the possibility of an international language for world-wide use, the mode of choice of such a language, its implications for the future of mankind—all highly controversial topics on which additional light needs to be shed.

While individual credits for the previously published articles appear on the copyright page, it is my pleasure to express my sincere appreciation to all the magazines, newspapers, and professional journals that have been kind enough to issue permission to reprint.

PART ONE

Language Origins

Language Origins

Language has a purpose and a history. The purpose is to serve you by conveying your thoughts to other human beings, and making their thoughts accessible to you.

The history consists of something more than an account of the doings of the speakers, a description of sounds and forms, and the evolution of individual words. There are seldom treated, relatively obscure areas in language history which are fascinating to explore, even though they may not always lead to definite conclusions.

How did language originate? No one really knows, but speculation abounds. Are there little bits of evidence that cast light upon the problem? Can we tell anything from the way in which sounds occurring in nature, which are universal and should be neutral, strike the human ear and are "echoed" in the speech of various groups?

In the matter of individual words of a non-echoic variety, is there the possibility of linking together, in a common origin, words of widely diverging form and meaning in different languages, or even in the same language? What does this indicate? Does the wording of widespread proverbs and sayings in many lands of diverse cultural backgrounds disclose startling similarities (or differences) in the thought processes of the various groups? What are the implications?

In the matter of words, the sources of our own language are reasonably clear. We know that English is basically a Germanic tongue, blending together the language of the Anglo-Saxons and the Scandinavian of the Danes who settled in the north of England; that upon this Germanic framework there is superimposed a Romance vocabulary brought in by the French-speaking Normans; and that from the early Renaissance to the present, thousands of words have been

11

added, lifted bodily from the Latin and Greek lexicons for purposes of literature, religion, science, technology, business, and politics. Beyond this, what has happened? We know that English has borrowed from every language under the sun. But in what measure? Are some lenders favored more than others? Is a contemporary popular writer on the English language justified in devoting six pages to the words that have come to us from India, and only six lines to those from Italy?

Our etymological dictionaries reveal that we know where most of our long, involved words come from. Are we equally certain with respect to the short, simple, one-syllable words of more frequent occurrence?

Let's explore some of these questions.

CHAPTER 1

Language and You

Can you conceive of a world in which no one speaks? A world in which people are unable to communicate, or make their thoughts known to one another? A world in which each individual is on his own, because he has no way to get together with his fellow man and plan any sort of joint action?

That happens now if you step outside your own country into another land that speaks another language. But in such a country, the natives understand one another, even if you don't understand them or they you. Life goes on around you, even if it bypasses you. And so far as you are concerned, you have many recourses: you can learn the foreign language, you can hire an interpreter, you can find someone who speaks your tongue, and if the worst comes to the worst, you can use a few elementary gestures.

But the languageless world we are asking you to visualize is one where everybody is a foreigner to everybody else, where there are no interpreters because there is nothing to interpret, where even gestures fail because they are based on ideas that are couched in language.

Language is the thing we most take for granted, the thing we think least about. Yet without it all concerted human activity (and in modern times all activity is 99 per cent concerted) would be paralyzed.

No language means little or no help or co-operation, and that in turn means that nothing really big or worth while can get done. Since most of the things connected with our civilization are big, they call for lots of help and co-operation, for the joint efforts of many people, all working intelligently together, each with a clear understanding of what the others are doing, and when, where, and how he must come in. The only thing that makes possible our sky-scrapers, our airplanes, our machines is the fact that the many people working on them understand one another. Take away that understanding, and they will all sink back into barbarism or savagery, because the means of transferring their thoughts to one another will be lost.

Language is primarily speech. The word *language* itself comes from the Latin *lingua,* meaning "tongue." Its original meaning is "that which is produced with the tongue."

A broader interpretation of the word *language* is "that which carries meaning." This permits us to speak of written language, gestural or sign language, and even the language of music, art, or mathematics. But the primary, basic form of language is speech, and it is an interesting thing that it is precisely speech that distinguishes the human being from the rest of animal creation. There is no human group, no matter how backward, that does not communicate by means of speech, though there are many such groups that have no writing. On the other hand, no animal species has ever succeeded in combining sounds and meanings into the sort of complex code that humans all possess in common. Some animals, like dogs or apes, can express with their voices emotions like joy, fear, hunger, anger, alarm, but are unable to go beyond that. Other species, like the myna bird, can imitate the sounds of the human voice, but are unable to link them to specific meanings.

The speech feature of the human being lies not so much in his ability to produce sounds as in his mental capacity to link the sounds with meanings which are accepted by other human beings so that there is a real transfer of thought from one mind to another. It is only in this sense that you have real speech and real language. The mere capacity to make nonsense sounds is not language. Neither is it real language when the sounds have meaning only to the one who makes them. Newborn babies make sounds which may have a meaning to them, but which their elders do not understand. Insane people sometimes make up words which they alone can understand. This is not language.

Language actually begins when two or more human beings decide that a certain sound or set of sounds shall have the same meaning to both or all of them. At this point a language is born.

No one knows how, when, or where language first began. There are many theories, but none can be proved. Imitation of sounds heard in nature, like the barking of a dog, the roar of a waterfall, the crash of a tree falling in the forest, sounds plausible, until you stop to think that no two languages reproduce the "natural" sound in the same fashion. What is "cock-a-doodle-doo" to an English speaker is *cocorico* to a Frenchman. What is "bow-wow" or "woof-woof" to us is *bu-bu* to an Italian.

But perhaps this very diversity in the way natural sounds are heard and reproduced gives us the clue to the problem of the many languages in existence. The human vocal organs are capable of producing many sounds, but it is only when a certain sequence of certain sounds is accepted as carrying a certain meaning by two or more persons that you really have language. If the chief of a small primitive tribe pointed to a dog, whose bark he heard as "woof-woof," and repeated the sound often enough to his followers until they grasped the fact that he wanted them to call the dog by that particular sequence of sounds, and if they obediently accepted his designation and began using it regularly, we would have the elementary understanding necessary for setting up the beginning of a language. But by the same token, the chief's order would not carry over to other tribes, which would set up their own separate designation for dog, and here you would have the beginning of two or more distinct languages.

Today, there are in existence approximately three thousand separate spoken tongues. Some, like English and Chinese, have hundreds of millions of speakers. Others are spoken by only a few thousand or even a few hundred speakers, like many of the native tongues of the North American Indians. Yet each tongue is fully meaningful to its own speakers.

Their differences are enormous, and it is a well-known fact that if the speaker of one language wants to communicate with the speaker of another, he must learn to speak all over again. Yet all languages have certain things in common.

Physically speaking, every language consists of sounds produced by the human vocal organs and received by the human ear. The human vocal organs are capable of producing hundreds, perhaps even thousands of separate sounds, but the average language utilizes only between twenty and sixty of these many possibilities. The fact that they don't all utilize the same sounds complicates matters, because if you have grown used to producing and hearing a certain set of sounds and you are then faced with the need of using another set, your ingrained habits will get in your way.

These sounds are arranged in certain sequences to produce words, as when d-o-g are lined up to give "dog" and c-a-t to give "cat." Here is where agreement among the speakers comes into play. English speakers are agreed that the sequence of three sounds in the spoken word *dog* shall symbolize in their minds the image of a particular animal, and if one speaker utters the word *dog* to another, his listener will automatically receive that image. But that particular sequence of sounds might be altogether meaningless to a speaker of French, whose sound symbol for the animal is *chien*, or to a Spanish speaker, who says *perro*. The situation here is similar to what happens with currencies. My dollar bill is valid for purchases all through the United States, because all Americans have agreed to accept it; but if I go to another country I find that my dollar bills are not legal tender and I have to change them into the currency of that country.

Lastly, the words have to be lined up in accordance with certain traffic rules, which are not the same in all languages. In English, if I want to indicate more than one dog, I add an -s and make "dogs," and my hearer understands that I have more than one dog in mind. Or I may change the order of my words and get a different meaning, in common with my hearer. "John sees George" is one thing. "George sees John" is another.

There is no language that does not have these three things: individual sounds; meaningful sequences of sounds, or words; and traffic rules, such as adding on an ending or arranging the words in certain set sequences.

Learning another language means: (1) acquiring new sounds; (2) learning to accept new sound sequences or words in given meanings; (3) learning new traffic regulations for the new words. Difficult? Yes, but you've done it all before, when you learned your own language. As a baby, you began to hear sounds produced by your parents, and then you tried to imitate them and produce the same sounds. You also learned to associate certain words with certain objects or actions, and to string your words along in a certain way, or make in them certain changes that would modify their meaning. What you did once you can do again.

Writing is a substitute for speech. It has two advantages over speech: it can be used at a distance, and it is permanent. Both of these advantages are rapidly vanishing today, when we have records and tapes in which actual speech can be shipped or stored.

Speech is a symbol of thought. Writing is a symbol of speech. This means that writing is a symbol of a symbol, just as a check is a symbol of money, which is a symbol of purchasing power.

Writing began as picture writing, the drawing of pictures to tell a story or convey a message. Many of the early cave paintings by primitive men in France and Spain, many of the American Indian pictorial histories of expeditions inscribed on the bark of trees remind us of a comic strip, with the characters appearing over and over again as the action unfolds.

But the pictures soon turned symbolic, as in the cuneiform clay tablets of the ancient Babylonians, the hieroglyphs of the Egyptians, and the Chinese characters. They still, however, represented ideas, and had little or no link with the spoken language. The big change came when the Phoenicians decided to let some of their characters stand, not for ideas, but for sounds. At this point the alphabet was born.

Language is forever changing, along with its speakers. Our English language is far from being the one of which we have the oldest records, but even in the scant fourteen centuries that have elapsed since its first recorded appearance, English has changed drastically. The title of an English king, Aethelstan, who lived slightly over one thousand years ago, runs: *Ongol-Saxna cyning and Brytænwalda eallæs thyses iglandes* ("King of the Anglo-Saxons and British ruler of all this island"). The only word you really recognize is "and."

Even four centuries later, in the "Cuckoo Song," popular in the days of Chaucer, you run across such difficult passages as *Ne swik thu nauer nu* ("Be thou not silent now"). Coming down to Shakespeare, here is a passage that could conceivably have been written in his times: "Daw, you have begecked me! I yuke to pingle with you and yerk you until you ghost!" ("Fool, you have cheated me! I itch to fight with you and hit you until you die!"). On the other hand, what would the Bard of Avon have made of this statement by one of his present-day producers: "Your play will be broadcast and televised on high frequency over this network by a coast-to-coast hookup"?

This tendency to change is inherent in all languages. The French and Spanish some boys are studying in high school were once the Latin that others are taking, while English and German were once one and the same language.

There are families of languages and family relationships, just as among people. Some connections are close, like that which exists among brothers, others more remote, like distant cousins. German, Dutch, and Scandinavian could be described as the brothers of English, while the first, second, and third-degree cousins include such tongues as Italian, Russian, Hindi, Persian, Armenian, Welsh. Then there are others for which relationship may exist but cannot be proved, like Chinese, Japanese, and Arabic.

Within what is supposed to be one and the same language there are cleavages, major or minor, known as dialects. An American and an Englishman will normally have little difficulty communicating with each other, and they both claim to use the same English language. Yet one can spot the other with ease, by the way he pronounces some sounds, or by the use of special words. If an English businessman asks his American counterpart: "Are you sending the shipment by lorry or by goods-waggon?", the American may or may not understand that the choice is between shipment by truck or by freight car. But even within the same nation we have dialectal differences. You normally know whether a person you are speaking with is from Brooklyn, Boston, the South, or the Midwest. These dialectal differences are what led in the past to the creation of separate languages out of a single tongue, as when English, Dutch, and German broke apart. They could conceivably lead to the creation of new separate languages in the future, if historical conditions were to favor that process.

But this is not very likely to happen under present-day conditions. It is far more likely that the dialects will tend to merge and disappear and that each major language will become more standardized and uniform than it is today. There is even the possibility that a single world language may eventually emerge, to take care of world-wide communications among people who are now hampered by lack of understanding because they speak different languages.

CHAPTER 2

Animal Voices

There are many theories, all unproved, as to how language began. Most picturesque among them is the "bow-wow" hypothesis, to the effect that men began to speak by imitating the natural sounds they heard, or thought they heard, around them.

The barking of a dog would strike the ear of the leader of a small band of primitive humans. It would sound to him like "bow-wow," and as he tried to imitate it, he would convey to the others, by pointing to the dog and repeating "bow-wow," that the creature that made that particular sound should henceforth be referred to as "bow-wow."

Too simple? Yet consider how often children spontaneously fasten upon some utterance produced by one of their number, and use it to designate him, pointing to him in derision as they do it.

The scientific name for this process is *onomatopoeia*, or "name-making." Less scientific but easier to pronounce and spell is "echoic word." You echo what you hear. If the fall of a big tree in the forest sounds to you like "crash," that is what you use to designate that type of sound. The noise produced by a bee may sound like "hum" or "buzz." Words like "click," "wham," "bang" all seem to be of echoic origin.

Different breeds of dogs bark in different ways, or the same sound may be differently interpreted and echoed by various human beings. This would account for "bow-wow," "woof-woof," "yip-yip," all appearing in the same language. If you have many languages, the differences may be far greater.

English has perhaps more echoic words than any other civilized tongue. Is this because we are more primitive and elemental? Or because our language runs more to monosyllables and avoids endings?

20

Or because we make greater use of comic strips, where the picture largely tells the story, but sound effects have to be graphically portrayed?

Yet the echoic word does not have to be monosyllabic, or even repetitive, especially if the sound it portrays strikes the ear as composite. Among early echoic words that are not repetitive are ancient Sanskrit *chish-chá*, denoting the "whiz" of an arrow in flight followed by the sound of its impact, and *kikirá*, to denote a palpitating sound, like our "pitter-patter" of the heart.

Both Greek and Latin had plenty of echoic words, a few of which, like Latin *murmur*, have been passed on to us. The Roman grammarian Quintilian describes Latin as poor in such sounds, but the facts don't seem to bear him out. However, both Latin and Greek are languages given to endings that denote specific parts of speech, so that many of what must have been originally one-syllable echoic words appear as two- or three-syllable nouns, verbs, and adjectives. For example, one of the Latin words meaning "to bark" is *baubari*, where the *-ari* ending is merely an infinitive suffix; the Roman "bowwow" was evidently *bau* or *bau-bau*, though it does not appear by itself in the literary records that have come down to us. "To neigh" in Latin is *hinnire*; here again the Roman speakers must have used the root *hinn-* when they wished merely to imitate the neighing of a horse.

The Greeks did better in leaving us records of bare echoic roots. To them the croak of a frog was *koax*, but that of a raven was *krō*. The grunt of a pig (our "oink") was *grū*, but the squeal of a small pig was *koi*. The bleating of a sheep (our "baa") was to them *beh*, and it is a joke among linguists that as the Greek sounds changed during the course of centuries, the same written word got to be pronounced *vee*, which does not at all sound like a sheep, thus proving that animal language remains the same though human speech changes. Even the speakers of Sanskrit have left us their idea of "splash" as represented by *bāl, p-hāl,* or *p-hāt*.

It is fairly evident by this time that different groups hear the same sound in different fashion. What to us is the "smack" of a kiss is to Spanish speakers *muá*. The "snip-snip" of a pair of scissors sounds like *krits-krits* to the modern Greeks, *su-su* to the Chinese, *cri-cri* to the

Italians, *riqui-riqui* to the Spaniards, *terre-terre* to the Portuguese. Our "bang" of a pistol may come out as *bam, pam, pan,* even *tau.* The "crash" of a tray of plates and cups falling to the floor is *kling* to the Danes, *krats* to the Finns, *chir-churr* to the Hungarians, *hua-la-la* to the Chinese, while the comic strip "wham" of someone sitting down suddenly and very hard is *pan* in French, *cataplúm* in Spanish, *catrapuz-bum* in Portuguese, *patatrac* or *patapunf* in Italian. Even the ringing of a phone, which to us is *ting-a-ling,* taken from an earlier echo of the tinkling of a bell, comes out as *dringh* in Greek, *drin* in Italian, *kili* in Finnish, *tlim* in Portuguese.

But along with this diversity there are widespread resemblances. The Latin *murmur,* which has come down to most Western languages, appears in very similar form in Armenian, Lithuanian, Greek, even Sanskrit, where *marmarah* means "noisy." Our "gurgle" is *glut-glut* in Latin, *glu-glu* in Italian. Even our "slap" has a close equivalent in Latin *stlop(pus),* from which, interestingly, Italian and Spanish derive their words for "shotgun" (*schioppo, escopeta*). The "ho-ho-ho" of the Jolly Green Giant is *khokhot* in Russian, *kakhat-* in Sanskrit.

Animals have proved their superiority over humans by achieving a primitive international language within their respective species. There is no convincing evidence that the braying of a donkey, the cackling of a hen, the quacking of a duck, or the mooing of a cow is any different in China or the Soviet Union from what it is in the United States. But there can be vast differences in human reception and rendition.

Most standardized, perhaps, among animal sounds is the cow's "moo" (it may, of course, be spelled *mu,* and French has an interesting variation, *meuh*).

Second in standardization is the cat's "meow" (here the spelling runs from Italian *miao* and French *miaou* to German and Rumanian *miau*). But Japanese has *nya-nya,* and Arabic has a double form, *nau-nau,* for ordinary meowing, but *maw-oom* for the cat's voice in the mating season. This unanimity does not extend to the cat's "purr," which Spanish imitates as *arroró-arroró* and French as *ronron.*

The bleating of the sheep gives rise to two renditions, one with *b*, the other with *m*. Greek, Latin, English, Spanish, Italian, Russian, Vietnamese favor the first (Russian has *bya-bya*, Vietnamese has *be-be*); German, Rumanian, Chinese, Japanese favor the *m* sound (*ma-ma or me-me*). French and Arabic use both.

The crowing of a rooster and the cackling of a hen have only one element that is internationally common, an initial *k* sound, often repeated elsewhere in the word; everything else is different. Corresponding to English "cock-a-doodle-doo" are French *cocorico*, Spanish *quiquiriquí*, Italian *chicchirichì*, German *kikiriki* (note that the last three, despite their different representations in spelling, sound very much the same: kee-kee-ree-KEE), Rumanian *cucurigu*, Russian *kukareku*, Arabic *ko-ko* or *qee-qee* (*q* in Arabic is a very guttural *k*, pronounced as far back in the throat as you can get it), Japanese *kokekkoko*, Vietnamese *cuc-cu*.

For the hen's cackle, English does not have a real echoic word (we make up for it by imitating a turkey's "gobble-gobble," which few other languages bother about). The "kadawkut" and similar forms suggested by correspondents seem to be purely local to southern New England, and are not registered in any dictionary, while "cluck" is robbed of some of its purely echoic quality by being used as a noun and a verb. Here French has *cot-cot*, Rumanian has *cotcodac*, Italian has *coccotè*, Arabic has *qa-qa*, Chinese has *ko-ko-ko*, Japanese has *kukku*, Vietnamese has *cuc-tac*. Even Latin had *co-co*, or, with greater repetition, *co-co-co-co*.

We lack an imitation of the horse's neigh, which Italian portrays very graphically with *ih-ih-ih-ih-ih*. Rumanian has *hi-hi-hi*, Arabic *hem-hem*, Japanese *hi-hin*, Vietnamese *hí*.

On the other hand, we have a donkey's "hee-haw." Here French has *hi-han*, Italian and Chinese share *i-o*, German and Russian share *i-a*, Rumanian has *i-hau*, Arabic uses *ham-ham* or *hee-hee*.

There is considerable internationality in the duck's "quack-quack." French uses *couac-couac* or *coin-coin* (the latter sounds like *kwan-kwan*). Spanish has *cuac-cuac*, Italian *qua-qua*, German shares *quack-quack* with us. Russian has *kva-kva*, Vietnamese, *cac-cac*. But Japanese begins to diverge with *ga-ga*, Rumanian carries it on to *mac-mac*, Arabic to *bat-bat*, Mandarin Chinese to *ya-ya*, and south China's Cantonese to *ap-ap*.

No language seems to have a real lion sound, though many use our own "grrr" for any kind of growl or roar. Arabic, which has some contact with lions in their native habitat, uses *ū*, which is a prolonged *oo*. Vietnamese has no lion sound, but with plenty of tigers in the land, the tiger's roar is imitated as *ham-hü* or *gam-gü*.

Animals have imitation words where they are well known to the people. The Nutka Indians of Alaska imitate the sound of a whale as *ᶜhw* (constriction of the throat, strongly uttered *h*, sound of *w*). Eskimo tribes prefer *peu-wu*.

Closest to our "oink" for a pig's grunt is French *oui-oui*, which means that in France the pig is forever saying yes. Quite remote are Russian *khru-khru* and Rumanian *guits-guits*. The "peep" and "chirp" of chicks and small birds is imitated as *pio-pio* in Italian, *piu-piu* in Rumanian, *cui-cui* in French.

The dog, who contributed one of his names to the "bow-wow theory," has the most far-reaching divergences, due perhaps to different breeds, but also to the fact that it was probably the first animal domesticated by man (the dog was the sole domestic animal of the North American Indians). Corresponding to our assorted "bow-wow," "woof-woof," "yip-yip," "arf-arf" we find French *oua-oua* (pronounced *wah-wah*); Italian *bu-bu*; Spanish *guau-guau*, or *jau-jau* (pronounced *how-how*); Rumanian *ham-ham* (with *a* of "father"); German *hau-hau* or *wau-wau*; Russian *vas-vas* or *vaf-vaf*; Arabic *ᶜau-ᶜau* (constrict the throat at the start); Vietnamese *gaugau*; Turkish *hov-hov*; Chinese *wang-wang*; Japanese *wan-wan*. Even ancient Sanskrit had *bhuk-bhuk*.

Kindred to echoic words are interjections, those exclamatory sounds that we use to express pain, pleasure, disgust, annoyance, joy, sorrow, or simply to call someone's attention. These come closest to the natural, spontaneous sounds made by animals. Some are surprisingly international, others surprisingly different. As a sample of the first, we find in the ancient Sanskrit of the Vedas all of these familiar forms: *ā, hā, hāhā, ahaha, hē, hāí*. But some can undergo amazing changes in meaning in the course of time. The Latin *bua* is described as "a sound made by infants to denote what they are drinking." The same word is used to and by children today in Italy but it means "to hurt," "to ache," "to have a sore spot," "to be ill."

To call someone's attention at a distance, we generally use "Hey!" The ancient Greeks used *eia,* the Romans *eho,* the modern Italians, particularly in Rome, *aò.*

I once asked a girl who was completely trilingual, having been brought up in New York, Paris, and Havana in equal measure, whether she had ever gotten her three languages mixed up. She thought and thought, then brightened up. "Yes! One time, on Varadero Beach in Cuba, someone stuck me with a pin, and I yelled 'Ouch!' instead of '*Ay!*' " On a French beach, she should have yelled "*Aïe!*" or "*Ouille!*" In Italy it would have been "*Aio!*"; in Hungary, "*Jaj!*" (pronounced *yoy*); in Finland, "*Boi!*"; in Japan, "*Itai!*".

We indicate disgust by using "blah" or "aak" ("phooey" is a recent borrowing from Yiddish). In Spanish it's *huy* or *uf,* in Italian, *uffa,* in French, *fi, pfutt,* or *zut,* in German *pfui.* In a good many of these, there seems to be some imitation of the sound of spitting. But Latin used *pro.*

Sorrow used to be indicated by "alas!", but this, save for the initial *a,* is not an echoic word. It comes from Old French *ah, las!,* "oh, weary (me)!" Our real international exclamation of sorrow is, historically, the "woe" of "woe is me!" This has wide range, from Latin *vae of vae victis* ("woe unto the conquered!") to Welsh *gwae,* Gothic *wai,* Armenian *vai,* Old Persian *avōi.* But Latin had, side by side with *vae,* also *eu, eheu* and *ei* (the last often combined with *mihi,* "woe is me!"). Greek used *pheu,* which is perhaps linked to German *pfui.* This *pheu* has come down into the college yell of Italian university students: "*Pheu, pheu; barú!*", "Alas, alas; way down in the dumps!" But the old sorrowful connotation is altogether lost, and the mournful Greek words have been turned into a happy rallying cry.

CHAPTER 3

Curious Couples

The story of words is endlessly fascinating; but the chroniclers of language are usually content to work their way back to Latin, Greek, or Anglo-Saxon and stop there.

There is, however, an earlier stage to the story—a time when Greek, Latin, Anglo-Saxon, and many other ancient languages were all one. This parent language is called Indo-European because later, when its speakers broke up and wandered away from one another, they covered most of Europe and parts of southwestern Asia as far as northern India.

Precisely when Indo-European was spoken is unknown, because writing had not yet come into being at the time. We may assume, however, that it flourished perhaps as much as five thousand years before Christ. Its speakers were probably centered around the shores of the Baltic, from which they spread out fanwise, in a general southerly direction, to northern India and the Iranian plateau, and to eastern, central, southern, and western Europe. Their speech diverged as they went, until it finally assumed such diverse forms as the Sanskrit, which appears around 2000 B.C., the Homeric Greek of 800 B.C., the early Latin of 500 B.C., the Gaulish, Old Irish, and Old Welsh which are the earliest Celtic languages, and the relative late-comers to the scene—the Gothic of Wulfila's Bible translation (about A.D. 400), which is our earliest record of a Germanic tongue, the Old Church Slavic of about A.D. 900, and Armenian and Albanian.

The diversification of an originally single tongue into such different speech forms as the ones listed above resulted from a process of migration followed by a complete break of communications among the various migrating groups. When communications are broken, language tends to split into dialects; when communications are restored, the dialects tend to come together again into a national language. But in the days of Indo-European migrations, there was no possibility of restoring communications. Hence, the process of diversification was drastic.

Yet it becomes obvious, when the earliest recorded languages of each of the eight Indo-European groups are laid side by side, that they were originally one. The grammatical structure of each appears to be the same. Basic words are shared in common—numerals, nouns of family relationship, names of animals, plants, and minerals, verbs of frequent occurrence. Even the sounds are identical, provided one makes allowance for certain regular shifts peculiar to a given group. For instance, where certain words begin with *p* in Sanskrit, Greek, Latin, Albanian, and Slavic, we find a consistent shift to *f* in Germanic, to *h* in Armenian, and a fall of the initial consonant in Celtic. This comparative method, similar in nature to that employed by paleontologists in reconstructing extinct animal and plant species from a few fossil remains, enables us to determine, at least hypothetically, what the originally Indo-European form must have been. In the case just cited, it is far more likely that the original Indo-European sound was the *p* indicated by five out of the eight groups than any of the other three sounds, which do not even coincide among themselves.

As a result of their painstaking analysis, the language scholars of the nineteenth century were finally able to establish a certain number (perhaps two thousand) of Indo-European root words which, by endless change and recombination, form the source of tens and even hundreds of thousands of present-day words in the various languages. This, in turn, leads to another interesting discovery. Many English words once thought to be completely separate really belong together and are intimately related. Some of them form curious couples, or even larger groups, with a single Indo-European root word as their common ancestor. But they have undergone vast changes of form and meaning.

Take "ankle" and "anchor." What do they have in common? "Ankle" goes back to Anglo-Saxon *anclēow*, which had the same meaning in the days of King Alfred that "ankle" has today. "Anchor" comes to us, through Latin *anchora,* from Greek *ankȳra.* But if we trace *anclēow* and *ankȳra* back to the Indo-European parent speech, we find a common root, *ank-,* which meant "to bend." The Saxons applied the bending idea to the flexible movement of the ankle, the Greeks to the curve of the appliance which served to hold their ships fast to the sea bottom.

Can there be any connection between "baby" and "barbarian," other than a far-fetched modern one taken from the comic strips? "Babe," of which "baby" is a diminutive form, is not recorded in Anglo-Saxon, but appears in Middle English, and seems definitely connected with "babble," the sort of incomprehensible speech a very young child produces. "Barbarian" goes back to Greek *barbaros,* which meant "a foreigner," "one who speaks an incomprehensible language." The Indo-European root word which gave rise to both was simply an imitation of the sound supposedly made by one whose speech we cannot understand: *balbal-* or *barbar-.*

A great many English words come from the Latin root *vid-* or *vis-,* "to see." "Vision," "visual," "visa," "visit," "view," "video" (a name for TV that is not as frequently used as when TV first came on the market) are only a few among them. Do all these words have a native English relative, a word that did not come from Latin, but appeared in Anglo-Saxon? To find it, we have to remember that words that in Latin have *v* and *d* usually appear in Anglo-Saxon with *w* and *t.* You've guessed it. The native English relative of Latin *vid-* is "wit." But, one may object, *vid-* has to do with seeing, "wit" with mental activity; in fact, the old meaning of "wit" (as shown by its archaic past tense *wot*) is "to know." True; but what better way of "knowing" is there than by "seeing" with your own eyes? If you want further proof, you'll find it in the *Vedas,* the old sacred writings of India. *Veda* has the same *v* and *d* as Latin, but the same meaning as English "wit"; it means "knowledge," "wisdom" (the latter, by the way, can be analyzed as *wits-dom*).

Can there be a possible connection between "judge" and "teach"? "Teach," the dictionary tells us, is straight Anglo-Saxon, and the Old English form was *tǣcean.* "Judge" comes from the French *juger,* which goes back to Latin *judicare.* But *judicare* is really a compound word, consisting of *jus-dicere,* "to tell the law." *Dicere,* the

Latin word for "say," "tell," and Anglo-Saxon *tæcean*, both go back to an Indo-European root word *deik-*, which means "to show" (notice again, by the way, that where Latin has *d*, Anglo-Saxon has *t*). The teacher is "one who shows"; the judge is "one who shows, or tells, the law."

The Indo-European parent language was particularly fond of a sound, represented by *bh*, occurring at the beginning of words. This *bh*, which remains unchanged in Sanskrit and even in modern Hindustani, generally became *b* in Anglo-Saxon, but *f* in Latin (Sanskrit *bhrātā*, English "brother," Latin *frater*, is an easy example). Now we have an entire series of curious couples, where the native English word starts with *b*, while the word that English takes from Latin begins with *f*.

"Bed"—"fossil": the ancient root word is *bhedh-*, "to dig." Anglo-Saxon has *bedd* (notice the digging idea in "flower-bed," "road-bed"). Latin has *fod-*, "to dig," with *fod-* turning into *fods-* or *fos-* in some forms. *Fos-silis* is "that which can be dug up"; in other words, a "fossil."

"Beetle"—"fission": here the root is *bheid-*, "to split." In English the idea of splitting goes on to include that of biting off, and we get the Anglo-Saxon verb *bītan*, "to bite," and the Anglo-Saxon noun *bitula*, the "biter," which is applied to an insect that bites, and eventually turns into "beetle." In Latin, *bheid-* becomes *find-*, *fid-*, *fids-*, *fis-*, but the meaning remains "to split." "Fission" is one of the products of the Latin root, and atomic fission is "the splitting of the atom."

"Bull"—"fool": the root is *bhel-* "to swell up." In Anglo-Saxon, the *bula*, which later became "bull," was originally a "swelled-up creature." In Latin *bhel-* becomes *fol-lis*, a "bellows," which, of course, swells up. But so does an inflated, stupid person, who is jokingly called a "bellows" (even today, we say that a person has a "swelled head"). Later on, the Latin *follis* turns into French *fou* or *fol*, which was brought to England by the Normans and became "fool."

"Bloom"—"foliage": the root is *bhlē-*, "to blossom, sprout up." *Bloom* is not Anglo-Saxon, but Scandinavian, brought in by the Danes, who occupied half of England in the days of King Alfred. Their language, like that of the Saxons, belonged to the Germanic branch of Indo-European, and they too had *b* from Indo-European *bh*. In Latin, the *bh* turned into *f*, and we have such words as *flos*, "flower" and *folium*, "leaf," from which we get "foliage."

"Break"—"fraction": *bhreg-*, "to break, crack," gave Anglo-Saxon its verb *brecan*, which in modern English becomes "break"; it gave Latin its *frang-*, *frag-*, *frac-*, which appears in *fraction*, *fragment*, and even "suffrage" (*sub-fragium*, literally "under-break," at first used in the sense of "intercession," "pleading," on behalf of someone, then a vote on his behalf).

Where Anglo-Saxon turned Indo-European *bh* into *b* and Latin turned it into *f*, Greek generally made it over into *ph*. Accordingly, we have the couple "beacon"—"photo," from the root *bha-*, "to shine," which in Anglo-Saxon gives rise to *bēacen*, "that which shines," a beacon light, and in Greek to *photos*, "light."

We do not always have to go to two different sources for our curious couples. "Boor" and "neighbor" both go back to Indo-European *bheu-*, "to dwell," but they are both of the Germanic branch, as shown by their initial *b*. "Neighbor" is the Anglo-Saxon *nēahgebūr*, "nighdweller," one who dwells near you. "Boor," which does not appear in English until the fifteenth century, was taken from Dutch, where it means "dweller on the land," "peasant," "farmer" (the Dutch spelling, by the way, is *boer*, and the Boers were the South African farmer-settlers of Dutch origin). Peasants are sometimes ill-mannered, and this gave rise to the special modern connotation of "boor."

"Duel" and "belligerent" are both Latin. In "belligerent" and "bellicose" we have the Latin *bellum*, "war." But the older form of *bellum* was *duellum*, formed on the root of *duo*, "two," a contest in which there were two participants.

"Cape," in the sense of an article of clothing, and "chapel" are originally the same Latin word, *cappa*, a cloak. According to tradition, St. Martin of Tours, who was an officer in the Roman army, was riding along a country road on a cold winter day when he was halted by a beggar asking for alms. Martin had no money with him, but noticing that the beggar was shivering with cold, he took off his military *cappa*, or cloak, cut it in two with his sword, and gave half to the beggar. The latter then revealed himself to be Christ, and requested that a shrine be erected on the spot where Martin had offered his half cloak. The shrine was duly built, and was called *cappella,* or "little cloak," from the fact that Martin's offering was kept there. The name soon came to be applied to any small roadside shrine, and *cappella* eventually turned into *chapelle* in French and "chapel" in English.

Philology makes strange bedfellows of our most common words. "Whiskey" and "biology" have one common element, which appears at the end of "whiskey" and at the beginning of "biology." The latter is Greek, and consists of *bios,* "life," and *logos,* "word," later "science." "Whiskey" is Celtic, and in its Gaelic form is *uisge-beatha,* "water of life." *Bios* and *beatha* both go back to the same Indo-European root word for "life."

These curious linguistic couples, though they have their origins in a tongue that has been "dead" for some seven thousand years, suggest that there's at least some life in the old language yet.

CHAPTER 4

The Big Mystery in Small Words

In the literary segment of every language there are words that stump the experts, both as to meaning and as to derivation. The Romans of the late Republic admitted they were puzzled concerning some of the words that appeared in their more ancient laws and treaties. "What did our ancestors mean?" asks Polibius in the second century B.C. Here, archaism and forgetfulness, coupled with ignorance of etymology, supply the explanation. For some of those words, we know more about their meaning and origin than did the Romans of the pre-Augustan age.

The medieval French ballads of François Villon contain dozens of words that are unclear to modern scholars. Here the fault lies with Villon's use of *jobelyn*, the thieves' cant of his period. It is likely that many of the words he used were unfamiliar even to the upper social strata of his own day.

Dante scholars have wondered for centuries about the meaning of the words Dante puts into the mouth of Pluto at the beginning of the Seventh Canto of the *Inferno: "Pape Satan, Pape Satan Aleppe!"* Pluto seems bewildered and unpleasantly surprised at the invasion of his nether realm by visitors from the world of the living, and the best bet is that he is calling upon his superior, Satan, to eject them. *Aleppe* is then interpreted as the Italian ren⌉ᵍ of *aleph*, the first letter of the Hebrew alphabet. This would give Satan the status of "number one" demon, head of the infernal hierarchy, but leaves *pape* unexplained. Could Dante, whose anti-papal leanings had led to his expulsion from Guelph-dominated Florence, be ironically comparing Satan to the Pope?

Ingenious, but utterly incredible, is the explanation supplied centuries later by Benvenuto Cellini. He states that at the Paris court, which he had had occasion to visit, the chief usher, or bouncer, was nicknamed Satan, and that Dante, who had also been to Paris, though at a much earlier period, was giving a covert italianized version of a French *"Paix, Satan, paix! Allez!"* ("Peace, Satan, peace! Go!").

Both the Bible and the eleventh-century French *Chanson de Roland* repeat at the end of stanzas words which make no sense. The biblical word is *selah,* given untranslated in the English King James version, which comes repeatedly in the Psalms and occasionally elsewhere, and to which Semitic scholarship has been unable to assign a meaning or derivation. Greek versions sometimes render it by *diapsalma,* "that which comes between verses," but this begs the question. The word is generally interpreted to be a musical direction indicating a pause or rest.

The *Chanson de Roland,* most famous of medieval French epics, reported to have been sung by William's men at the Battle of Hastings, often makes use of a similar word, *aoi,* at the end of its *laisses,* or stanzas of unequal length. Is this just a vocalization, meant to be intoned by the *jongleur* for musical effect? Is it a nonsense word designed to mark the end of a *laisse?* If so, why is it not universally used throughout the poem? Why does it appear in no other contemporary or subsequent work? Above all, does it have a meaning? Theories abound. One of the most elaborate is that *aoi* is the continuator of Latin *avoco,* "I am calling away or off," "I am interrupting," and that it gives rise to our nautical "ahoy," which most sources list as a mere interjection. But it must be mentioned that "ahoy's" first recorded appearance is in 1751, a trifle late for connection with the *aoi* of the late eleventh century.

When we leave the rarefied atmosphere of literature and step down among the common words of everyday usage, we are amazed at the large number of such words, most of them monosyllabic and high in the frequency scale, which have no known origin or source. Dictionaries of word etymologies are always at pains to tell us what our big, long words come from, and what their original meaning was. They just as regularly avoid telling us about the short words of common use. They are merely following the course of least resistance. Some measure of uncertainty attaches to terms like "dream," "drama," "tube," "small," "boss," "kiss," "gay," "ask," "to mean." We can trace them easily enough to their immediate source, Greek, Latin, or Germanic. Beyond that, we are in doubt, because the Greek, Latin, or Germanic root has no cognates in the other Indo-European branches, as it should have. This raises the possibility that the particular language in which they first appear may have borrowed from outside the Indo-European family. Could, for example, Greek have taken "drama" from Semitic? Could Latin have done the same with the word which gives us "tube" and all its derivatives? Could the Pan-Germanic "dream" root be of Semitic origin? Could there have been an earlier, unrecorded link, or even a downright affiliation, between the Semitic and our own Indo-European languages?

There are, of course, plenty of Semitic words in the tongues of the West. Many of them, like "alcohol," "algebra," "cotton," "alkali," "zenith," "syrup," "assassin," came in from Arabic during and after the Crusades. Others are the good old biblical words from Hebrew and Aramaic which spread with Christianity and the Bible, words like "amen," "abbot," "jubilee," "sabbath" and "sabaoth," "seraph" and "cherub," "hosanna" and "hallelujah." Normally, their formation and meaning are crystal-clear, though they do lend themselves to the process of folk etymology, the type of legend whereby "sirloin" is attributed to a mythical king who liked loin of beef so much that he knighted it and said: "Rise, Sir Loin!" Actually, sirloin is just the French *sur longe*, "above the loin."

Sabaoth is the Hebrew plural of *saba*, "army," used in a possessive relation, so that "Lord Sabaoth" means "Lord of hosts." "Hosanna" is the Aramaic *hoshi ah nna*, "pray save us now." "Jubilee," despite legends to the contrary, comes from Hebrew *yobel*, "ram's horn," which seems to give rise even to our "yodel" and "yowl." "Hallelujah" is the Hebrew *hallelu-yah*, "praise ye Jahweh"; but the Italian folk legend would have it that at the time when Christ's body lay in the sepulcher, it was guarded by three Roman legionaries who happened to be, respectively, a Roman, a Piedmontese from northern Italy, and a German mercenary. When Our Lord rose from the dead and stood before them, they were at first stricken speechless. Then the Roman broke out into a single exclamation of amazement: "Ha!" The more articulate man from Piedmont cried out: "L'è lü!", which in present-day Piedmontese dialect means: "It's him!" The German could only stammer out his agreement: "Ja!" And so "hallelujah" came into being.

Among words of this type there is one, not biblical, concerning which doubt lingers: "abracadabra." It is attested in both Greek and medieval Latin, but does not appear in English until 1696. One version, supported by the appearance in Greek of the variant *abrasadabra*, takes the word back to Abrasax, a name devised for the Lord of Heaven by Basilides the Gnostic, who lived and taught in Alexandria in the second century of our era. More plausible, perhaps, is derivation from Aramaic *abhadda kedabrah*, "vanish at this word," a suitable incantation for warding off maladies or other evils.

It is easy enough to construct a list of words of one syllable whose origin is mysterious. But first let us look at a group of three words of purely American and quite recent origin: "blizzard," "jitney," and "sundae." Earliest recorded appearance of "blizzard" is in 1829, but with the meaning of "sharp blow." It is only in 1870 that it assumes the sense of a snowstorm accompanied by high winds and sub-zero temperatures. The Oxford English Dictionary tentatively suggests affiliation with an English dialectal "blizzer," ultimately associated with "blaze," while Eric Partridge, in his *Origins*, offers "blizz" and "blaze" with an "-ard" suffix which is usually derogatory. The Random House Dictionary, most recent on the market, carries it back to Anglo-Saxon *blysa*, "torch," and *blysian*, "to burn," but does not seem too sure of itself. Webster's Third International gives up and labels its source "unknown." It does the same with "jitney," which first appears in 1915. Here Random House calls it "slang for five cents," which still tells us nothing, and only Partridge ventures to connect it with Old French *geter*, modern *jeter*, "to throw," and its modern derivative *jeton*, "coin-shaped token." For "sundae," first recorded in 1904, Random House says nothing but "special use of Sunday," Webster's Third calls it an "alteration of spelling," Partridge suggests that it may originally have been served only on Sunday, and Oxford offers the entrancing theory that sundaes were made up of what was left over from Sunday sales of ice cream and related items. Another, unofficial, source claims that the sundae arose in a Puritanically-minded Midwestern town where the sale of ice-cream sodas was forbidden on the Sabbath, but unfizzed ice cream was allowed, even if doctored up with other food ingredients. The peculiar spelling, paralleling that of the feminine name "May," "Mae," could be attributed to American creativeness in orthography (after all, it was Andrew Jackson who said that it was a mighty poor mind that couldn't think of more than one way to spell a word).*

Two more words of two syllables may be mentioned before we plunge into our monosyllabic list: "bogus" and "baron." The first is of relatively recent appearance (1827). Both Oxford and Webster's Third agree that it was first applied to an apparatus for producing counterfeit money, but beyond that Webster, Random House, and Partridge link the word to "bogie" (or "bogey," or "boogie") of "boogie man" (goblin), which in turn goes back to *bug*, a Middle English word of uncertain provenance, possibly borrowed from Welsh. Partridge further offers a dialectal English *tankerabogus*, meaning goblin, of which the first element is altogether obscure.

"Baron" has a long and honorable history. It appears in early Middle English, but long before that it had made its bow in the Romance languages, especially French, where it has as much the meaning of "hero" as that of "nobleman," and Spanish, where it means "male," "masculine" (*un niño varón*, "a male child"). Beyond that, it is anybody's guess. There is in Latin a word *baro* (the root is *baron-*),

---

* Norman A. Riggle of Trona, California, sent me the following notation concerning one of his ancestors: "James Baird Porter (1869-1939) . . . Invented ice cream sundae. It is an interesting bit of American history, publicised by the Literary Digest and the 'Strange as it May Seem' newspaper column, that Jim Porter invented the popular delicacy known as 'ice cream sundae' and gave it its name. The name was first used in 1898. Jim's soda fountain clerk had found that the tasty concoction was very popular with a group of youthful customers who frequented his place at times, especially on Sunday afternoons. They began to call for this combination of ice cream with fruit dressing on it as 'a Sunday.' So the firm (Mr. Porter was both a druggist and an ice cream manufacturer in Tulsa, Okla.) picked up the name. But Jim Porter, a faithful Presbyterian Elder, felt it was a sacrilege to publicise his popular product under the name of the Lord's Day, so he changed the spelling to 'Sundae'; and so it stands today throughout the nation—and sells all over the world."

but it means a "simpleton." There is a Germanic *bar* or *baro,* meaning "free man." Some say the two words may have gotten crossed, or that the Latin "simpleton" may have been borrowed from the Germanic "free man" (but the Latin word appears as early as Cicero, which makes borrowing from Germanic unlikely). There is the further supposition that the Germanic word may be related to the root of "to bear," and that the Germanic free man, coming into the Roman armies, may have been used as a porter, man of all work, and therefore a simpleton. But aside from the fact that Germanic mercenaries were somewhat of a rarity in the Roman armies of the first century B.C., the word would have had to undergo a dramatic enhancement of meaning to transform itself into the he-man of Spanish and the hero of Old French. The mystery deepens when we find that Italian has, side by side with *barone* (which it seems to have borrowed from French), also a *baro* that means a "cheat," and on which the verb *barare,* "to cheat at a game," is based. How to reconcile all these varied and contradictory meanings?

Here are twenty common English monosyllables, each of which poses a problem: "bad," "big," "blab," "boy," "brave," "bronze," "chat," "cut," "dad," "fit," "fog," "fun," "girl," "job," "jump," "lad," "lass," "put," "slum," "tot," and, for good measure, "zinc."

"Bad" starts its career as the thirteenth-century Middle English *bædde* or *badde,* which has no direct counterpart in Anglo-Saxon (*yfel,* the ancestor of "evil," is the regular word there). There are, however, such Anglo-Saxon words as *bæddel,* "hermaphrodite," *bædling,* "effeminate," and even a word *bædan,* "to defile." Could it be that *bad* itself simply did not have the good fortune to be recorded in any of the Anglo-Saxon writings that have come down to us? Or should we listen to Partridge's enticing alternative of derivation from Celtic *bados,* "wide open" (to evil ideas)?

"Big" is Middle English *bigge,* but again does not appear in Anglo-Saxon. Here the general theory is that it may have been a Scandinavian importation from the days of the Danelaw and King Cnut. There is a Scandinavian *bugge,* meaning "important man," which would give our "Mr. Big" an archaic flavor. Partridge complicates the matter with the possibility of relationship to "bug," to Latin *bucca* ("cheek," "inflated cheek"), and even to Celtic *beccus,* "beak."

"Blab" is the late Middle English *blabbe,* said to be derived, by the process of cutting off the ending, from *blæberen,* which gives us "blabber." But *blæberen* itself is said to be an "echoic" word, one coined on the basis of the sound produced by the object, which again injects a note of uncertainty (does blabbering really sound like *blabber?*).

"Boy" is late Middle English, and here we have a wide choice of possible origins. Partridge and Random House are in substantial agreement in pointing to Frisian *boi,* "young gentleman," Old High German *buobe* (modern German *Bube*), and Old Norse *bófi* or *bófa,* "rascal," "rogue." Partridge points to the similar semantic development of our "knave" and German *Knabe,* where the boyish and roguish ideas are intertwined. Oxford rejects all this, and claims that "boy" came in from Old French *abuié,* "fettered," "chained," which would make the boy originally a slave. Webster further brings in the possibility of baby talk for "brother" (note the equivalence of American "Oh, boy!" and "Oh, brother!"). Random House also brings in the Germanic proper name *Boia,* which arouses another fascinating parallel: Italian has *boia* for "hangman," but also popularly for "rascal," particularly "young rascal"; this word is derived from Latin *bojae,* a leather collar worn by captives and slaves, which ties up with the Oxford *abuié* cited above. So you pay your money and take your choice. In any case, our boy has traveled far.

"Brave" first appears in English in 1485, and Oxford derives it from Italian *bravo.* But *bravo* itself makes its first appearance in English in 1597; should it not have shown up first? Random House and Webster prefer derivation from Latin *barbarus,* through an unattested Vulgar Latin *brabus* and an attested Old Provençal *brau.* If this is so, we are carried all the way back to Greek *barbaros* and Sanskrit *barbara,* "babbler" or "stammerer" (the Greeks labeled as "barbarians" or "babblers" all who spoke languages other than Greek, as fine a sample of linguistic egocentrism as history has to offer). But there is another possibility, advanced by Menéndez-Pidal and involving a complete semantic reversal. Latin *pravus* (from which we get "depraved") meant in origin physically "crooked" or "twisted." The word was later used exactly like English "crooked" and "crook," and by the time of Cicero we find it applied to Catiline and his conspirators, who were morally depraved, but for that very reason had to train themselves to endure all sorts of hardships so they could carry out their scoundrelly plots against the Roman state. The man who is a thoroughgoing crook must have some courage, and this we find enhanced in the medieval Italian *bravi,* hired retainers or gangsters. These courageous scoundrels were handy to have around, and in your pay, when danger impended, and gradually the quality of courage took the upper hand over the more unsavory characteristics until it alone remained. It was left for modern times to invest *bravo* in Italian and *brave* in French (but only when used before the noun) with the connotation of "good," "kindly," "easygoing," the precise opposite of the original *pravus;* in fact, *brave homme* and *brav'uomo* are occasionally used ironically of husbands who easily allow themselves to be deceived. In Spain, *bravo* was primarily applied to fighting bulls, and *toros bravos* means something more than "brave bulls"; it means rather mean, vicious bulls, retaining some of the original content of *pravus.* Any doubt on this subject is removed by the Spanish expression *ponerse bravo,* applied to a man, which means not "to get brave," but "to get mean, vicious, violent."

"Bronze" is a latecomer to English (1721). Random House and Webster derive it from *(aes) brundisinum,* "brass from Brundisium," the modern city of Brindisi on the Adriatic (but there is no indication that a better grade of brass or bronze was produced in Brundisium than anywhere else). The form *brundium* appears in late Latin, and the Italian *bronzino,* side by side with *bronzo,* might lend some credence to the *brundisinum* theory. Partridge, however, offers an alternative derivation from Persian *birindj,* "alloy," and in this he is supported by various European scholars.

"Chat" is Middle English, and said to be a cut-off form of "chatter," first attested in 1540. This in turn is said to be an echoic word, formed on the basis of the sound striking the ear, like "blab." Perhaps so.

"Cut" has Middle English precursors that take the forms of *cuten,* *cutten,* even *kitten,* and Random House gives a hypothetical Anglo-Saxon ancestor *cyttan,* unfortunately unattested. Swedish forms, like *kotta, kata,* and Icelandic *kuti,* "little knife," lend support to Oxford's theory of a Germanic root *kut,* of which we have no direct evidence. Partridge, however, prefers a French source, *escurter,* modern *écourter,* "to cut off, cut short, curtail" ("cutty pipe," "Cutty Sark" seem to support this). If we accept this view, the ultimate source is Latin *curtus,* "short."

"Dad" first appears in 1500. All agree that it is child talk, and that it has a very wide range (Irish *daid,* Welsh *tad,* Latin, Greek, Sanskrit *tata,* Gothic *atta,* Slavic *otets*). The best guess seems to be that the child is trying, in all these languages, to utter the word *pater* or something similar (the *pater-father* root is practically universal in Indo-European), and substitutes a dental for a labial in the first syllable, either because the dental is easier to articulate or because he is anticipating the dental in the second syllable. What concerns us is from which of these sources English took its "dad." On the basis of both form and chronology, Irish or Welsh would seem to be the most likely candidates.

"Fit" (in the sense of "a fit of anger," not that of "to fit a dress") goes all the way back to Anglo-Saxon *fitt,* where it has the meaning of "strife." Random House suggests a secondary meaning, "a round of a fight." The question then arises whether *fitt* is linked to Anglo-Saxon *feoht* and *feohtan,* which give us "fight" as a noun and as a verb. The evidence for the link is not as clear as it might be.

"Fog" does not show up until 1544, in the form *fogge.* A Scandinavian source seems most likely. Danish has *fog* as "spray" or "snow," Old Norse has *fjuk* in the same sense, *fuka* as "sea-fog." Again the time element comes into play. Is this a relatively late borrowing from Danish, or did it come in with the pre-Hastings Danes and lie unrecorded until the sixteenth century?

"Fun," too, is late (1685), and is at first used only as a verb, *to fun,* meaning "to cheat, hoax, cajole, make a fool of." Partridge alone links it to *fond,* which he derives from Middle English *fonned,* the past participle of *fonnen,* "to be silly, make a fool of." Beyond that, he suggests Celtic origin (Irish *fonn,* "pleasure," "folly"; Welsh *gwan,* "feeble," "faint"). To a modern observer, it is interesting to note how a word which in origin was a verb turns into a noun, then into an adjective ("fun dress," "fun party," even "Fun City").

"Girl" is given as Middle English and obscure by both Oxford and Webster. Random House links Middle English *girle, gurle* with Anglo-Saxon *gyrlgyden,* "virgin goddess," and with Low German *göre,* "young person" (some Scottish dialects still use *girl* to refer to the young of either sex). Partridge admits this possibility, but also advances Anglo-Irish *girleen* and the hypothesis of a borrowing from Irish *caile, cailin* (the word familiar to most as *colleen*).

"Job," from 1557, seems at first to have had the meaning of "lump" (a lump of work?), and Webster definitely links it to *gob.* If this is right, then it goes back to Old French *gober,* from which we get *gobble* and even *gobbledygook.* French in turn gets it from Welsh-Breton *gob,* "snout" or "beak." So far as English is concerned, the semantic link seems weak, and we can't really blame Random House for rejecting it.

"Jump," from 1511, is described as echoic by Oxford (does one necessarily make a sound when jumping, and if so, does it sound like "jump"?). Webster links the word with Swedish *gumpa* and Low German *gumpen,* while Partridge claims a medieval Latin *jumpare.* We have been unable to find the latter, but are in a position to offer Partridge the colloquial Italian *zompare,* which could well have come from the form he claims, and means precisely "to jump." Italian etymological dictionaries claim, like the English, that their word is echoic.

"Lad" is Middle English *ladde,* originally meaning "serving man." Both Random House and Partridge, however, advance the Anglo-Saxon proper name *Ladda* as a possible source.

"Lass" appears in Middle English in the form *lasce.* Oxford theorizes that this may be linked to Swedish *lösk kona,* "unmarried woman," while Partridge suggests that *lasce* or *lasse* may be a cut-down form of *laddesse,* "lad" with a feminine suffix.

"Put" is generally linked to Anglo-Saxon *putian, potian,* "to thrust, push, goad," and Old Norse *pota,* "to thrust," is advanced by Random House. Partridge alone suggests that it may be echoic.

"Slum" is a quite modern word, first appearing in 1812, and labeled "cant" by Oxford. There is general silence as to its derivation save from Partridge, who says it may come from "slumber," in the sense that slum areas, being unknown to lexicographers, who took good care not to wander into them, may have unjustly acquired the reputation of being sleepy and quiet.

"Tot," first attested in 1725, draws no theories from Oxford or Webster. Random House suggests derivation from "totterer," but also envisages a possible link with Anglo-Saxon *totrida,* "a swing," where the *rida* is "rider" and the *tot* betokens a projecting part, as in Icelandic *tota,* "toe of a shoe." Partridge cites Danish *tommeltot,* and runs the last part of the word back to Old Norse *tuttr,* "dwarf." It may be mentioned that "tot" refers to a small drink as well as a small child, and in this connection we have the "toddy" of "rum toddy," from 1609, which is taken from Hindi *tari,* "a drink." Could "toddy" have been cut down to "tot"? The relative chronology of the two words in English would permit this hypothesis.

Our supernumerary "zinc" is directly taken from German *Zink.* Beyond that, Random House suggests a link with German *Zinn,* "tin"; Webster makes the link with Old High German *zinte,* "point" or "barb," by reason of the jagged formation assumed by zinc when smelted; Partridge makes the same link with *Zinker,* "spike," and further suggests a connection with *Zahn,* "tooth," which would place "zinc" squarely in the very large Indo-European family of "tooth," "dent-," and "odont-."

These elements of mystery and doubt connected with our shortest and most common words could easily be duplicated in every language. That they are most numerous in English is perhaps due to the extremely varied sources from which we have obtained our vocabulary. They also account for the tendency of our popular etymologists to deal with words like "rhododendron" and "sesquipedalian" in preference to "fog" and "girl." But there is an added psychological trait that enters the picture. The long words we have to think about. The short ones we use without thinking.

CHAPTER 5

Parallel Proverbs

Proverbs are among the most ancient of human institutions. Numerous proverbs appear in the tongues of which we have the oldest existing records—Egyptian, Akkadian, Chinese, Sanskrit, Greek, and Latin. The Hebrews have contributed to the Bible an entire "Book of Proverbs." Yet, though most countries teem with popular sayings, a few groups have none. Literacy and culture seem to have nothing to do with it. The African Negroes have many proverbs, the American Indians none.

Criticism of life, in brief and pithy form, is characteristic of proverbs, while their popular philosophy is, indeed, proverbial. "Proverbs are the wisdom of peoples" goes an Italian saying. This is perhaps an exaggeration, but there is no doubt that much of a nation's folk philosophy gets into proverbs, along with the spice of national customs and, above all, the peculiar flavor of the nation's language and phraseology.

How did proverbs originate? No one knows exactly, but if the Greeks have given us a correct etymology in their word for "proverb" (*paroimia*, "by the roadside"), then they are sayings that have grown up "along the road." The Latin equivalent, *proverbium*, means "a word uttered forth" or "publicly." Proverbs are generalizations of human experience, condensations of oft-repeated occurrences of the trial-and-error variety. Above all, they are the fruit of observation and inductive reasoning, two of the great faculties of the human mind.

A sage of ancient Babylon, Palestine, Greece, or Rome, watching the infinite variations of events taking place around him, yet noticing that similar sequences led more or less inevitably to the same outcome, was undoubtedly the one who first spun the generalization.

43

Then he offered it, as the Greek word implies, "along the roads," to anyone who cared to listen. The saying caught on, became popular, was passed from mouth to mouth, from generation to generation. Ultimately it became an integral part of the group's folklore and was referred to whenever the situation it described recurred.

"Language," says an Arab proverb, "is a steed that carries one into a far country." But for proverbs a distant journey is hardly necessary, because "many minds with but a single thought" is often highly appropriate. Proverbs prove that human nature is one, whether in New York or Moscow, Peking or Timbuktu. If there is an element of common vicissitude, then many languages will be sure to "have a word for it."

Some sayings are almost prehistoric, others quite modern. "What is healthy to a Russian is death to a German" sounds like something manufactured during the three winter campaigns of the Second World War. Actually, it goes back several centuries and is the Russian way of saying that "one man's meat is another man's poison."

"You can't fool all of the people all of the time" is attributed to Lincoln. It received a vivid demonstration in Fascist Italy, where Mussolini's followers were trying to force their own manufactured slogan down the people's throats: "Mussolini is always right!" "Particularly when he's wrong" was the addition made by an unknown native wit. And that was the way the slogan stuck, to plague the Fascists.

It was not the first time, for Italians specialize in taking internationally known bromides and giving them a humorous twist: "Silence is assent; but if you keep your mouth shut you're not saying anything"; or "Slow but sure—and you never get there."

Many sayings are international, proving that "great minds run in the same channel," even if the minds are anonymous. But the same idea can be expressed in different ways. Witness our "Too many cooks spoil the broth"; in Russian it runs, "With seven nurses, the child goes blind"; in Persian, "Two captains sink the ship"; in Japanese, "Too many boatmen run the boat up to the top of a mountain"; in Italian, "With too many roosters crowing, the sun never comes up." We "call a spade a spade," but the Spaniards "call bread bread and wine wine." We say, "Don't bite the hand that's feeding you," while the Russians say, "Don't defile the well; you might want to drink from it," and the French, "Don't spit in the air; it might fall back on you." "Pray to God and keep your powder dry" is in Russian "Pray to God, but row toward shore."

"Don't put the cart before the horse" has a counterpart in Finnish "Trees are climbed from the bottom, not from the top." "Don't bite off more than you can chew" is paralleled by Rumania's "Don't stretch yourself till you're longer than your blanket." "Setting a thief to catch a thief" is in Hungarian "Setting a dog to watch the bacon." "To have one's cake and eat it" is in Russian "Keeping one's innocence and accumulating capital." To the Russian "A fly in the ointment" is "A spoonful of tar in our cask of honey"; "When in Rome do as the Romans do" is "When living with wolves, howl like a wolf"; "To hit the nail on the head" is "To smite not on the brow, but in the eye"; "To have a heavy heart" is "To have cats scratching on your heart." The old Latin proverb "In the land of the blind a one-eyed man is king" is curiously paralleled by Korea's "Where there are no tigers, a wildcat is very self-important."

Every proverb tells a story and teaches a lesson. "If the pitcher hits the rock, or the rock hits the pitcher, it's too bad for the pitcher" is a Spanish warning that you should not pit yourself against superior forces. China says the same thing in these words: "Don't set out unarmed to fight a tiger." Our American Southern counterpart is "The worm is wrong when it argues with the hen." "The palest ink is better than the most retentive memory" is China's admonition to "put it in writing," while Spain urges, "Don't sign papers you don't read, or drink water you don't see." Portugal, in the same vein, reminds you that "Caution and chicken broth never harmed anyone."

Proverbs are often cynical, especially in money matters. "The coal-man is black, but his money is white" says a Portuguese proverb. "The poor man dies waiting for the rich man to make up his mind" is an Albanian expression of skepticism, while Rumania has it: "The rich man makes a mistake, and the poor man hastens to apologize." "When it rains oatmeal, the poor man has no spoon to catch it with" is Sweden's contribution to pessimism, while the Italians assert that "Those who have bread have no teeth, and those who have teeth have no bread." Czechoslovakia sagely advises: "If you have no money, don't go to the inn." Surprisingly, it is Japanese, not Russian, that has the most rabidly anti-capitalistic saying: "A rich man and a spittoon grow dirtier as they accumulate." Japanese further shows its contempt for earthly wealth by saying: "There is no instance of a naked man ever losing anything."

Cynicism appears in other connections. "Those who die are at rest; those who live set their hearts at rest" is Italy's rather bitter reflection on life and death. France is more lighthearted: "You can't make an omelet without breaking eggs." "The pleas of the mighty thunder out like commands," say the Swiss. America says: "When luck gets to running your way, sawdust is as good as brains," and Russia concurs with "Be born neither wise nor fair, but lucky." Highly pessimistic are Russia's "Good luck disappears like our hair; bad luck hangs on like our finger nails," and Spain's "Welcome, evil, if you come alone."

Proverbs of various countries are sometimes contradictory. "To trust is well, but not to trust is better" says Italian, but Spanish counters: "If you lose a knife that doesn't cut, or a friend that doesn't lend, you're not losing much." "Three tenths according to a man's ability; seven tenths according to his clothes" is China's way of saying that "Clothes make the man"; but Spain denies this: "Though the monkey wear silk, it's still a monkey." Contradictions may even appear in the same tongue. "A wife and a floor mat are good when fresh and new" and "A wife and a kettle get better as they grow older" are both from Japan.

Most proverbs were born at a time when civilization was agricultural and earthy; they seldom speak of machines, often of farm animals. "A big ox plows a crooked furrow," says the Czech. "A donkey's braying does not reach heaven," says the Italian. "Seat a pig at the table and he'll put his feet on it," says the Russian. "Why make an ox or a horse of yourself for posterity?" inquires the Chinese.

There is scarcely any contingency of life that is not covered by some national saying. "With words alone, you don't make the soup" is Rumania's way of reminding you that "Deeds talk louder than words." The Italian equivalent, "Deeds are masculine, words feminine," has been borrowed, untranslated, as the motto of the State of

Maryland. China has it: "Talk cooks no rice," and our Southern Negroes say: " 'Mean to' don' pick no cotton."

"A swimmer's real skill is knowing how to keep his eye on his clothes," warns Spanish; and Chinese gently admonishes: "Don't lean against a bamboo fence; lean against a wall." "Better to be waited for than to wait" is the Japanese excuse for being late to an appointment, while Arabic has a typical lazy man's proverb: "It is better to walk than to run; better to stand than to walk; better to sit than to stand; better to lie than to sit." Czech has a good slogan for salesmen: "When you're trying to catch a bird, sing to it nicely"; while Macedonian warns you to "Be a man, not a mouse" in these words: "If you turn into a lamb, the wolf will eat you up."

Volumes of philosophy are at times wrapped up in one saying. The Arabic "Birth is the messenger of death," the Rumanian "What man fears he cannot escape," the Italian "Graveyards are full of after-wisdom" are cases in point. For sheer moral grandeur, it is hard to beat Finland's "Fire cannot destroy the truth," Switzerland's "Conscience is a better guide than science," or China's "Those who follow that part of themselves which is great are great men; those who follow that part of themselves which is small are small men." A Spanish proverb runs: "God says: 'Take what you want, and pay for it.'" From our South Carolina mountaineers comes: "We ain't what we want to be, and we ain't what we're goin' to be, but we ain't what we wuz."

Philosophy is often interlarded with humor. The Czechs, for intance, say: "Real suffering is not working on a mountaintop; it's working among people." "The cat knows perfectly well whose chops he's licking," say the Portuguese. And the Chinese, with their Confucian background, have this to offer: "The good man, doing good, finds the day too short; the evil man, doing evil, likewise finds the day too short."

God and the devil play conspicuous roles. "The doctor examines you, but God makes you well," says a Polish proverb. "God does not pay off on Saturday, but by Sunday everything's paid up" is the Italian tribute to divine justice.

The devil of proverbial utterances is an imp. "Man makes fun of man, and the devil makes fun of all of them," says Rumanian. "Man is fire; woman is firewood; the devil comes along and blows on them," says Spanish. Albania believes in appeasement: "Light a candle to the devil too, so he'll do you no harm." But Macedonia thinks it's no use: "The devil doesn't listen to sermons."

Woman is all-powerful in some proverbs. "Man is the product of the women he has known" and "What woman wants, God wants," says the gallant Frenchman; and the Italian agrees by saying: "A woman's hair pulls more than a yoke of oxen." But there are limitations: "The prettiest girl in the world can only give what she's got" is another French saying (the Italian counterpart is "The cask can give only the wine it holds").

The fickleness of woman is celebrated in song and saying. "When she says no, a woman shakes her head lengthwise," say the Japanese; but out of fairness they add: "A man's heart is as changeful as the autumn sky." The Chinese add a touch of domestic cynicism: "Two women in one room are one too many." The Russians are nasty: "A dog is wiser than a woman; it doesn't bark at its master."

Love and marriage, of course, have their innings. "Keep your eye on people in love, because they are all stone blind," says Portugal. "If you hanker to be a martyr, lead a rich wife to the altar," says Switzerland. "When the bride is in the cradle, the bridegroom should be old enough to ride a horse" is Russia's idea of the proper age difference between the sexes. The Poles are bitter about marriage: "The woman cries before the wedding; the man cries afterwards." But the Russians think they know what to do about it: "Love your wife like your soul, and beat her like your fur coat."

The Dutch are pessimists about remarriage: "To marry once is a duty; twice, an act of foolishness; three times, lunacy." To which the French add: "Divorce is the sacrament of adultery."

The upbringing of children appears not only in our "Spare the rod and spoil the child"; the Danes say, "Give to a pig when it grunts and to a child when it cries, and you will have a fine pig and a bad child."

Both fools and sages are the object of ridicule. "Giving advice to a fool is like giving medicine to a dead man" is an old American proverb. "A fool can ask more questions than seven wise men can answer," says a German proverb. But a Spanish proverb counters: "There is no foolishness that is not sponsored by some sage." Our "A word to the wise is sufficient" is elaborated by the Czechs: "To a wise man, just whisper; but to a fool you must spell out everything."

Gossips also come in for their share. "He who knows little soon repeats it," say the Spaniards, and the Turks add: "Who gossips to you will gossip about you."

Some proverbs make you feel like arguing the point. Hungary's "Good wine needs no publicity" is quite at variance with America's "It pays to advertise." One could also dispute Albania's "Better to suffer misfortune quickly than to wait too long for good fortune," or Arabia's "All that is hidden is sought after."

"Don't get 'American stomach' by eating too fast" is the gist of several proverbs in many languages, like Italy's "At table you don't grow older," or China's "Work may be hastened, but not food."

In addition to proverbs, there are picturesque similes. "For eating, like a wolf; for working, like a log" is Rumania's way of describing some people. "Lucky like a dog in church" is Italy's description of bad luck. "As nice as soot is white" is Russia's expression of disgust, while the Arabic reply to a sympathetic inquiry as to how things are going is "like tar!" and the Chinese puts it: "Seven kinds of mess, eight kinds of disorder." If you want to be in a desirable spot against the wishes of those in control, you are said by the Italians to be trying to "get into Paradise in spite of the Saints." Other people are said to be "looking for work and praying to God they won't find it."

There is a Hungarian saying to console those who have to listen to long-winded speakers: "Even the longest speech has to end in a single word." For this, there is a Hindustani parallel: "The longest journey begins with a single step."

Proverbs of ultra-modern application appear where you least expect them. A principle that has been put to use by our picture magazines lies in the Chinese proverb "One picture is worth many thousand words."

National characteristics often get into proverbs. Here are three Russian ones to prove the point: "The Russian is strong on three foundations: 'perhaps,' 'never mind,' and 'somehow'"; "If you drink, you die; if you don't drink, you die; so you'd better drink"; "Those who know a lot are our friends; those who know too much are our enemies."

Proverbs are generally, but not always, anonymous. One coined some years ago by Dizzy Dean of baseball fame runs: "Lots of people who don't say 'ain't' ain't eatin'."

It is fashionable in some quarters to describe certain groups as backward, ignorant, illiterate. There may be mechanical justification for these epithets, but you certainly cannot prove mental inferiority or lack of philosophical perception by the language or proverbs of many of these groups. Take, as a single example, the Swahili of East Africa. "To speak is good, and not to speak is good" parallels the European "Speech is silver, silence is gold." "He who is there above, await him below" sounds very much like our "Pride goes before a fall." "He who is not here, and his business is not here" reminds you of the Italian "The absent are always in the wrong." There is a world of earthly wisdom in "Whether the cock crows or not, it will dawn"; "Drunkenness takes away sense"; "Whether you have little or much, be content." And what has the West to offer that surpasses this triad in philosophical content:

"Profit surpasses pride"

"Understanding surpasses property"

"As for dying, we shall all die"?

There is little question that proverbs have historical and cultural value. Often, as we have seen, they tell a story that is directly traceable to the story of the group that uses them. Even more often, they are a reflection of group habits and points of view.

Do proverbs and sayings also have a psychological value to their users? This question is more difficult to answer. The proverb has a great deal in common with the cliché, which may be described as a capsule of predigested thought. Whatever writers like Bergen Evans may say, clichés are used because they are available and easy to use. They seem to fit exactly into certain situations. They describe accurately what one would otherwise have to describe in his own words. They are timesavers and effort savers. If a cliché (or a proverb) offers you the idea you want, why look further? Why rack your brain?

So the proverb survives and the cliché flourishes. Both are expressions of human thought—not necessarily on the highest plane, but freely offered, like the tidbits of a smörgåsbord. Very little in the field of human experience is original in the sense that it has never happened before. Why should the thought that summarizes the experience be original? In fact, if it was first formulated ten or twenty centuries ago, does it not lend vigor and strength both to the experience and to its description? And is one man not entitled to use the thought of another, when it can be simply, economically, and pithily transferred in terms of language?

CHAPTER 6

Some Foreign Contributions
to the English Vocabulary

Language being a tool of human thought, the loan words that find
their way from one tongue into another are in the nature of cogs and
bolts, screws and gaskets, many of them relatively unimportant, in
the vast machine that constitutes human speech.

But etymology has also been defined as the history of human
progress reflected and expressed in language. Viewed in this light,
the loan words that have passed from one language into another
lose their mechanical characteristics and assume the role of witnesses
to the absorbing interchange and interflow of culture and civilization
that has gone on through past centuries and is still going on.

English is the world's greatest borrower of words. Starting with an
original Anglo-Saxon vocabulary of probably not over fifty thousand
words, it went on to appropriate what it needed. Its first borrowings
were both from its kindred Germanic language, Danish, and from
the Latin and Greek of the early Christian missionaries who had
been sent to convert the Anglo-Saxon tribes. Later, in 1066, William
the Conqueror brought to English not only an army of French-
speaking Normans, but also a veritable host of French words, most
of which had come from Latin, some from Greek, others from Germanic dialects akin to Anglo-Saxon, yet different from it.

From the Norman Conquest on, the English language adapted to
its own use droves of new words, of all origins and sources. The great
majority of these, constituting perhaps three fifths of the total present-day English vocabulary, are later borrowings from French and
learned borrowings from the classical tongues, Latin and Greek.

Then, having become firmly set in the habit of borrowing, English began to take in words from all over the globe. Italian, Spanish, Portuguese, Dutch, German, the Celtic, Slavic, Semitic, Oriental, and African tongues, even the languages of the Australian aborigines, have contributed to the present English vocabulary.

The question is, in what measure? A word count based on the rather extensive vocabulary of the author's *The Families of Words** indicates that after the Germanic, French, Latin, and Greek elements, leading roles are played by two additional Romance tongues, Italian and Spanish. We shall therefore undertake to examine the contributions from these two sources in detail.

* Harper & Row, 1962.

CHAPTER 7

Contributions from Italian

Every word tells a story, and from the linguistic treasures that a nation like Italy has poured with an unstinting hand into our English tongue we may be able to derive a fairly accurate idea of the vast parallel contribution made by Italy to Anglo-Saxon civilization, a contribution which began in the days of the Romans, continued throughout the so-called Dark Ages, attained sublime heights in the centuries of the Italian Renaissance, and goes on unabated, in unvaried rhythm, in our own times.

It was imperial Rome that offered the primitive inhabitants of Britain the *castrum* that give rise to the innumerable "-casters," "-cesters," and "-chesters" of present-day Britain and America, and the *strata* that becomes our modern "street," as well as the *moneta, pondus, uncia,* and *caseus* brought by the missionaries of Christian Rome to the idol-worshiping Anglo-Saxons, which eventually became transformed into the "mint," "pound," "inch," and "cheese" of modern English. Then there were the thousands of words brought into Gaul by Rome's legions, giving rise to the Old French that was absorbed by the Normans, and later came to England with William the Conqueror. But I propose to limit myself to those words which came directly into English from Italian when the latter had already ceased being the classical Latin of Cicero or even the Vulgar Latin of Gregory the Great, and had triumphantly entered upon a new phase of its existence under the lofty guidance of Dante.

Even with these self-imposed limitations, the field is vast. An actual word count of the English vocabulary shows that the Italian element in English is outstripped only by the native Anglo-Saxon and Scandinavian, the French of the Normans, and the revivified Latin and

54

Greek that make up so large a part of both our common and our scientific vocabularies. With these four exceptions, the Italian participation surpasses all others: German, Dutch, and modern Scandinavian, which are most closely related to Anglo-Saxon; Spanish and Portuguese, whose contributions have been considerable; Slavic and Semitic (the latter includes both Hebrew and Arabic); and all other Asian, as well as African, Pacific, and native American Indian languages put together. It is therefore quite surprising that a well-known popularization of the English language and its present and future role should devote five pages to contributions coming to us from the languages of India, and only six lines to those stemming from Italian.

The Italian contingent extends from Renaissance borrowings that have assumed a thoroughly English form, such as "sonnet," "gazette," "balcony," and "infantry," to words in which the Italian form has remained altogether intact, as is the case with "incognito," "broccoli," "impresario," and "marina." It includes not merely words of Latin stock, but words originally stemming from a dozen oriental languages, such as "cotton," "taffeta," "pistachio," and "bergamot," which were picked up in foreign ports by the daring sailors of Pisa, Genoa, and Venice at a time when those maritime republics ruled the waves, and by them transplanted to English soil. It reaches out into every nook and cranny of every walk of life, of every form and type of civilized activity, as an undying testimonial to the mighty force of penetration of Italian culture into the life and ways of a once alien race that has been utterly transformed and reformed by the perennial light of civilization that is diffused over the world by Rome the Immortal and her most direct descendant.

From the loftiest areas of art, music, literature, and science to the most vulgar regions of colloquialism and slang, from the innermost recesses of the home and kitchen to the stately functions of the court and the wide-open spaces of the salty ocean, we find our English vocabulary and our Anglo-Saxon civilization invaded and pervaded by the graceful, picturesque, and ubiquitous influence of Italy, an influence that our highest and lowest classes would in vain attempt to shake off, since it sweeps from the "pastel" in the "dilettante's studio" to the "cartoon" in the "jovial magazine," from the "andante cantabile" of the "coloratura soprano" to the "capricious finale" of a "burlesque" show, from the "gala masquerade" of an "ambassadorial salon" to the "carnival carrousel" of Coney Island, from the "stanza" of the "improviser" to the "bambino" of the "sporting gazette," from the "cash deposit" of the "banker" to the "partisan ballot" of the "isolationist," from the "stiletto" of the "assassin" to the "musket" of the "sentinel," from the "cant" of the "pedant" to the "Boloney!" of the "populace," from the "caress" of the "Romeo" to the "jealous chagrin" of the "marquise," from the "marconigram" of the "pilot" to the "flu" that "attacks" us as a "group."

The field of art is one in which Italy has ever excelled. Here the contribution of Italian to the English vocabulary is as extensive and varied as has been Italy's contribution to the world's artistic endowment. Words denoting forms, styles, or methods of painting, such as "chiaroscuro," "fresco," "aquarelle," "aquatint," "mezzotint," "miniature," "profile," "sketch," impasto," "contrapposto," "tondo" have in part become generalized (a "sketch" or "profile" may be written as well as drawn, while the "mini-" of "miniature" has been extended out of all proportion, to apply even to skirts). There are learned words descriptive of artistic or historical epochs: "trecento," "quattrocento," "cinquecento," with derivative adjectives in "-ist." There are forms of sculpture, such as "torso" and "bust"; names of colors, such as "magenta," "solferino," and the misspelled "sienna," which should have only one *n*; artistic materials, like "bronze," and artistic products, such as "medal," "cameo," "intaglio," "alto-," and "basso-rilievo." There are words of general artistic connotation, such as "dilettante" and "dilettantism," "replica," "model," "studio," and two proper adjectives that have won their place in Webster's: "Raphaelite" and "Sistine." In connection with some of these words, the vast extensions of meaning they have acquired testifies to their popular use and penetrative power. We speak today not merely of an artist's "model" and an artist's "studio," but of a "model" son, an example on which to "model" our behavior, a Hollywood motion-picture "studio," and a photographic "studio." It is characteristic of many Italian loan words that although originally adopted with a specific, technical meaning, they have acquired such vogue as to become current in everyday speech.

Passing from the field of art to that of music, we are faced with a unique situation. The English musical vocabulary is over three-fourths Italian, and the words, for the most part, have been permitted to retain their Italian form without a vestige of anglicization. This is a mighty tribute to the far-reaching influence Italian music has had upon the world in general and the Anglo-Saxon lands in particular. Almost every known form of musical composition bears an undiluted or slightly modified Italian name: from "concert" (or "concerto") to "opera," "operetta," and "opera-bouffe"; from "barcarolle" and "serenade" to "oratorio," "sonata," "passacaglia," "scherzo," and "caprice" (or "capriccio"); from "aria," through "cantabile," "largo," "intermezzo," and "recitative" to "ritornello" and "finale." Even the military "tucket" comes from the Italian *toccata*. Practically the same situation exists in the field of musical instruments. The Greek "orchestra," passing through Italy, has given rise to its English counterpart and derivatives, "orchestral," "orchestrate," "orchestration." The Italian "spinnet" has given way to the equally Italian "piano" (or "pianoforte"), which is accompanied by the Italian "piccolo," "trombone," "viola," "violoncello" (or "cello"), "mandolin," and "violin" (the last-named may be a "Cremona" or "Stradivarius": *Strad'* for short), and is occasionally supplemented by a "concertina." As for the performers, they are all Italian: "basso" (whether or not "profundo"), "contralto," "soprano" ("coloratura" or otherwise), "mezzo-soprano," and "tenor." The "prima donna," who is a "diva" and a "virtuosa," has been trained by an Italian "maestro" and is directed by an Italian "impresario" (this has even given rise to a semi-slang "comprimario"). Her "trills" (or *trilli*) and "cadences" are hailed by shouts of "Brava!" and "Viva!" (provided she does not strike a "falsetto" note), and "bravura" denotes the quality of her singing. No matter in what formation the performers choose to sing, the group will receive an Italian name: "solo," "duo" or "duet," "trio," "quartet," "quintet," even "sextet." The notes of the musical scale, from "do" to "si," are the invention of Guido d'Arezzo, who may possibly have been French, but certainly worked in Italy. Musical directions are 90 per cent Italian: *adagio, allegro, andante, crescendo, da capo, con brio, diminuendo, forte* and *fortissimo, legato, maestoso, moderato, obbligato, piano* and *pianissimo, pizzicato, presto* and *prestissimo, rallentando, sostenuto, staccato, tremolo, volta, più forte.* There is one linguistic gem, "*glissando*," which has a French root and an Italian ending. Among musical terms that defy classification are "libretto," "scenario," "tempo," "counterpoint," and the verb "improvise" with its many derivatives. Again it may be remarked that many of the Italian musical terms have received an extension of meaning that makes them current words in fields other than music. We speak of the "concert" of powers and "concerted" action, a "crescendo" of noise, the "staccato" rattling of a machine gun, "Presto" self-rising flour, a "tremolo" quaver in a person's voice, a "trio" of rascals, a "falsetto" shriek, the "scenario" of a photoplay, the "tempo" of recovery, the "cadence" of a dialect, the "improvising" of a speech.

Only a step removed from the operatic stage is the spoken drama. In the theatrical field we find a legion of words testifying to the inroads made by the Italian Commedia dell'Arte into England. "Ballet," "prima ballerina," "burlesque," "buffoon" and "buffoonery," "mountebank," and "fiasco" on the one hand, "Harlequin," "Columbine," "Scaramouche," "Pantaloon," and "Punchinello" (the latter, by the way, gives rise to England's favorite humorous periodical, *Punch*) are typical examples of this penetration. One Italian word that has come directly to America is derived from the puppet show, or Teatro dei Piccoli (Children's Theater), the last portion of which was erroneously seized by American producers and foisted by them upon the public to denote the puppets themselves. Note the extension of "fiasco" (the "fiasco" of a summit meeting) and the peculiarly American outgrowth of "burlesque," originally "funny."

Equally far-reaching are the ramifications of Italian influence in the vocabulary of literature. From typically Italian forms, such as "canto," "stanza," and "inferno" (not merely Dante's poetic creation, but also the "inferno" of modern warfare) we go to thoroughly anglicized words: "lampoon," "novel," "sonnet," "madrigal." From adjectives like "macaronic" and "Dantesque" we pass to proper names that form part of English literary history, such as Antonio, Bassanio, and Romeo ("he is a veritable "Romeo" with the ladies"). Little did Spenser know when in writing his *Faery Queen* he devised *Braggadocchio* as one of his characters that the term "braggadocio" would survive to the present day as the personification of boastfulness.

To what extent the architectural world is indebted to Italy is shown by the host of Italian words that enter every phase of present-day construction, from cellar to roof: "portico," "arcade," "banister," "colonnade," "corridor," "cornice," "façade," "gallery," "mezzanine," "balcony," "casement," "rotunda" among the details of architectural construction; "dado," "niche," "pedestal," "pilaster" among forms of decoration; "camposanto," "campanile," "cupola" in religious building; "belvedere," "casino," "pergola," "terrazzo," "piazza," "villa," "esplanade" in rural construction; "baroque," "Romanesque," "Moresque," "arabesque" in the domain of style. "Stucco" and "mosaic" among the building materials, "vista" among the beneficial results of well-planned architecture, testify to the debt that the real estate world owes to Italy. "Campagna" and "maremma" are applied to features of the Italian countryside, but "marina" has been generalized to denote any improved stretch of seacoast.

Military science, of late much in vogue, owes much of its terminology to the land of the *condottieri*. In the field of military construction and fortification we have "barrack," "barricade," "camp," "canteen," "citadel," "parapet," "post," "redoubt," "stockade," and the originally Arabic "arsenal." Among styles of combat, we find "ambush" and "ambuscade," "attack" and "campaign," "espionage" and "reprisal." The "cannon" and its by-products, "cannonade" and "salvo," the "carbine," the "musket" and the "scimitar" are of Italian origin. So are "battalion," "regiment" and "brigade," "cavalry" and "infantry," "escadrille," "squad" and "squadron," "sentinel," "carbineer," "musketeer," and "sapper"; even the Hungarian "hussar" may be an outgrowth of Italian *corsaro*. Army ranks, from "corporal" through "captain" and "colonel" to "brigadier" and "generalissimo," are Italian. The verbs "spy" and "espy," though originally Germanic, are lost to Anglo-Saxon and return by way of Italy, as does the military command "Halt!" The originally military "alert" has been extended far beyond its primary meaning, and we have only to refer to televised speeches of prospective candidates to realize how far "campaign" and "attack" have strayed from their once straight and narrow path. "Commando" is perhaps the most recent addition of this type, passing from Italian to Dutch at the time of the Boer War in South Africa, then gaining big vogue in the Second World War.

The courtly life of Renaissance Italy has given rise to a myriad festive terms that today form part of our common linguistic heritage. "Confetti," "costume" and "rocket," "gala" and "motto," "compliment," "vogue" and "punctilious," names of places where people gather for merrymaking, including both "salon" and "saloon," names of dances and other forms of festivity, from "tarantella" to "masquerade," from "quadrille" to "carrousel" and "carnival," from "travesty" to "cortege"; court "intrigue" and court "personages," from "cavalier" to "majordomo," from "paladin" to "page"; titles of nobility, such as "marquis" and "marquise"; the noun "escort" and the verb "to escort," all come directly or indirectly from Italy. More specifically Italian and literary are terms like *doge, messer, cortigiano, podestà*.

Many of our games and gaming terms come from Italy, from the "gambit" of chess to the card game called "casino," from the innocent "dominoes" and "lotto" to the "lottery" until recently illegal and the "punt" of games of chance. The word "sport" itself being a variant of the "disport" derived from the Italian *diporto*, it is not surprising that many of our sporting terms are of Italian origin. To select three widely different fields, we have the "racket" of the tennis player, the "duel" of the swordsman, and the "regatta" of the boating club. *Palestra*, the general Italian word for "gym," has been appropriated as the name of the Philadelphia sports palace.

It is only natural that Italy, home and center of the Christian religion, should have given us many of our religious terms. "Limbo" and "madonna," "catacomb" and "cassock" come from Italy. So do the names of most monastic orders, the Capuchins, the Carmelites, the Franciscans among them; and various ranks of the church hierarchy, from "fra" to "monsignor" and from "nuncio" to "cardinal." "*Aggiornamento*" (not adjournment, but bringing up to date) is quite recent.

The art of printing did not originate in Italy, but many of our most current press terms did. In the printer's shop we have "agate" and "paragon" type, "italics" and "italicize," and the paper unit "ream," which goes back to an Italian *risma* borrowed from Arabic; while among the finished products of the printing industry we have "gazette," "bulletin" and "magazine," "cartoon" and "caricature."

The land of Machiavelli, a name that has given rise to "Machiavellian" and "Machiavellianism," could not fail to supply us with a large number of terms pertaining to politics and statesmanship. "Ambassador" and "embassy" are of world-wide application, as is "league." "Manifesto" and "portfolio" retain in whole or in part their Italian form, but "ballot," "partisan," "revolt" have been anglicized almost beyond recognition. Historical and political names could be cited aplenty; suffice it to mention "Guelph," "Ghibelline," "Rinascimento," "Risorgimento," "Irredentism" and "Irredentist."

In the field of crime, the vocabulary contribution far outstrips the dubious participation which statistics show has been furnished by Italy; a unique situation, considering that in the other fields the opposite seems to be true. Linguistically, practically every field of crime shows traces of Italian influence: from "vagabond," "charlatan," and "ruffian," through "brigand," "bandit," and "corsair," to "bravo" and "assassin" (the last, however, is originally Arabic); from "contraband" to "brigandage" and "vendetta"; from the exclusively Italian *Camorra* and *Mafia* to the American "Mano Nera," "Cosa Nostra," and "racket"; from the "stiletto" that serves to perpetrate a crime to the "bagnio" that punishes it.

Our modern system of banking, credit, and finance had its inception in the great medieval merchant centers of Florence, Genoa, Venice, and Milan. It is therefore not surprising that many of the current words of the banking world had a similar origin. Not only the coinage of literature ("ducat," "florin," "piaster," "sequin," and "pistole"), but even the "valuta," which came to us via Russia and Germany, originated in Italy. "Cash" and "cashier," "debit," "credit," and "deposit," "bank," "banker," and "bankrupt" testify to the influence of those Italian financiers whose memory is immortalized by London's "Lombard" Street ("lumber," by the way, is a derivative of "Lombard"). In the related world of business we have "accredit," "firm," "mercantile," and "mercantilism," the originally Arabic "tariff," the "tontine" form of annuity, and such assorted terms as "agio," "banco," "tale quale," and "del credere." American financial circles sometimes euphemistically refer to Wall Street as the "Rialto."

International trade, once practically the monopoly of Genoese, Venetian, and Pisan navigators, is heavily endowed with Italian terms. The "lingua franca" of the Mediterranean Orient is supplemented by hosts of shipping terms which prove to what extent navigation was an Italian prerogative back in the days of sailing ships and sailing skill: "bark," "brig" and "brigantine," "frigate," "galley," "skiff," "tartan," as well as "pilot," are Italian. Nor must we forget the Venetian "gondola," which should be stressed on the first syllable, along with its "gondolier." To a lesser degree, overland transportation bears an Italian earmark from the days when horses had not yet turned into horsepower: "barb," "cavalcade," "gallop," "vault" are samples.

Navigation and commerce go hand in hand with industry. Italy, land of textiles, has given us not only the imported Persian "taffeta" and Arabic "cotton," but also "plush" and "poplin," "satin" and "shagreen," "velvet" and "floss," along with a color, "beige," that is peculiar to woven goods. Among the finer, semi-artistic products we find "terra cotta," "majolica" and "porcelain," "filigrain" and "filigree"; among the less refined, "Leghorn" straw and "lumber"; but the "carton" in which our cigarettes come, the "laundry" to which we send our wash, the "cafeteria" where we eat lunch, along with its "manager" and "management," are also Italian, as is the "artisan" who works at skilled trades, and the "milliner" whose output, "millinery," so delights the gentler sex. Of course, the verbs "to launder" and "to manage" have acquired numerous extended meanings. Recently, the term *piccolino* to describe a type of junior costume made its appearance in the advertising pages of the New York *Times,* while "credenza," as a household word, tends to displace the native "sideboard."

The food industry is the one in which Italian has made the vastest and most durable impact, particularly in America. *Pasta* (or even *pasta asciutta*) has become an all-purpose word in American English, as in Italian. But think of what it includes! *Ravioli, spaghetti, vermicelli,* and "macaroni" will immediately come to the reader's mind; but let us not forget that earlier derivative of the Italian *maccheroni,* the "macaroon." To these have been added of late dozens of other varieties: *cannelloni, lasagne, rigatoni, fettuccine,* all to be cooked *al dente. Semolina* and *farina,* the ingredients for *pasta,* have made vast strides. So have *pizza* and the *pizzeria* where it is produced and sold. All should be preceded by the appropriate *antipasto. Chianti* is the best-known of Italian wines, but we have also *Moscato* (or "Muscatel"), *Barbera* and *Barberone,* and the generic *spumante,* which Italian importers prefer to "champagne" for Italian sparkling wines. Other drinkables include *maraschino* and the once Arabic "syrup." A land that specializes in excellent cheeses has given us *Gorgonzola, Bel Paese, mozzarella, ricotta, provolone,* "Parmesan" (or *Parmigiano*) and *pecorino* (or *Romano*). *Bologna* sausage has really penetrated the American vocabulary, to the extent of giving rise to "boloney," even in a slangy sense. American supermarkets now stock and label *prosciutto, salame, peperoni, coppa, capocollo.* Our vegetable markets are filled with authentic Italian produce, from the originally Greek "celery" and "chicory" to the anglicized "endive," "radish," and "artichoke," down to the latter-day and uncorrupted "broccoli" and "zucchini." In fruit stalls we find not only Arabic "oranges" and Persian "pistachios" that come to us by way of Italy, but also "cantaloupes" from Cantalupo in Calabria, as well as three linguistic gems that shyly peep out at us from amid the greenery: the "Jerusalem artichoke," a corruption of Italian *girasole,* "sunflower," to whose family it belongs; the Teutonic-looking "kohlrabi," which is *cavoli-rape* in disguise; and a product resembling celery in appearance, but squat and with a bushy green top. Its proper English name is "fennel," but the greengrocer won't understand if you call it by that name. He will spell it *phinochi* and pronounce it, correctly enough, *finocchi,* one of those unfortunate cases where the ear has proved mightier than the eye or the dictionary. *Ceci,* along with Spanish *garbanzos,* tends to oust the native "chick peas." For dessert, there is "pastry," derived from *pasticceria,* along with *spumone* and *zabaione,* and if you "stretch your coffee break" with chewing gum, it may turn out to be "tutti-frutti." Condiments like *basilico* and *oregano,* styles and sauces like *Fra Diavolo, cacciatora* and *marinara,* dishes like *caponatina, scaloppine* and *scungilli,* bread products like *grissini,* the Italian-style *caffè espresso,* and even the *macchinetta* for making it at home, publicized in the advertising pages, round out the picture.

Italy's contributions to the world of science seldom receive the recognition they deserve. Yet a mere glance at the dictionary shows us their extent and range. The mathematical, chemical, and astronomical lore of the Arabs was diffused by Italy, as proved by such terms as "algebra," "cipher," "zero," "alchemy," "elixir," "zenith." Medicine's debt to Italy transpires in a series of proper adjectives: "Eustachian," "Fallopian," "Malpighian," "Pacinian"; of technical and semi-technical terms: "petechiae," "mattoid," "tarantism," "pellagra"; of semi-popular, popular, or even slang forms: "lazaret," "malaria," "malarial," "influenza," and "flu." In archaeology, the Pompeian "graffiti," the Sardinian "nuraghe," and the royal Egyptian "cartouches" testify to Italian participation. In pedagogy, we have not only "pedant," "pedantry," and "pedantic," but also a "Pestalozzian" system and a "Montessori" method. In mineralogy, besides the originally Arabic "amber" and the Greek "emery," we have "agate," "travertine," "granite," "lava," "tufa" and "pozzolana," "soda," "sodium," and "manganese." In geography, in addition to the originally Greek "archipelago" and "gulf," and the surveying instrument known as "stadia," we have "cape," "rivulet," "volcano," "grotto" and "lagoon." In zoology, Italian has given to English not only the Arabic "gazelle" and "giraffe," but also "buffalo," "parakeet" and "parrot," "popinjay" and "tarantula," "jackanapes" and "Leghorn" hen, while in botany the contributions range from Arabic "saffron" and "tamarind" and Turkish "bergamot" to "rosemary," "pimpernel," "palmetto," and "belladonna." In the physical sciences, "Torricellian," "marconigram," "galvanic" and "galvanize," "volt," "voltmeter," "voltage," and "megavolt" bear witness to Italian inventive genius.

The household is indebted to Italy for the Arabic "mattress" and "sofa," as well as the native Italian "credenza" of very recent importation; the businessman for his "desk"; the traveler for his "valise." Among articles of apparel we find "garb," "pants," "jeans," and those two indispensable articles in a land of sunshine and rain, the "parasol" and the "umbrella."

So far, classification has served us. But there is a host of words that defy attempts to catalogue them into definite fields. Some of them bear a purely Italian form, like "ghetto," "gusto," "imbroglio," "incognito." Others show signs of change, like "ditto" and "mustachio," or the more anglicized "mustache." Still others have taken on a thoroughly English form, like "attitude," "bagatelle," "bizarre" (originally derived from the mysterious language of the Basques), "brave," "brusque," "caprice" and "capricious," "carcass," "caress," "cascade," "chagrin," "disgrace" and "disgraceful," "dispatch," "fracas," "grandiose," "grotesque," "group," "guide," "isolate" (with "isolation" and "isolationist"), "jargon," "jealous" and "jealousy," "jovial," "pinion," "poltroon," "populace," "race," "rebuff," "scaffold," "schedule," "tirade," "cant," "caper," "gambol," "infuriate," and the Greek "scope."

Italian influence does not stop at mere words. It penetrates our tongue to the extent of giving it two productive suffixes, "-ade" and "-esque," as well as many phrases and expressions: *al fresco, in petto, poco a poco, mano a mano, dolce far niente.* The motto used by the State of Maryland reads: *Fatti maschi, parole femmine* ("Deeds are masculine, words feminine").

Italian influence does not stop at literary or even standard language. It penetrates the innermost recesses of colloquialism and slang, and contributes such expressions as the "bimbo" and "bambino" of sporting circles, and the ever-present "Boloney!" that Al Smith brought into vogue. The "Dear me!" that today is mildly colloquial is attributed to a corruption of Italian *"Dio mio!"*, and while there is no direct proof, such American expressions as "And how!" and "You're telling me!" sound suspiciously like literal translations of the far older Italian colloquialisms *"E come!"* and *"Lo dici a me?"*

Lastly, tribute must be paid to Italian influence in the field of proper and geographical names. "Fiorello," popularized by politics, appears as the title of a musical comedy. "Gina" and "Dino," to mention only two popular first names, have been popularized by screen and television. "Levant" and the "canton" of Switzerland are of Italian derivation. "Montenegro" is a literal Italian translation of Slavic *Crnagora*, "Black Mountain." "Venezuela" is a Spanish translation of "Little Venice." "Colombia" in South America is a tribute to the greatest of Italian navigators, like our own "Columbia" and the many cities named "Columbus." The very name of "America is Italian. There is a "Tontitown" in Arkansas, but within the borders of New York State itself we find "Rome," "Florence," "Venice," "Naples," "Milan," "Turin," "Genoa," "Ravena" (it should really be spelled "Ravenna"), "Modena," "Palermo," and "Syracuse," not to mention "Buffalo," which is an Italian word, though it has no counterpart city in Italy.

While this discussion is far from exhaustive, it points up the vast cultural and linguistic contributions made by medieval and modern Italy to Anglo-Saxon civilization.

CHAPTER 8

Contributions from Spanish

What role did the tongues of the Iberian peninsula play in the massive task of building up the vocabulary of a tongue that is probably richer in words than any other on earth, and that is, among the major languages of the world, the most thoroughly international in its word origins?

We must consider not merely words of originally Spanish and Portuguese stock, but also those which the Hispanic tongues themselves borrowed, first from Arabic, later from the American Indian languages with which the Portuguese navigators and the Spanish conquistadores were the first to come in contact, and which they later transmitted to English, either directly, or indirectly, through French or Italian. The sum total of these words justifies us in claiming that the Hispanic contribution to the English vocabulary is one of the most varied, abundant, and important.

In examining this massive word transfer, we must, however, realize that in contrast with the Scandinavian, French, Latin, and Greek loan words, which begin very early in history, the Hispanic contribution is a relative latecomer. Very few words of assured Hispanic origin appear during the Middle English period, and even the fifteenth century, which saw the discovery of America, has little to offer. The Hispanic tide really begins with the sixteenth century, continuing unabated through the seventeenth, diminishing in the eighteenth, then, in the nineteenth and twentieth, shifting its course from the homeland of English to the North American continent.

Secondly, many of the loan words we shall enumerate have question marks attached to them, indicating lack of agreement among authorities in the language field. Numerous words are described in-

67

differently as coming from the Spanish or from the Portuguese. In the case of others, notably words originally Arabic, there is some doubt whether they came directly into English, arrived in England via Spain, or passed from Arabic into French and Italian, and thence into English.

To exemplify both points: "hazard" is a word that first appears in English during the Middle English period, that is to say, before 1400. There is no doubt as to its Arabic origin (*al zahr* or *azzahr*, "the die," of which the plural is "dice" that serve for gambling purposes). According to some authorities, it came into English through Spanish, according to others through French. On the other hand, authorities are agreed that "almanac," also a word of Arabic origin first appearing in English during the Middle English period, came through Spanish. Other early borrowings from Spanish are "jennet" (derived from *jinete*), which first appears in 1463, and "marmalade," which some consider of Spanish, others of Portuguese, origin (*marmelo*, "quince," is common to both languages), first appearing in 1480.

It was no doubt the contact born of rivalry in the voyages of discovery and exploration that opened up the dikes and permitted words of Hispanic origin to flood the English-speaking world. Since this period extended through the sixteenth and seventeenth centuries, it is here that the majority of our Hispanic words is concentrated, with a noticeable dwindling in the eighteenth century and a new peak achieved in the nineteenth by reason of the American settling of the West and the extensive contacts between speakers of American English and speakers of Mexican Spanish which that historical era brought in its wake.

As for the nature of the borrowings, it would be extremely difficult to assign them as a whole to any specific category. It cannot in any way be said that they favor one sphere of human activity over another. It is, of course, possible to classify some of them. Bullfighting, for instance, is peculiarly a Hispanic activity, and its vocabulary has been heavily drawn upon in direct rather than translated form. Hence, English dictionaries contain such words as *corrida*, *torero* (or "toreador"), *picador*, *matador*, *espada*, *banderilla*, and even a recent borrowing, *aficionado*, which in some intellectual American circles replaces the native "fan" (a cut-down form of "fanatic"), not merely in the sense of one who regularly attends bullfights, but with the more generic meaning of one who is fond of any given activity (an "aficionado" of the prize ring, or even an "aficionado" of painting).

In like manner, there are certain forms of entertainment, particularly music and the dance, which by reason of their Spanish origin retain their Spanish form in English. *Fiesta* is a term known to all English speakers. Even more general, though somewhat disguised, is "parade," from Spanish *parada*. "Castanets" are Spanish. So are such dances as the "fandango," the "bolero," the "seguidilla," the "flamenco" style of dancing, even the "conga" (which Cuban Spanish adopted from the name of the African country Congo), and the "saraband." English musical terms are for the most part taken from Italian. Italian itself, however, took the name of one musical form from the Spanish *pasacalle* and italianized it into *passacaglia*, and it is in this form that English finally appropriated it in 1659 (the etymological meaning is "a song that passes through the street," a "street song").

Certain titles and forms of address are thoroughly Spanish, yet appear in all English dictionaries. *Señor, señora, señorita, caballero, don, doña* (with its variant *dueña*, which in English assumes the antiquated spelling "duenna"), even *hidalgo* (a late sixteenth-century borrowing) are familiar to most English speakers, and Webster's Collegiate Dictionary goes so far as to list *gracias*.

Some of our terms refer to articles of attire, and here begins a double division which accompanies us through most of our categories. Certain words are used in English, but only with reference to articles worn in Spain or in Spanish-speaking countries (*mantilla, sombrero, serape*, even the sixteenth-century *sanbenito* are in this class); others, like the "morion," which was borrowed in 1554, have thoroughly lost their Hispanic connotation and denote an object which acquired complete citizenship in the English-speaking world. Similarly, we find coins like the *real*, "doubloon," *peso*, and *peseta*, which are obviously Hispanic, but we also find a metal like "platinum," which few English speakers will connect with its true origin, the Spanish *plata*, "silver."

Most political, military, and historical terms that have come to

English from Spanish reveal themselves by their form or use (*alcalde, armada, caudillo, infanta, junta, camarilla, Cortes, Carlist, insurrecto, incommunicado, presidio, ley de fuga,* even the *Rurales* of Mexico, the *Guardia Civil* and *Carabineros* of Spain and the *vigilantes* of the old Southwest); some, however, have come into such common use that their Spanish form is, if not forgotten, overlooked; such is the case with *guerrilla*. Others have acquired an English or French form which effectively disguises them ("squad," "squadron," "escadrille," and "filibuster," which represents an originally Dutch *vrijbuiter*, "freebooter," acquired by Spanish as *filibustero*, then passed on to English). A word like *cinchona* represents a proper name, that of Cinchón, a Spanish governor of Peru in the seventeenth century. English even has a word that distinguishes itself as Spanish or Portuguese by the shift of a single vowel (*auto de fé, auto da fé*). One recent and curious loan translation from Spanish is "fifth column," a rendering of the *quinta columna* of General Mola as he advanced upon Madrid with four columns, boasting that he had a fifth one working for him within the city.

One of the most productive sources of borrowings from Spanish is the food field. Here we have on the one hand a series of originally Spanish dishes and items with which English speakers have become acquainted (*cocido, paella, arroz con pollo, puchero, tortilla, frijoles, fritos, vanilla*; particularly interesting is the English "olla" or "olio," which goes back to the Spanish *olla podrida*, first appearing in English in 1622). On the other hand, there is a whole array of foods originating with the American Indians, brought by the Spanish explorers to Europe, then passed on to English. Taino, an Indian tongue of the Antilles, seems originally responsible for "potato," "maize," and "barbecue," as well as "tobacco," which is not properly a food; the Nahuatl of Mexico, through Spanish, brought to English "chocolate," "tomato," "tamale," and "cacao"; "tapioca" seems to come from the Tupi-Guaraní of Paraguay; doubt attaches to many other food names, such as "banana," "pompano," and the fruit appearing variously in English as "papaya" and "pawpaw." "Tabasco" sauce seems to owe its name to a Mexican locality. Some doubt attaches to "anchovy," which could be either Spanish or Portuguese, and to "nougat" and "caramel," which some authorities ascribe to Spanish, others to Provençal. There are names of wines and other alcoholic and non-alcoholic drinks, like "sherry" (from Jerez de la Frontera), which first appears in English in 1608, the *manzanilla, alicante,* and *amontillado* of Spain; the *pulque, tequila,* and *mescal* of Mexico; the "sarsaparilla" that goes back to 1577. One very recent addition is *sangría,* the cooling drink made of red wine from Rioja, sliced fruits, sparkling water, and ice.

English has taken from Spanish a certain number of literary terms ("quixotic," "picaresque," "Gongorism"; *bodega* is partly literary, from the novel by Ibáñez, partly directly derived from Hispanic grocery stores in American cities); names of literary characters ("Sancho Panza," "Rocinante," "Don Juan," "The Cid"); even items of linguistic terminology, like *tilde, cedilla* and *Ladino.* There are geographical expressions, such as *llano, pampa* (originally Quechuan), *arroyo, cañón,* which is modified into "canyon." There are names from the animal world, like "alligator" (*el lagarto*), "cockroach" (*cucaracha*), "mosquito" (appearing in the sixteenth century in such varicolored forms as *muskite, muskito, muscato,* and *moscheto*).

There are words current in the American Southern states, though they are not nearly so numerous as those of the West. "Quadroon," for example, represents a Spanish *cuarterón.* "Creole," first appearing in 1604, is the Spanish *criollo.* "Key" in the sense of "island" (Key West, or Cayo Hueso) is originally a Taino Indian word, disguised to resemble a common English term. "Pickaninny" is variously ascribed to Spanish (*pequeño niño*) or to Portuguese (*pequenino*). There is the "cannibal" which represents Columbus' *caríbal,* a Carib Indian. There is the "bagasse" which seems to represent a Spanish *bagazo,* though the form is French. There is the "gringo" which is used as a popular slang term for an American in some Spanish-speaking countries (it is said to come from the opening line of a song sung by American troops during the war with Mexico, "Green grows the grass"). There is the "lagniappe" which some authorities claim is Louisiana French, while others describe it as coming from *la ñape,* an originally Quichua term appropriated by the Spaniards in South America.

Many English terms that are Spanish in origin are so cleverly disguised in the borrowing process that it takes considerable research to unscramble their source. "Jerked beef," for instance, sounds very English; yet the "jerked" is the Quichua *charquí*, passed on by Spanish, and not at all from English "jerk." "Buckaroo" represents an originally Spanish *vaquero*, which itself appears in the English dictionaries. "Calaboose" and "hoosegow" are Western adaptations of *calabozo* and *juzgado*. "Lariat" is *la reata*, displaying the ancient phenomenon of the article telescoped into the noun. There are such Western vulgarisms as "savvy" (*sabe*), "vamoose" (*vamos*), and probably, from a cut-down version of the latter, even "mosey." "Horse wrangler" is said to take its second word from a Spanish *caballerango*, but the difficulty here is that one cannot find the Spanish word in Spanish dictionaries, even of a comprehensive variety. One word that shows wide migrations is the slang "wop" by which an Italian is occasionally designated in American English. This seems to be an English adaptation of *guappo*, which in the language of the Neapolitan underworld means "fine," "handsome," "brave." The Neapolitan word itself, however, is a borrowing from the Spanish *guapo*, of obscure but probably Germanic origin.

"Negro" is an English borrowing, either from Spanish or Portuguese (it first appears in English in 1555). With it go a host of other words that retain their Spanish spelling and, to some extent, their Spanish pronunciation: *embargo, siesta, Hispano* and *Hispanidad, plaza, yerba, padre, casa*. U.S. Western contacts probably bring into English such words as *esparto, peón, hacienda, rodeo, burro, loco, corral, desperado, mesquite, chaparral, bronco, mesa, tornado, patio, sierra, adobe, bonanza, vigilante, poco, pronto, hombre, machete, pinto, chaparejos* (or *chaps*), even picturesque expressions like *mañana* and *quien sabe*. A "placer" mine, though it sounds as though it came from the English verb "place," goes back to Spanish *placer*. "Stampede" is *estampida*, "cinch" and "chinch" are *cincha* and *chinche*. "Lasso" is *lazo*, and "mustang" is *mesteño*.

There seems to be no doubt about the Spanish origin of "cask" (*casco*), "cigar" (even though the suffix of "cigarette" is French), "risk" (a word that Spanish took from Greek), "sassafras," "carapace" (*carapacho*), "ladrone." There is doubt about such words as "capstan," "caparison," "caravel," "contraband," "emery," "paragon," "romance," and "savanna" (the last seems to come from a Taino Indian word which merges, by reason of similarity of form, with Spanish *sábana,* while the others are variously attributed to French, Provençal, and Italian, as well as to Spanish).

It has already been stated that Spanish passes on to English many words that it takes from American Indian languages and from Arabic. There are even a couple of Basque words, like "bizarre" and "vega." Among the Indian words are the Carib "canoe," the Taino "hurricane," the Arawak "hammock," the Nahuatl "coyote," the Tupi "jaguar," the Araucanian "poncho," the Quichua "quinine," "alpaca," "llama," and "vicuña."

Arabic, that great source of additions to the peninsular vocabularies, presents the difficulty of determining whether its words were passed on to English by Spanish or by other Mediterranean languages, such as French or Italian. Among the doubtful words over which authorities clash are the early "jar" (it first appears in English in 1592), "alcohol," "algebra," "alkali," "caliber," "magazine" (Arabic *makhzan* would seem to oppose the theory of borrowing through Spanish *almacén,* which carries the Arabic article). Among words of Arabic stock for which there is little or no doubt concerning Spanish transmission we have "carafe," "alcove," "tariff," "tamarind," "alcazar," "algarroba," "alkanet," the previously mentioned "almanac," and the "alforja" which first appears in English in the form "alforge" in 1611. "Popinjay" is a Middle English word, and if some of our authorities are correct, it comes from *papagayo.* Some of these migrating words have picturesque histories. "Bizarre," for instance, means "strange" or "queer" in English, as it does in modern Spanish, but the earlier Spanish meaning was "strong," "manly," and the Basque original means "beard"; this gives us a curious parallel with the Rumanian word for "man," *bărbat,* which goes back to Latin *barbatus,* "bearded" (a beard is characteristic of a man, and a man is manly and strong, even to the point of being queer). *Alcázar,* despite the fact that it comes from Arabic and has a decidedly Arabic appearance, is not at all Moorish in origin; the Arabs borrowed the Latin *castrum,* "camp" or "fort," and turned it into *kasr,* prefixing their article *al-*; in Palermo, Sicily, there is a seafront drive called *il Cassaro,* which shows the Arabic *kasr,* borrowed from the Latin *castrum,* without the prefixed article. *Alcázar* appears in English, incidentally, as far back as 1615.

The borrowing process does not limit itself to mere words. There are suffixes which are occasionally taken over from one language into another, and a few of them become productive of new words in the borrowing language. Such is the case, for instance, with the ending -*ería*, which originally came into English through *cafetería*. This suffix became so popular in English as an indication of the fact that the customer serves himself that it was attached to words having no connection with Spanish, such as "booketeria" and "valeteria." Other suffixes are perhaps not productive in the new language, but appear in a sufficient number of borrowed words to warrant separate discussion in a complete English dictionary. This is the case with the -*illa* of "guerrilla," "camarilla," "mantilla," "seguidilla," "cedilla," "vanilla," "sarsaparilla," etc., along with its French modification -*ille* of "escadrille," "quadrille," and the masculine form that appears in "Negrillo." It may be said for both -*eria* and -*illa* that they are aided and abetted by identical suffixes from languages kindred to Spanish (Italian -*eria* of "pizzeria," Latin -*illa* of "Camilla" and "Priscilla"). Where a Spanish suffix does not obtain such international cooperation, its extension is limited to personal and place names (the -*ito*, -*ita* of "mosquito," "bonito," "Negrito," "manzanita," for example, goes on to such names as "Juanito," "Juanita," "Anita," "Bonita," but it could plausibly be argued that these personal names are independently borrowed and do not represent an English extension of a Spanish suffix).

This brings us to the matter of personal and place names. The former include family names of a historical variety that have become household words in the English-speaking world, names of painters like Velázquez and El Greco (the latter, however, is a combination of the Spanish article with the Italian form of the national adjective); of explorers like Cortés, Pizarro, Coronado, Ponce de León, de Soto (or was he a Portuguese de Souto?), even a nickname like Cabeza de Vaca; of statesmen and leaders like Bolívar, Martí, Villa, Alemán, Franco, Castro; even of chess players like Capablanca. They also include widely used personal names of Spanish origin (Inez, Dolores and its diminutive Lola, Ferdinand, Elvira, Alphonse (or

Alfonso, or Alonso), Mercedes, Carmen, Consuelo, Mona, Linda, along with Spanish forms of names that have an English equivalent but are occasionally used in the English-speaking world (Carlos, Juan, Diego or Jaime, Francisco, José, Pablo, Pedro, Miguel, Guillermo).

Place names are of different varieties. There are those that give rise to names of objects ("granadine," from Granada, or "majolica," which is an Italian adaptation of Mallorca, but comes into English as early as 1555). Others are simply attached to names of articles as adjectives to indicate derivation ("Castile" soap, "Cordovan" leather, "Toledo" blade; the last, after its initial appearance in 1598, was often used in the form "Toledo" alone, with the blade understood).

Next we have Spanish place names from outside English-speaking areas that are so familiar to English speakers that even their meanings are known: Tierra del Fuego, Valparaíso, Vera Cruz, Venezuela ("little Venice," because the natives dwelt in houses erected on stilts over the water, reminding the Spanish explorers of the canals of Venice). All English-language geographies indicate the Sargasso Sea, whose name is Spanish, and the Ladrones Islands, so named by Spanish navigators who found the natives inclined to steal. Corregidor is in the Philippines, but Americans have reason to remember it.

But far more widespread is the use of Spanish names in those areas of the United States that were long subject to Spanish influence, such as New Mexico and Arizona. Alamo, Los Alamos, Alamogordo are widely scattered U.S. place names, and even "alameda" is accepted as a common noun by American dictionaries. We have names of states, like Florida, California, Nevada, possibly Montana; rivers, like the Perdido of Florida, the Cimarrón of Oklahoma, the Brazos of Texas (its full name is Brazos de Dios, "Arms of God"); mountain ranges, like the Sierra Nevada, Sierra Madre, and Sangre de Cristo; cities, like Las Vegas, Sacramento, Santa Fe, Las Cruces, Los Angeles, San Diego, Santa Barbara, San Francisco, San Luis Obispo, and others far too numerous to mention (note also the adjectives *Angeleño* and *Barbareño,* used in local English to denote inhabitants of Los Angeles and Santa Barbara); coastal spots, like the former Cape Canaveral, Boca Grande, and Boca Ratón, all in Florida; islands like Key West (a corruption of Cayo Hueso, as has been stated) and all the other Florida "keys," as well as Catalina in California; translated names, like St. Augustine, even names of imaginary localities, like Eldorado. There is a Mount Diablo in California. New Mexico, where Spanish is still one of the two official languages of the State Legislature, boasts such place names as Gallina, Algodones, Servilleta, Quemado, Rincón. There is even an Elsinore which comes not from Hamlet's castle in Denmark, but from El Señor. Picturesque to the point of being amusing are the names bestowed upon three dangerous rocks along the coast of Alaska, one of the most recent American states, by the Spanish explorers who first charted those waters: Abreojo, Alárgate, and Quita Sueño ("Open your eyes," "Get away," and "Stop sleeping").

What of the sister language of Spanish, Portuguese, and its contributions to English? We have already seen that many English borrowings leave the experts in doubt as to whether they come from one of the Hispanic languages or from the other. Among English borrowings from Portuguese concerning which there is agreement are such words as "albino," "aril," "apricot," "bayadere" (*bailadera*), "fetish" (from *feitiço*), "mandarin," "albacore," "maraca," "carioca," "caste," "mango" (taken by Portuguese from the Tamil of India), "junk" (in the sense of a Chinese sailboat), "joss" (this represents the Portuguese *Deus*), and even the Zulu throwing spear called *assegai*, which represents a Portuguese form (*azagaia*) of a word originally taken from the Berber of North Africa.

This description of Spanish influence upon English would hardly be complete without some reference to the mixed languages that grow up in regions where the speakers of Spanish and English intermingle. In Cárdenas, Cuba, are families that came from the United States generations ago, settled down, and became Cuban citizens. One of them still writes its name as Jones, but pronounces it Spanish fashion, so that in English transcription is appears as HAW-nays. It is well known that the Puerto Rican settlements in New York have adopted and adapted many English words from their new environment (*champú, fanfurria, estor,* and *marqueta,* for instance, represent the English "shampoo," "frankfurter," "store," and "market," though why the last two should have been necessary in the face of Spanish *tienda* or *bodega,* and *mercado* is a little mysterious).

It is particularly along the U.S.-Mexican border, however, that a mixed language called *Pochismo* has developed. New Mexican Spanish tends to be conservative of old Spanish forms, so that words like *agora, naidien, trujo,* and *escrebir* are still heard. What it has borrowed from English, however, is far more colorful: *lonchi, blofero, grimbaque, jatqueque, esteque, olraite, jamachi,* and *charape* are described by Mencken in his *The American Language* as being what borderline speakers have done to English "lunch," "bluffer," "greenback," "hot cake," "steak," "all right," "how much," and "shut up."

In this fruitful interchange and cooperation of the languages, is there not a lesson for what concerns the interchange and cooperation of the people that speak them?

PART TWO

Language Curios and Language Problems

Language Curios
and Language Problems

The linguists have coined the term "paralinguistics" to betoken all those things which, though not truly part of language, nevertheless carry meaning—gestures, inflections of the voice, coughing, giggling, sneering, smiling, bodily postures, movements of the eyes and facial muscles.

In addition to paralinguistics, there are other semantic elements which are difficult to classify, but which round out the total picture of human expression. By what words or other means shall you convey to your interlocutors of different language backgrounds that your attitude toward them is one of politeness and courtesy? Conversely, how may you successfully insult them?

Are there words, forms, pronunciations, attitudes which give you away, and reveal to the person you are speaking to what you would perhaps wish to conceal? Do names have psychological values that transcend those of mere numbers, such as appear on your Social Security or credit card? Do colors have a symbolism, and is it universal? Religion plays an important part in the lives of most of us, but does it have a symbolic language of its own?

The geographical distribution of languages is always a fascinating theme. What languages are you likely to encounter in any given area, be it a huge one, like the Western Hemisphere south of the Rio Grande, or a relatively small one, like Manhattan Island?

We strive for realism in many fields—literature, art, music, stage, screen. Should we strive for realism in language in connection with any and all of these? Or should we supinely accept a version in the language that is accessible to us as the symbolic representative of the one actually used in real life?

These issues may not be as important as those of good usage or accurate translation, which is perhaps why they are so seldom mentioned in the linguistic manuals. But they are undoubtedly part of the general semantic picture, and I propose to discuss them, even if they can't be solved.

CHAPTER 9

How to Be Impolite in Twenty-seven Languages

According to one story, the trouble began in the later days of the Roman Empire, when there got to be two emperors, one in Rome, the other in Constantinople. Until then, there had been only one way of addressing a single person—*tu*, corresponding to our archaic "thou." Republican Rome used *tu*, whether to a consul or a slave; *vos*, like Bible English "ye," was used only in speaking to more than one person.

But with the two emperors, a curious custom arose. People addressing the Emperor in Rome began to use the plural *vos*, on the theory that they were really addressing both rulers. At that point our "polite" difficulties began. Those wishing to flatter men with imperial ambitions, or even petty officials, started addressing them in the plural. Barbarian chieftains, pouring into the Empire after Rome's fall, demanded imperial honors for themselves. Soon anybody of any consequence was *vos*. The polite address vogue arose in every language that came into being out of Latin or was influenced by it. Today most Western languages have at least two forms of address: one reserved for the family, intimate friends, children, pets; the other for formal use, in speaking with reserve, deference, politeness, or merely addressing a stranger. The use of the wrong form marks you as a boor.

English has always distinguished itself by being practical. It wavered for a time between "thou," "thee" and "ye," "you," in dealing with one person. Then "you" got the upper hand and soon became the sole form of address except among Quakers and in a few dialects of England. Only those who have started out with a lan-

83

guage which required them to decide at what point of acquaintance-ship it is safe to drop the formal and assume the familiar can realize what this means in the way of putting you at your ease.

Take, for instance, the case of the Italian judge who found himself faced with a man of decent and cultured appearance who was ac-cused of theft. To address him with the familiar *tu* would have been brutally humiliating; the intermediate *voi*, generally used to servants, would have had a touch of condescension; the fully polite *Lei* was too much for a man accused of a common crime. The judge tried to solve the puzzle by avoiding all three. "So, it seems we have stolen a watch," he said to the culprit. "Perhaps *you* have, Your Honor," came the haughty reply; "*I* certainly haven't!"

Interestingly enough, Esperanto, a scientifically constructed arti-ficial language spoken by several million internationalists, follows the comfortable English usage with a single form of address, *vi*, for both familiar and polite duty. But in one respect English and Esperanto have a disadvantage in the lack of distinction between the singular and the plural "you." Southerners try to remedy this by using "you-all" when addressing more than one person, and some Easterners by using a plural "youse." Neither usage, however, has official sanction.

Most other languages do not suffer from this disability. They suffer from, if anything, a super-abundance—what the French would call "an embarrassment of choice."

French has the familiar singular *tu,* and a *vous* which can be either a plural or a polite singular. There is a word in French, *tutoyer,* which means "to thou and thee somebody," to address some-one familiarly. To use the form when you shouldn't is a fairly grave breach of etiquette, and some of our most recent French grammars for beginners try avoid the pitfall by eliminating the familiar form altogether; but for an American doughboy to address his comrade-at-arms *politely* would be almost as grave an impropriety, and might lead to his being classified as a snob.

However, French usage is simple when compared with that of the other Latin tongues, in which the discriminating process has gone much farther. Italian, Spanish, and Portuguese all came, at various times, to the realization that the mere plural "'you" had become so widespread as to lose its polite force, whereupon they went to work to remedy the situation.

Italian developed such expressions as *Vostra Signoria* ("Your Lordship") and *Vostra Eccellenza* ("Your Excellency"). These expressions called, naturally enough, for the third person singular of the verb (like English "Your Honor *is* mistaken; I was going only thirty miles an hour"). But they were long and cumbersome. First they were contracted to *Vossia, Voscenza* (words which greeted the first GIs to land in Sicily, where they are still used); then it was deemed best to eliminate them altogether and replace them with a pronoun. But the nouns "Lordship" and "Excellency" in Italian are feminine. So the pronoun used to replace them was *Lei,* "she." The result is that today the fully polite way of saying, even to a man, "You are very kind" is "She is very kind." This is a bit bewildering when you are speaking to a six-foot *carabiniere,* but there's no help for it, and he cheerfully replies in kind.

The Fascist regime, impelled perhaps by an uncomfortable feeling of effeminacy in this matter of "she," tried to decree its abolition and a return to the older *voi.* The Italians smiled, used *voi* in their official correspondence, and kept right on using *Lei* in their conversations. The habit of politeness was too ingrained.

Not all Italians are cultured enough to be polite, however. Some jumble up their three forms of address, without apparent rhyme or reason. In Naples and among the aristocracy, *voi* is the polite form. In the heel of the Italian boot, strangely enough, it is *tu.* An army officer was once trying to break local conscripts of the habit; they innocently argued, "Nothing can be more respectful than *tu;* it's what we use when speaking to God."

In Spanish, the old plural *vos* was used as a polite form down to the time of Columbus and beyond (it is still in current use in some South American countries). Then, like the Italians, the Spaniards decided to go super-polite. The forms evolved were *Vuestra Merced* ("Your Grace") and *Vuestras Mercedes* ("Your Graces"). Here again there was a contraction to *usted, ustedes.* A great many Spanish speakers carry the process on to the point of using nothing but *ustedes* in the plural. It sounds a bit funny to hear a mother, who would address any one of her children individually as *tú,* saying to them collectively, in effect, "Your Graces have been very naughty today, and consequently Your Graces will go to bed without their suppers."

Expressiveness is added to Spanish by a sudden shift from *tú* to *usted*. Bosom friends, if they happen to quarrel, will switch to the polite form, which conveys a subtle shade of bitterness and irony. Portuguese advanced one more step, which is reminiscent of congressional usage: "the gentleman (*o senhor*), "the lady" (*a senhora*), "the young lady" (*a menina, a senhorinha*). "Does the gentleman speak Portuguese?" is the way you will be addressed in Lisbon or Rio.

Among the Teutonic languages, German and Danish, after using a plural "you," moved on to "they" as a polite form, even when speaking to a single person. Swedish, more rugged, retains "you." Dutch has a whole welter of forms, of which the most polite is *U*.

Russian has "thou" and "you," from the days of the czars. When the Soviets got into power, they made no attempt to abolish the polite "you," as might have been expected. They did, however, concentrate on the old "sir" and "madam." What you get today is "comrade," "citizen," "citizeness," but with a polite "you." The same thing happened, by the way, in France at the time of the Revolution, but it didn't last long. The French were too fond of their *Monsieur, Madame,* and *Mademoiselle* to give them up permanently.

Czech and Serbo-Croatian, like Russian, have "thou" and "you," though in Czech there used to be an old polite "they," built up under German influence but later discarded. Polish is without doubt the most polite of the Slavic languages. *Pan* ("sir"), *pani* ("madam"), *panna* ("miss") are used at the slightest provocation. "Has Sir some roast chicken?" says the customer to the restaurant waiter. And the reply is: "We have, may it please Sir."

Hungarian has a familiar "thou" and two polite forms (*ön* and *maga*), and the game is for would-be speakers of Hungarian to decide which one to use. Rumanian likewise has a familiar "thou" and two polite forms, *Dumnea-ta* ("Thy Lordship") and *Dumnea-voastră* ("Your Lordship"), and the choice between them is not easy.

Some oriental languages have peculiar distinctions. Arabic uses a different "you" according to the sex of the person addressed. Extraordinary effects can be obtained by using the wrong gender. A teacher in an Arab country relates that on one occasion his pupils had grossly violated the rules and knew they deserved summary and severe punishment. He calmly addressed them for ten minutes in the feminine, till they visibly wilted and begged for anything but that.

Persian and Malay show respect by using the plural for the singular "you"; Hindustani has a super-polite "they" which reminds us of German; Siamese shows politeness by using "slave" for "I."

Not too much in the way of polite forms of address appears in Chinese, though "he" is sometimes respectfully used for "you." Japanese on the other hand, has a familiar, a polite, and a super-polite or honorific way of speaking. The last must be used with circumspection, for it may, on occasion, denote sarcasm. The story goes that when a German military mission visited Tokyo, the Japs did not like the crudeness of the Nazis, and the cruder the latter became the more the Japs turned on the honorifics. By the time the visitors left, the super-honorific *gozaimasu* was echoing and re-echoing in their ears.

In addition, the Japanese verb is impersonal, which means that instead of saying "I am going," "you are going," "he is going," a form is used which really means "there is a going," with who does the going left generally to the hearer's intelligence. The oversensitive Japs are offended by Western insistence upon *who* does the action.

In most of the languages using a polite "you," it is customary to capitalize the "you" in writing. "I," on the other hand, is capitalized only in English. Foreigners accuse English speakers of egotism when they see "you" spelled with a small letter and "I" with a capital.

Forms of address make up only a fraction of the possibilities of impoliteness. You can use the correct form and still violate a "formula." "I want," which we use with rather brutal frankness, is shunned in most languages; "I should like" is preferred. In Spanish, you must be especially careful not to say "I want you," because the same word is used for "want" and "love." "Give me" sounds a bit crude and grasping in some tongues; Italian prefers to say "Favor me with."

If you are speaking of a person's close relatives, it is better in Latin countries to prefix "Mr.," "Mrs.," or "Miss" to the relationship: *Mon-*

sieur votre père, "Mr. your father." In this regard, Japanese goes to extremes, using entirely different words according as the relative is mine or yours.

German adds the word *schön*, "beautifully," to "thank you" or "please," making a "pretty please" out of the latter and using it regularly in the sense of "Don't mention it."

The Poles, with their customary politeness, have a hyperbolic formula for asking a lady her name: "*Jak Pani godność?*" which literally means "How is Your Ladyship?" An American traveler who knew some, but not enough, Polish, on being asked this question at the customs house, innocently replied: "Very well, thank you."

Arabic, which shares with Hebrew the beautiful salutation "Peace be unto you!" (to which the equally poetic reply is "And unto you be peace!"), also has a formula to be used by unexpected male visitors when entering a house. It is *taghattu*, "cover up," and serves as a warning to the ladies of the household that they must veil their faces. Neglect of this may lead to dire consequences.

The most elaborate formulas of politeness are to be found, of course, in Japanese. They include the hiss or sucking in of the breath which greets you when you are introduced, and the *o* (incorrectly translated as "honorable") which is placed before names of inanimate objects. *O mizu kudasai* does not mean "bring the honorable water," but rather "you, honorable person, bring the water."

A friend of mine who resided for ten years in Japan describes one of his early *gaffes* in the following words: "The first time I was invited to dinner at a fine Japanese home, the lady of the house, at the end of the meal, uttered the customary formula to the effect that it was a very wretched meal to have been offered to so honorable a guest. There is, of course, an appropriate reply to the effect that the humble guest is honored by the gorgeous meal. But with my then limited knowledge of Japanese, I uttered one phrase I did know, which fitted most occasions: '*sayō de gozaimasu*,' which in good American means 'It sure was!' I shall never forget the amazed expression on the good lady's face."

Chinese, which does not sin too much on the polite side, has some negative formulas which amount practically to taboos. It is the height of impoliteness, for example, for a son to use the second character of his father's given name, or for a subject to use the characters in his sovereign's name.

Ludicrous indeed are the effects that can be obtained with words having a similar sound in two different languages. A missionary to Malaya had a son named Bobby. He soon noticed that the Malay children avoided Bobby as though he had the plague. A little investigation revealed that "Bobby" sounded like *babi*, which is Malay for "pig." The Malays are Mohammedans, and abhor the pig; to call one a pig in a Mohammedan country is the most deadly of insults. The Malay children figured that anyone whom his own parents would call "pig" was unfit to associate with. Bobby straightaway became Robert, and the ostracism ceased.

There is a long list of harmless English words which have practically the same sound as Hungarian words that are not so innocent. Do not use these words within hearing range of a Hungarian if you can possibly help it: "bus," "fuss," "pitch," "boss," "pin," "huge," "closet," "toy." They have somewhat the same effect as the "Amgot" which our Administration had to relinquish as the name of one of its overseas agencies because of its connotation in Turkish.

Then there are words which seem to be good translations, but are not. When I first began to attend an American school at the age of seven I was asked why I had been absent one day. The teacher smiled, the whole class giggled, and I wondered why when I replied that I had been constipated. In the Latin languages "to be constipated" means to have a cold in the head. A Mexican song about a guitar-playing Romeo who urges his ladylove to come out on the balcony has the maiden replying: "No; if I come out into the night air the wind will give me a cold." These simple words, in their Spanish version, always draw howls of laughter from American listeners who know some Spanish. They are: *"Si salgo yo, me van los céfiros a constipar."*

Don't say "No thanks; I'm full" to your hostess in France when she offers you a second helping; "to be full" has in French the same slang meaning as "to be soused" in English. And don't say, as an army chaplain did, *"Que Dieu vous préserve!"* for "May God preserve you!" for *préserver* means "to pickle."

Spanish is a language of pitfalls which work both ways. "I can't come out with you tonight; I'm compromised," said a *señorita* to a doughboy. He opened his eyes wide, but all she was trying to say was that she had a previous engagement (*comprometida*). Another ludicrous situation arose when a young lady from Cuba remarked that she had dreamed with a certain man of her acquaintance the night before; English says "to dream of," but Spanish uses "to dream with." On the other hand, an American woman relating an experience to Spanish-speaking friends drew polite and half-covered snickers when she said *"estuve muy embarazada."* She means she was greatly embarrassed; but *embarazada* also means pregnant.

Then there are what might be described as "dictionary blunders." You look up a word in the dictionary, find half a dozen foreign equivalents for it, and pick out one at random. A young man writing a letter in what he thought was Swedish to a lady of his acquaintance searched for "dear" for his opening line and drew *älskling*. He wondered why she never answered him; *älskling* is *the* word between lovers.

There is one last way to insult foreigners, and that is to affiliate them with racial or national groups other than their own. Hungarians foam at the mouth when they hear themselves described as "Slavs" or their language as "one of the Slavic tongues." Some Bulgarians feel the same way. "Call us Turks, Tartars, Mongols, but not Slavs!" was the way a Bulgarian statesman protested to some western European diplomats who had suggested that the Bulgars might get together with their "fellow Slavs," the Serbs. The Slovaks like to hold themselves and their language aloof from the Czechs, though there is about as much difference between Czech and Slovak as between General American and the King's English.

The Danes and the Norwegians once used the same literary language; then the Norwegians developed a written tongue of their own out of their local dialects; today they feel quite touchy about being linguistically lumped with the Danes. When writing a book on languages I submitted the Norwegian section to a native. He discovered that I had unwittingly used a Danish form. "This is Danish, and the Danes can keep it!" was the indignant annotation I received.

The Portuguese-speaking Brazilians are a polite but haughty people. If there is one thing that burns them up it is to see themselves referred to as "Spanish-speaking."

English is definitely among the languages in which you can be insulting. There are local taboos as in Chinese ("bloody" is one), which are definitely "out" in some sections of the English-speaking world. There are flippant local expressions which may not be well received in other sections, like the Canadian "gridiron" for "Old Glory," "rebel picnic" for "the glorious Fourth," "unbleached American" for "colored person," "improved Britisher" for an Englishman who has resided some time in the Dominion. Some of our grosser terms for referring to foreigners of various nationalities are well known ("Dago," "Wop," "Greaser," "Kike," "Polack," "Bohunk," etc.). They have counterparts in other English-speaking countries: Australia uses "Dingbat" for Italian, "Pommie" for Englishman, "Chow" for Chinese, and New Zealand has "homey" for Englishman. In the case of certain terms ("Chinaman" for "Chinese," or uncapitalized "Negro") the insulting connotation is so illogical as to place the offending word in the taboo class.

Is there a way of not being unwittingly impolite? There is, but it's a hard one. Don't speak.

CHAPTER 10

Betraying Words

During the Second World War, immigration authorities had their hands full preventing American and Canadian draft-dodgers from losing themselves on opposite sides of the border. They looked, dressed, and talked alike—with one small difference. American schools teach the last letter of the alphabet as "zee"; British and Canadians say "zed." When suspects were asked to recite the alphabet, this was their undoing.

Similarly, on the other side of the world, another language test was being applied by MacArthur's men in the Philippines, where Japanese infiltrators, posing as Chinese or Filipinos, were trying to penetrate the defenses of Bataan and Corregidor. Suspects would be asked to pronounce "hula-hula." Chinese and Filipinos have no difficulty pronouncing *l*, but Japanese have no *l* in their language, and when faced with a word containing it in a foreign language, they use the sound closest to it, *r*. Unable to pronounce *l*, the Japanese said "hura-hura" and thereby spelled their own death sentence.

These were repetitions of a historic method of telling foe from friend. An ancient case occurs in the Book of Judges, where the Gileadites, at war with the Ephraimites, a kindred Semitic people speaking an almost identical language, had routed their foes, then trapped them at a ford. But here they found it difficult to identify their enemies from their own men, the language and dress of the opposing forces being about the same. A wise leader hit upon the trick of making every suspected person pronounce the expression for "ear of corn," which in the speech of the Gileadites was *shibboleth*, in that of the Ephraimites *sibboleth*. Those who pronounced the *sh* correctly were allowed to cross; those who used *s* instead of *sh* were forthwith put to death.

Several other historical instances of language "shibboleths" are on record. In the thirteenth century, the French under Charles of Anjou had occupied Sicily. Their highhanded methods aroused the Sicilians to revolt, and a massacre of the French ensued. It was known as the "Sicilian Vespers" because the church bells tolled vespers as a signal for the outbreak. The French had been in control of the island for many years, and many of them had acquired the Sicilian brand of Italian well enough to pass for natives. But there is one sound of Italian which a Frenchman practically never acquires to perfection, the sound of *ch*. He tends to use *sh* instead. When faced with doubtful cases, the Sicilians compelled suspects to say "*Cicero Ceci.*" If it came out "Cheechero Chechee," all was well; but "Sheeshero She-shee" branded the speaker as a hated Frenchman, to his undoing.

In the nineteenth century there was a war between the Turks and the Egyptians. The latter, headed by Ibrahim Pasha, invaded what was then the Turkish province of Syria, but there found themselves faced by the Druses, wild, hard-fighting mountain tribesmen. The latter captured many of Ibrahim's men. Among the captives were Syrian fellow countrymen of the Druses, for Ibrahim had recruited far and wide. It was the desire of the tribesmen to spare their fellow Syrians, even if they wore the hated Egyptian uniform, but as soon as their intention became known, every prisoner claimed to be a Syrian. Both Syrians and Egyptians speak Arabic. This time the pass-word was *gamal*, the Arabic for "camel" (in fact, our own "camel" is derived from the Arabic word). Egyptians pronounce it *gamal*, but Syrians say *jamal*. Only the *jamal*-speakers got by.

During the Chinese revolution of 1911, which led to the freeing of China from the Manchu imperial dynasty and the setting up of Sun Yat-sen's Chinese Republic, members of the Manchu ruling and official class were hunted down and put to death. These Manchus had lived long years in China and had mastered the Chinese language, with the exception of one sound, the *ehr*, which is like a good Midwestern rolled *r*. The nearest Manchu equivalent for this sound is *l*. The Chinese, when faced with doubtful cases, asked for the word for "little dog," *chüan-ehr*. If they got *chüan-ehl*, there was one less Manchu.

The word "shibboleth," from the earliest of these incidents, is defined in Webster's as "criterion; test; watchword that distinguishes one party from another; some peculiarity in things of little importance."

It is that, and more. It is the earliest recording of man's natural and universal tendency, when acquiring another language, to substitute for all the unfamiliar sounds of the new language, close but not identical sounds from his native tongue. It is, of course, a form of laziness, and can be overcome with the use of effort. But not all people are willing to exert the effort and learn to produce a sound that does not occur in their native tongue. It is this "lazy" tendency that gives immigrant dialects their peculiar flavor. The immigrant replaces all English sounds that do not occur in his own speech pattern with sounds that do, and that are close enough to pass muster. Hence "kink" for "king," "seet" for "sit," "ze" for "the," etc. If you laugh at the way a Frenchman sounds when he speaks English, remember that you sound just as funny when you speak French, even though you may not be, as Milton puts it:

> Without reprieve, adjudged to death
> For want of well pronouncing shibboleth.

CHAPTER 11

What's in a Name?

The baby is a boy. You wonder what to name him. Why not settle for John? It's a fine name, proudly borne by four or five million other Americans. And don't think that all those people are called John just because their parents could think of nothing else, or didn't care. Some chose it as a manly name, others because of a saint whose virtues they admired. The Roman Calendar of Saints lists no fewer than sixty St. Johns. When the baby grows up, he will thank you for John, but not for Galahad, Terwilliger, or Elbridge.

The baby is a girl. Well, what's wrong with Mary? The U.S. has about six million Marys, so you have plenty of support in selecting that name. Your daughter will like Mary; she might not be happy over Delight or Daisy.

America is not alone in its predilection for John and Mary. The same names, in different forms, are also popular in all Christian countries, including those behind the Iron Curtain. Ivan and Maria (John and Mary) are the leading Russian names. But while Maria generally remains the same in most languages, John can assume the forms of Jean (French; often combined with another name: Jean-Albert, Jean-Paul, even Jean-Marie); Juan (Spanish; diminutive Juanito); Giovanni (Italian; diminutive Giovannino, or even Nino); Johann (German; diminutive Hans, Hansel). Ivan's diminutive form is Vanya. Portuguese has João, Polish has Jan, Hungarian has János, Irish has Sean, Serbo-Croatian has Jovan, Finnish has Juhana.

In this country, well over twenty million men have the names of Charles, James, George, and William. As Paul J. Phelan once observed, every Tom, Dick, and Harry is not named Tom, Dick, and Harry. But Charles may appear as Karl, Carlos, Carlo, Karel; James as Jacques, Jaime (or Iago, or Diego), Giacomo, Yakob. George may take the form of Jorge, Giorgio, even Jerzi (Polish) and Jiri (Czech). And William can give you Wilhelm, Guillaume, Guillermo, Guglielmo, and many additional forms.

Side by side with these "international" names, there are others that seem peculiar to a certain ethnic group, though they may be borrowed untranslated: French Gaston, Yves, Monique, Odile; Spanish Eloy, Ruy, Alvaro, Gonzalo, Carmen, Consuelo; Italian Alfio, Dino, Marisa, Silvana, Concetta; German Siegfried, Helmuth, Horst, Brünnhilde, Gretchen; Russian Boris, Igor, Olga, Tatiana; Scandinavian Olaf, Hjalmar, Kirsten, Ingrid; Serbo-Croatian Stojan, Dushan, Zoran, Ljuba; Polish Waclaw, Jadwiga; Hungarian Béla, Géza, Zsazsa; Czech Jaroslav; Arabic Ali, Hassan, Fatima; Hebrew Chaim, Abba.

There's more in a name than one might think. People had first, or personal, names for centuries before they had clan, or family, names. In the most primitive societies, the individual has a single name; this is still true today of Indonesian, where Sukarno or Prawoto constitute the person's entire name. Long before it became necessary to identify a person by referring to his ancestry, tribe, occupation, or personal characteristics, the individual had to be personally named. As far as we know, God did not bestow a family name upon Adam and Eve.

Biblical names from the Old Testament are generally inspired by a strong religious spirit. This is true of the many Hebrew names ending in -el, which means "God" or "of God." Emanuel, for instance, is "God's servant"; Michael is "like unto God"; Daniel, "God is my judge." But Old Testament names show considerable variety. Adam is "man" and Eve is "life." Abraham is "father of a multitude," Jacob and its English descendant James means "supplanter." Esau is "hairy," while Thomas means "twin." Mary (Miriam is the original Hebrew form) is "bitter." The name of Jesus Christ is the Greek translation of Hebrew Joshua Messiah, "savior anointed."

The Greeks and Romans, as well as the Germanic tribes that overran the Roman Empire, bore first names that often betrayed pagan origin. Marcus, Martius, and Marius were derived from Mars, Roman god of war, and Martin literally means "warlike." Philip in Greek is "horse lover," and Hippocrates "horse ruler." Gerald is Germanic for "spear wielder." But in the early Christian era many of these names gained a new connotation because they were borne by saints. Thereafter they became "Christian" names. However, the custom of using saints' names in baptism, thus placing the recipient under the protection of a patron saint, did not come into full vogue until after the tenth century. Before this, in the sixth, seventh, and eighth centuries, Germanic proper names had become widespread in countries penetrated by the Germanic invaders after the fall of the Roman Empire. Documents of the period show us such gems as Chioberga, Childeberchthus, Bertegisilus, Helmegaudus in France; Adaloald, Wolfrit, Liutprand, Theodelinda in Italy; Argemundus, Eggisenda, Ermenegildus, Lovesindus in Spain.

Many of those names are still with us. "Bert," at the beginning or end of Germanic names, means "illustrious," or, more literally, "bright." Albert is "honor-bright"; Robert (or Rupert, or Rupprecht), "fame-bright"; Herbert, "army-bright" or "glory of the army"; Lambert, "land-bright"; Bertram or Bertrand, "bright raven." The root appears all by itself in Bertha, which is an exact counterpart of Latin Clara.

Other Germanic names concern animals. Bernard and Eberhard are "hardy as a bear" and "hardy as a boar." The *-olph* ending of Adolph and Rudolph is really "wolf," used in the sense of "hero." This makes Adolph "noble wolf" and Rudolph "famous wolf." The Latin name Lupus, which became widespread at the time of the Germanic invasions, was probably a translation of Germanic "wolf." It survives today in such place-names as Saint-Lô, Saint-Leu, Saint-Loup in France, Cantalupo in Italy. But the Romans may also have developed it all by themselves, because they had previously used other animals names, such as Leo, "lion," and Ursus, "bear."

Louis, Lewis, Ludwig, Italian Luigi, even Hungarian Lájos, are all variants of an originally Germanic name meaning "bold warrior." The old Germanic form, as it appears in the documents of Merovingian France, is Chlodovechus, later contracted to Clovis, who was the first king of the Franks to be converted to Christianity. He was the founder of a long line of French kings who bore the name of Louis, including the saintly leader of the Crusades, Louis IX; Louis XI, who unified France; Louis XIV, the "Sun King," who tried to conquer all of Europe even before Napoleon; and the unfortunate Louis XVI, who lost his head under the guillotine.

Another Germanic root for first names is *Theo-*, "people." Theodoric, king of the Ostrogoths who invaded Italy, was "mighty among the people," and his name appears today under the various forms of Thierry, Terry, and Dietrich. But the Germanic *theo-* can easily be confused with another *theo-* that comes from Greek and means "God"; Theodore and Dorothea, for example, both mean "God-given" or "God's gift."

Ed-, which means "wealth," is a Germanic root that was particularly favored by the Anglo-Saxons in names like Edward, Edgar, Edmund, Edwin. Edward is one who "stands guard over riches." Its diminutive form in England is Ted, which Americans use more frequently as a short form of Theodore.

Germanic feminine names are numerous. Adeline is "of noble birth." Gertrude is "spear-maiden." Matilde (or Maud) is "mighty battle-maiden."

Among Greek names, Stephen is "victor's wreath" (it may appear in various lands under the forms Etienne, Esteban, Stefano, Stepan, Istvan, Stiobhan). Irene is "peace." Napoleon is "forest lion." George is "husbandman," "farmer." Ulysses is "hater." Barbara is "strange," "foreign." Nicholas is "leader of a victorious army," which makes it practically a synonym of Latin Victor.

Among Latin names of interest are Caesar ("born through a caesarian operation, from *caedo*, "to cut," which appears also in "incision"); Agnes, "lamb-like," with its Spanish variant Ines or Inez; Mandy, an abbreviation of Amanda, "lovable"; Calvin, "bald"; Claude, "lame"; Paul, "small"; Ursula, "she-bear."

The Celtic languages (Irish and Scots Gaelic, Welsh, Breton) make considerable contributions to our roster of names. Arthur is Celtic for "noble," Brian for "strong," Llewelyn for "lightning," Kenneth for "leader," Owen for "young warrior," Bridget for "strength," Gwen for "white."

Old French gives us Algernon, "bewhiskered," Roy, "king," Amy (either from *amie*, "girl-friend" or from *aimée*, "beloved"), and the diminutive ending *-on* of Marion and Madelon. Among names that come from ancient Persian are Cyrus, "sun"; Darius, "preserver"; Esther, "star"; Roxana, "dawn."

Not all languages place the "first name" first. The Hungarians, like the Japanese and Chinese, regularly and conversationally place it last, as it would appear on an index card. Chiang Kai-shek is Kai-shek of the Chiang family. The Hungarian liberator whom we know as Louis Kossuth is Kossuth Lájos in his own land.

Where first names do not follow the Christian calendar, strange situations may occur. With some primitive peoples of the South Seas, the name is so intimately bound up with the individual's personality that it becomes practically taboo, and is seldom if ever used. Among many African tribes, names are not divided into male and female. This state of affairs has a curious parallel in America, particularly in the South, where names like Pearl, Marion, Leslie, Beverly, Dana may be used for either sex. A motion picture's plot was once based upon the circumstance that in it Clifton Webb's first name was Lynn.

Among some American Indian tribes, such names prevail as "Place-in-the-West," "When-they-weave-something," "Early-part-of-sunrise." As feminine names we find "Yucca-with-broad-leaves," "Water-with-wind-blown-spray," "Cold-moving-mist." Indians do not hesitate to bestow picturesque names on distinguished visitors. The actress Diana Lynn was "adopted" by the Florida Seminoles with the name Ch-Tuk-Nup-Hut-Kee, or "White Silver." Admiral Chester Nimitz was known to the Ottawas as Be-Ka-Na-Ge, or "The Winner." The Otoes gave Eamon de Valera the name of Irah-Ri-Turah-Hi, "Good Friend from across the Sea." Cardinal Spellman was inducted by the Oglala Sioux as Wanbli Ohitika, or "Chief Brave Eagle"; but one of his fellow prelates, taken into the tribe at the same time, got a name which may be freely translated as "Chief Smooth Talker."

Japanese names are often descriptive of virtues, like Tadeshi, "Righteousness." Others are numerical, like Ichiro, "First Boy." Girls' names often end in -*ko*, "child," or are of a poetic nature, like Tori, "Bird."

Mencken, in his *Supplement* to *The American Language*, illustrates American creativeness in the matter of coining first names with a long list from the Texas-Oklahoma region that starts with Alapluma, and goes on through Covadonga, Earthel, Townzella to Xmay, Yondah, and Zzelle. In sixteenth- and seventeenth-century England Philadelphia was a popular name for girls, while Humility, Hate-Evil and Kill-Sin were among the first names handed out by the Pilgrim Fathers.

In more recent times, a family labeled its fourteenth child Finis. Difficulty arose when a fifteenth child came along, but it was solved with Postscript. Invasia and Dee Day were names bestowed on girls born at the appropriate time in the Second World War, while Tootall was bestowed upon a boy in Kentucky who later actually grew to the height of six and a half feet.

Under American influence, the inhabitants of the upper Amazon jungles widely took up Frigidaire as a first name for girls, while a South African tribe that had somehow gotten hold of a publisher's catalogue bestowed upon its chieftain the sonorous name of Oxford University Press. When Fiorello La Guardia took over the direction of the distribution of American relief in Korea, many Korean babies got the name of Lee Mi Wah, a literal translation of "Little Flower."

It may at times be worth while to investigate the meaning of names in the language from which they are taken. Do you really want to name your little girl Ethelinda or Ophelia? The first means "noble snake" in its original Germanic, the second is "serpent" in its original Greek. Mona is Spanish for "she-monkey," but since it has the secondary meaning of "cute" it can get by.

In the Catholic countries of southern Europe, little attention is paid to birthdays, which are often glossed over with a mere wish ("A hundred of these days," say the Italians). The day that really counts, and is joyfully celebrated with festivities and presents, is the person's name day; that is, the feast day of the person's patron saint after whom he or she is named. Curiously, the same custom prevails in a few predominantly Protestant countries on the shores of the Baltic, notably Estonia. This is perhaps a throwback to the days when they were Catholics, and still believed in the Roman Calendar of Saints.

Do names have a psychological value to their bearers? Of this there is no doubt. Family names accompany family pride, pride of lineage, and pride of tradition. First names fulfill these functions to a more limited degree. Certain first names are traditional in royal and noble families, so that the bearers sometimes have to add numbers or qualifiers for positive identification (George V, Ivan the Terrible, George Jones, Jr.).

Where the name does not bear any exalted connotation, it may nevertheless be invested with psychological factors. It has been pointed out that boys may not be grateful for names bestowed upon them by their parents which, rightly or wrongly, convey ideas of overrefinement or aloofness (Cuthbert, Dudley, Lancelot; but these connotations may change from time to time, and from place to place). Names are sometimes bestowed in commemoration of a political figure or historical event, which may turn out to be almost meaningless forty years later. Kim, a Korean name, was popular for American girls born at the time of the Korean "police action." There was a rash of Benitos in Mexico at the time of Benito Juárez, another in Italy at the time of Benito Mussolini. Whether the Italian recipients of Benito are happy with it today is a moot question.

There seems to be something homey and good-fellow about masculine names that lend themselves to easy and common abbreviation, as Bill, Joe, Jack, Ted, Bob; something ethereally feminine about such girls' names as Daisy, Violet, April, Mae, June; something subtly sexy about Susie, Hedy, Janice, Candy. Will the homey connotation be relished when Bill gets to be President of the United States? Will the flowery or sexy connotation be appreciated when June and Susie are in their fifties?

But these estimates represent only the writer's personal reaction. A recent survey and poll conducted by Barbara Buchanan and presented at the American Psychological Association Convention in Washington clearly indicates that young adults dislike Ferd, Isidore, Eugenia, and Beulah, and favor Michael, James, Linda, Susanne, and Kim. Male students polled considered Adam, Mac, Samson, and Bart as most "masculine" but women students preferred in that capacity Dave, Kirk, Michael, and James, with Valentine, Claire, and Shelley at the bottom of both lists.

Men considered Sue, Elizabeth, and Linda as most "feminine," but women picked Yvette, Sophia, and Cheri. Least feminine, in men's judgment, were Sydney, Ronnie, Jerry; in women's, Lou, Alfreda,

Billie. To men, "active"-sounding masculine names were Bart, Johnny, Dave; to women, Sargent, Kirk, James. To men, "active"-sounding feminine names were Bobbie, Patty, Bridget; to women, Deirdre, Jody, Tobi. Least "active" male names to men were Percival, Isidore, Milton, Valentine; to women, least "active" feminine names were Pansy, Prissy, Agnes, Violet, Rose, Mona.

Fortunately, every one is free to make up his or her own list. Even more fortunately, there is in most civilized countries the possibility of a change of name, by legal decree or even by unofficial preference, when the possessor of a name becomes old enough to make his or her own decisions. I honestly do not know why a good friend of mine, whose first name is John, chooses to be Richard to his family and close associates, but so far as I am concerned, Richard he is.

CHAPTER 12

The Language of Holidays

"Don't abbreviate Christmas to Xmas in writing. It's irreverent!"

How true is this? Not true at all. The X of Xmas is indeed an abbreviation, but it is no mark of disrespect. It is the Greek letter X or chi, the first letter of the Greek *Christos,* meaning "anointed" (a translation of the Hebrew *Messiah*), used since the early days of Christianity even by illiterates, who in making their mark with an X in the place of their signatures called upon Christ to witness their good faith.

Christmas itself is "Christ's Mass." The early Christians named the daily sacrifice of the Mass after the saint whose feast day was being celebrated, or a distinctive part of the ritual, as shown by such ancient feast-day names as Michaelmas (the feast of St. Michael) and Candlemas (the Mass, or feast, of candles). "Mass" itself is the English development of the Latin *missa,* "that which has been sent, or sped on its way," toward God. Its original use is to be seen in the closing words of the ceremony, addressed by the priest to the faithful, "*Ite, missa est,*" "Go, it has been sped on its way."

Among the world's chief Western languages, only Dutch accompanies English in calling this celebration of the birth of Christ "Christ's Mass" (the Dutch form is *Kerstmis*). French and Italian prefer expressions (*Noël, Natale*) which come from the Latin *natalis,* "pertaining to the birth." Spanish *Navidad* is a slightly contracted "Nativity"; but in wishing you a "Merry Christmas" Spanish shows a curious confusion of Christmas and Easter; *Felices Pascuas,* literally translated, means "Happy Easters." *Pascua,* the Spanish word for "Easter," like Italian *Pasqua* and French *Pâques,* is derived from the Hebrew *Pesach* or "Passover." The word in Spanish came to mean religious holiday in general, and if a Spaniard wants to be really precise he will say "*Felices Pascuas de Navidad*," "Happy Easters [i.e., holidays] of Nativity." In like manner, a Rumanian might say "*Sărbători Fericite*," "Happy Holidays."

The Russian *Rozhdestvo Khristova*, the modern Greek *Khristougenna*, the Esperanto *Kristnasko* are all, literally, "the Birth of Christ." Polish *Boże Narodzenie* is "the Birth of God," and Serbo-Croatian *Božić* is an abbreviation of the same expression, putting stress on "God." German *Weihnachten* and Czech *Vánoce* are "the Night of Consecration Masses."

So far, we have remained within the Christian-Hebrew tradition. But we must not forget that the Christmas period also coincides with the ancient pagan festivals of the winter solstice, and the final stowing away of gathered harvests. In this period the Romans held their Saturnalia, or feasts of Saturn, the most ancient and indigenous god of Italy, and this was an occasion for rejoicing accompanied by revelry. Some historians claim that the early Christians, uncertain as to the exact day of Christ's birth, decided to make it coincide with the Saturnalian festivals, so that there would not be too much of a break in the traditions and habits of Roman populations accustomed to a lengthy period of festivities around the close of the year.

The Germanic tribes had a similar pagan tradition in their Yule-tide celebrations, characterized by the burning of the Yule log. When they adopted Christianity some of them retained the old name, and *Jul* remains to this day the word for Christmas in the Scandinavian languages, spreading from them to the nearby Finns, who call the feast *Joulu*. The Slavs, who were not converted to Christianity until the ninth century, had a feast of the winter solstice which they called *Korochun* or *Korachon*. This they gave up in favor of the more Christian names we have seen above, but they passed on their own ancient word to two non-Slavic peoples, the Hungarians and the Rumanians, who to this day call Christmas *Karácsony* and *Crăciun*.

In the word of good wishes that accompanies Christmas there is a difference, too, in the various languages. English "Merry" and German *Fröhliches*, French *Joyeux* and Spanish *Felices* are all in the same class, but many languages prefer plain "good" (Italian *Buon*

Natale, Norwegian *God Jul,* or the comparatively little-used Rumanian *Bun Crăciun*).

As varied as the forms of expression are the customs that surround Christmas and the symbolical figures of the bearer of gifts. Our Santa Claus is of Dutch origin for what concerns the immediate past, but the San Nikolaas or Klaus of the Dutch goes back to a very ancient figure, that of St. Nicholas, bishop of Myra, who lived in the late third century and about whom there are infinite legends. That he was a friend of children is indicated by a medieval French play, the *Jeu de Saint Nicholas,* in which the good bishop brings back to life three little children who had been foully butchered by an innkeeper. There is also a story about his having bestowed surreptitious dowries upon three poor girls who could otherwise not have been married, and this is supposed to supply the connection between Santa Claus and gift giving with the original custom of giving secret presents on the eve of the feast of St. Nicholas. But Germanic countries then transfer the custom to Christmas. Teutonic lands are the only ones where Christmas is connected with gift giving, with a single Romance ramification in France, where children receive their gifts, not from Santa Claus, but from *le Père Noël,* "Father Christmas." Non-Germanic northern countries, like Russia, have their Father Frost, or Father Winter. In Holland, where our Santa Claus originated, it is indeed St. Nicholas who brings the gifts, but he brings them on his own feast day, December 6. It is perhaps significant that a pagan festival was celebrated on December 25 by the Anglo-Saxons and called *modranecht,* or "Mother's Night"; it is mentioned, but not fully described, by the Venerable Bede. Could gift giving have formed part of its ceremonies? The Puritans looked upon Christmas festivities as a survival of paganism, and forbade them, making Christmas a day of fasting, not feasting. Some of their spirit appears perhaps in Scrooge.

The Romance countries generally transfer the gift giving to New Year's Day or Epiphany (Twelfth Night). Epiphany is originally the "apparition" of a divine being, the "making manifest" of Christ. At first it was celebrated as the spiritual birth of Christ, but later it was confused with the coming of the Magian kings, who bore gifts. In Italy, the gift day for children is the Feast of the Kings, January 6, and the presents are brought down the chimney by an old woman, *La Befana,* whose name is a corruption of *Epiphania* or "Epiphany."

The Christmas tree is of Nordic and pagan origin, though it has recently spread to southern countries. The typical Christmas decoration in the more traditionally Christian Mediterranean countries is the *crèche,* a display of tiny figures showing the manger of Bethlehem, the Christ child, His Virgin Mother, St. Joseph, the Magian kings, the shepherds, the animals, and the star. The word *crèche,* though French, is of Germanic origin. It has a native English variant in *crib,* and also an older form borrowed from French, *cratch,* meaning "a crib or rack for fodder," which Dickens symbolically used in the name of the Cratchit family in his *Christmas Carol.* But Spanish and Italian use instead the Latin *praesepe,* likewise meaning "crib," which becomes *pesebre* and *presepio.*

Easter is in origin the spring festival of the Teutonic tribes, dedicated to Eoster, the spring goddess. April is *Ostarmanoth* in Old High German, *Eosturmonath* in Anglo-Saxon ("Easter's month"). Only German accompanies English in calling the festival by its pagan name (*Ostern* is the modern German form). Other Germanic languages go over to the Hebrew-Greek-Latin form which starts with Hebrew *Pesach* ("passing over," as did the angel who visited death upon the children of the Egyptians but passed over and spared the Jewish homes), to Aramaic *Pascha',* to Greek *Pascha,* to Latin *Pasqua,* most faithfully reflected in Italian *Pasqua* and Spanish *Pascua.* Danish today has *Paaske,* Dutch has *Paasch,* Welsh has *Pasg,* Russian has *Paskha.*

Sunday is still the pagan "day of the sun" for Germanic languages (German *Sonntag;* even *Sonnabend,* or "sun eve," for Saturday), but "day of the Lord" to Romance speakers (Latin *dies dominica,* French *dimanche,* Spanish *domingo,* Italian *domenica*). Since it is a weekly commemoration of Christ's resurrection, it is actually "resurrection" in Russian (*voskreseniye*). *Khristos voskrez,* "Christ has arisen," is the Russian Easter greeting.

CHAPTER 13

The Language of Colors
Is Not International

"Black is the color of mourning"; "Red symbolizes danger, violence, bloodshed, or radicalism"; "Green is symbolical of envy"; "When you're depressed, you're blue"; "If you're afraid, you're yellow."

Not at all. At least, not outside the English-speaking world. In China and Korea white, not black, is the color of mourning. In Russia, even under the czars, red stood for beauty and life; in fact, the Russians use a single root for "red" and "beautiful"; white, on the other hand, is the color of the frozen Siberian wastes, the color of death, and in the Russian civil war this color symbolism gave the Red Guard a tremendous psychological advantage over the White armies of Denikin and Kolchak. In France, "to be green to someone" means not to bear him a grudge, and to be depressed is "to have a black humor." In Italy and Germany, you're yellow with envy, not with fear.

The symbolism of colors is anything but universal. For a few items, like "black heart," "rosy hopes," "white innocence," you have some measure of international agreement, mainly because languages have borrowed the clichés from one another. But our "to be in the pink of condition," "parlor pink," "brown study," and dozens of other expressions involving color would be meaningless elsewhere. We would be equally at a loss before French expressions like "to tell a blue story," which means a "tall" story, or "to give a green reply," which is a tart reply. We would be stuck before the Italian "to have a blue voice," which means a crooning voice, or the Russian "black laborer," which means not a Negro, of whom there are few in the land of the Soviets, but simply a manual laborer.

What could be more opposite than red and green? Yet the Italian expression for "to be in the red" is "to be in the green," because Italians choose to view green as the color of hope, not of envy, and hope remains when all else is lost.

"Blue Monday" spells washday to the American housewife, and a tough accumulation of work to the office worker. But in German "blue Monday" means an extended weekend, a "holiday Monday." "Green Thursday," on the other hand, is to the French and Germans what our British cousins call "Maundy Thursday."

This disagreement on colors appears even in the case of concrete objects, about which there should be no argument. What is "red cabbage" to us is "blue cabbage" to the Germans and "black cabbage" to the Italians (German, by the way, uses "brown cabbage" for broccoli). The Italians occasionally speak of "red wine," but just as often call it "black wine," while the Spaniards call it "colored wine" or more precisely "tinted wine" (*vino tinto*). What is a "black eye" to us is a "blue eye" to the Germans, who also call the king of spades not the "black king," but the "green king." The yolk of an egg is the "yellow" of the egg to the Russians, French, and Germans, and can be either the "red" or the "yellow" of the egg to the Italians.

The symbolism of colors as applied to political ideas is exemplified by our "black Republicans" and our "Reds" and "Pinks." The medieval English had their civil War of the Roses (white rose for the House of York, red rose for the House of Lancaster). The Irish have had their troubles over the Orange and the Green. The Italians of Dante's time split wide open over the issue of the Pope vs. the Emperor. Followers of the Pope styled themselves "Guelphs" or "Blacks," adherents of the Emperor "Ghibellines" or "Whites." Dante himself was exiled as a "White" when the "Blacks" took control of his native Florence. In the province of Tehuantepec, Mexico, the local Conservatives and Liberals call themselves "Reds" and "Greens," and the joke is that it is the Conservatives who are the "Reds." Uruguay has it straighter: the "Whites" are the Conservatives and the "Coloreds" or "Reds" are the Leftists.

The theory of Nordic supremacy, with yellow-haired people as the Herrenvolk, far antedates Hitler. In a French poem of the twelfth century, we find the heroine endowed with a name which, freely translated, means "Golden One of Love." In the course of a soliloquy, she cogitates over the "golden" or "yellow" part of her name, and declares that "golden" (or blond) is the color of the best people."

Some of the color angles are based on material reality, past or present. To the extent that they are so based, they are international, provided always that the experience of one ethnic group gets across to the others. This accounts for such international expressions as "blackmail," "blue stocking," "blueprint," "blue ribbon," "white slave." But some of these word combinations have interesting and conflicting histories. "Bluestocking" was put in vogue in England around 1750 by a group that met at Montagu House for the purpose of literary discussions. The story goes that some of the members, including Lady Montagu herself, deliberately wore blue worsted stockings instead of black silk ones in order to give the gatherings an air of informality. It is a fact, however, that the term had already been used by a similar group in Paris around 1590, and still earlier in Venice, about 1400. At any rate, "Bluestocking" had also been applied derisively to the Puritan Little Parliament in the days of Cromwell and Charles I; Puritans, too, wore blue worsted instead of black silk stockings.

Other similar expressions have not gained international acceptance, largely because the object designated is local. Here we have such things as "greenback," "bluegrass," "red-light district" (as opposed to the more recent red light used as a traffic signal). "Green corn," "blue-pencil," "out of the blue," "whitewash," "whitecap" still have a basis in objective reality. So has Italian "green carpet" for gambling table. Beyond that, symbolism begins. "Black tie" and "white tie" have literal meanings; they are also applied to social affairs at which certain forms of dress must be worn. I can still recall being on a lecture tour in Delaware and being asked to a private theatrical performance where the invitation specified "black tie." I did not have my tuxedo with me, and there was no time to borrow or rent one. The man at whose home I was staying offered me a black tuxedo tie and suggested that I wear it with my charcoal gray business suit. No one batted an eyelash at this literal application of the term.

Much of the color symbolism has a partly literal and even historical foundation, if you happen to know it. "Blacksmith," for instance, was used as far back as the fifteenth century for one who works in iron (the "black" metal), in contradistinction to the "whitesmith" who works in tin (observe that even today, the French expression for tin is *fer-blanc*, "white iron"). "White elephant" comes to us from Siam. The white elephant of Thailand is a rare and delicate animal, and very expensive to support. The kings of Siam made presents of white elephants to those of their subjects whom they wished to ruin financially. One could not, of course, sell or otherwise dispose of a royal gift without incurring the charge of treason. "Blue-sky laws" seem to have been influenced, linguistically at least, by the German expression *blauer Dunst*, "blue haze," used idiomatically but understandably for "humbug" or "swindle." "Red tape" was used to tie up legal and other official documents as far back as 1696; the transition from the literal to the figurative meaning may appear in a passage from Washington Irving: "His brain was little better than red tape and parchment." The white, red, blue, black, and other books of different colors used in international diplomacy take their names from their bindings. A "Green Book," for instance, used to be an official report of the government of British India. Earliest among them for England (thirteenth century) seems to be the "Red Book" of the Exchequer. But "White Book" (*Liber Albus*) had already appeared in medieval Latin. Then there is the "black novel" or whodunit (*roman noir*) of French, paralleled by the "yellow novel" (*romanzo giallo*) of Italian, both of which take their names from the jacket or cover color of favorite thriller series. German "blue letter" for an official letter of dismissal was in origin just that—a letter that always came in a blue envelope and was written on blue paper.

"Blackout" is idiomatic but makes sense. So does the French and Italian "white night" for sleepless night (a night spent in the light, as opposed to the darkness). "Green finger" (or "green thumb") is elliptical, but the meaning is clear, considering that its possession leads to the sprouting of green things. "White lie" is justified only by opposing it to "black lie," where black is symbolic of evil, as it is in a whole list of expressions that include "Black Friday," "Black Hand," "black list," "black market," "blackmail," "blackguard," the *cronaca nera,* or "black news items," used by the Italian press to describe accounts of crimes of violence. *Bête noire,* which we have borrowed untranslated from French, lies in the twilight zone. But some of these "black" terms have curious histories. "Blackmail" was originally rent paid in labor or produce, as opposed to "white rent," paid in silver. "Blackguards" were at one time the cooks and scullions of royal and noble households, later of the army. Perhaps the semantic transition is indicated by a passage from the year 1696: "Satan placed his blackguards there." Unlike "white" and "black lie," "white" and "black magic" have a history that goes beyond symbolism and runs into the field of linguistic confusion. *Necromantia,* or necromancy, was the Greek term for foretelling the future by consulting the spirits of the dead (*mantis* is a soothsayer, and the *nekro-* root that means "dead" appears also in *necropolis* and *necrosis*). In medieval Latin, the word was misunderstand as *nigromantia* (black soothsaying). "Black art" appears in English as far back as 1590, but "white magic" has to wait until 1651.

Symbolism accounts for "white voices," used by Italian to describe male soprano choirs, the "green wine" of Portugal, which is merely new wine, the "green old man" of Spain, which means an old reprobate, the "green tale" (spicy story) of France. In all of this, we depend on our western convention that white is the color of good and innocence (extending to women and children), that green can symbolize, among other things, novelty, youth, freshness, hope (but there is a reverse to green's medal in its symbolization of jealousy, envy, or the Italian pennilessness). Idiomatic symbolization pure and simple attends our "strike me pink" and "talking a blue streak," German's "blue wonder" for seven-day wonder, and our "once in a blue moon" (French would speak of a "week of four Thursdays").

It is not at all necessary for us to leave our own language area to discover contradictions in color symbolism. A "redcap," who to us is a porter in a station, is to the British a military policeman. This is justifiable: our porters and their M.P.s wear red caps; their porters and our M.P.s do not. Then there is our 1929 "white-collar worker" (with "blue-collar" for an opposite number), who is to them a "black-coated worker." To us, "the blues" signify either a state of melancholy or a type of music; to them, capitalized, the "Blues" are the Royal

Horse Guard. In fact, we don't have to cross the ocean to get logical contradictions: would you rather be "red-blooded" or a "blue blood"? The first is literal, and requires no explanation; the second, too, is literal in the long run, but it is a long run. The expression, which is now fully international, originated in Spain, where some noble Castilian families asserted they had *sangre azul,* meaning that there was in them no Moorish or Jewish admixture. But why "blue" blood? Because the veins stand out blue when their possessor is fair-skinned.

One of our favorite symbolic colors is blue. We are subject to fits of "the blues" (here French and Italian would call it "black humor"), or we can simply "be blue" (French would say "be gray" or "be black"; "to be blue" in German would mean to be badly intoxicated, our "soused" or "stiff"; in French, one is "blue" with anger). Diverse as these national expressions are, they have something in common. Blue, which since 1500 has been with us the color of constancy ("true blue"), acquired a little later, around 1550, a secondary connotation of fear, anxiety, and low spirits, due to the superstitious belief that a completely blue flame, without a red glare, betokened the presence of ghosts or the devil. By 1787, we have "the blues" used in substitution for the "blue devils" that one sees, along with pink elephants, when he is suffering from delirium tremens. "Till all is blue" is an old English way of describing the effect of drink on the eyesight. This gives us a clue to the German "be blue" (intoxicated) and the French "blue" with anger, as well as to our "blue funk," in which French accompanies us with *peur bleue;* for strong emotions as well as hard liquor can disturb the eyesight. It even explains the connection between our "blue Monday" and the German "blue Monday" described earlier as a holiday Monday, for the expression, used at first for the Monday before Lent, when people still made merry, was then extended to any Monday when the workers stayed off the job and got drunk.

Our "blue laws" are without parallel, and have to be explained to anyone with a foreign background. The original ones seem to have been passed in New Haven, Connecticut, in the eighteenth century, but they go back to the political coloring of the Scottish Presbyterians or Whigs, as against the royalist reds or Tories. Why did the

Whigs choose blue? Because it's the color of constancy and steadfast faith.

Consider our "black and blue," which to us sounds fairly literal; German would call it either "green and blue" or "brown and blue"; Malay would call it "blue discolored." Our Blue Cross, which serves civilian medical and hospital needs, is to the Germans a form of poison gas, along with Green Cross, which is the Italian version of S.P.C.A.

Black is another of our favorite symbolic colors, following a precedent which goes all the way back to the Greeks and Romans. Its funereal symbolism extends across all Western nations, but with interesting variations. The Russians used to speak of the "Black Hundred," the pogrom mob stirred up by czarist rabble rousers to exterminate the Jews. They still speak of "black stairs" and "black entrance" for our back stairs and back entrance, but these are usually less well lighted than the ones out front. "To ride black" in German is to ride in a stolen car. The "black laborer" who is a manual worker in Russia is a non-union worker in Germany (he's a "yellow," however, if he belongs to a non-affiliated union). The Papal aristocracy is to the Italians the "Black Aristocracy," black being the color normally worn by churchmen. Our police wagon, "Black Maria," is in Austria *der grüne Heinrich,* "green Henry" (here there may be reference to the actual color of the vehicle; the shift in gender is interesting).

Gray is a color we use in symbolism only to a limited extent. It is perhaps worth noting that where we generally speak of a person as "gray-haired," other languages are more frank and use "white-haired." French, which seems to like the color, speaks of "having the grays" (or "giving someone the grays") for having, or giving someone, a hard time. "Making a gray face" at someone is French for giving him the cold shoulder. "To be gray," or "to get gray," is to be or get drunk; here the imagery is explained as having to do with getting enveloped in billowing gray clouds. On the other hand, a pretty, young working girl is a *grisette,* or "little gray one." The term was originally applied to the cheap gray material out of which were fashioned the dresses and smocks worn by the working girls; the transfer from the fabric to the wearer comes early in the eighteenth century;

overtones were added later. German paints a "gray picture" of someone or something where we would paint a "black picture." German also speaks of the remote past and the distant future as "gray antiquity" and "the gray to-come."

White lends itself to strange uses and a few contradictions. To the Russians, the wide world is the "white world"; this seems due to a secondary connotation that the Russians attach to white, that of vastness and grandeur, as attested by the "White Czar of All the Russias." "Fish in white" means to the Italians plain boiled fish served with oil and lemon juice. They also speak of someone or something being as "rare as a white fly" (we might occasionally use "black swan" in that connection, but with greater justification; there are black swans). In French, to "show a white paw" means to offer one's credentials, or identify oneself; this goes hand in hand with "to be white," which means to have a clean police record.

Where we "put something down in black and white," most other languages put "black on white." Italian *di punto in bianco* (literally, "from point to white," or "from dot to blank") means "suddenly"; the seemingly equivalent Spanish *de punto en blanco* means "from head to toe," "in full regalia." "White weapon" (*arma bianca*, or *arma blanca*) is to the Italians and Spaniards a cutting or stabbing weapon, as opposed to a firearm (which is never referred to, however, as a "red weapon," as it well might be). A strident contradiction appears in the designation for the bull's-eye of a target, which is "the black" in German, "the white" in French and Spanish; but this may be due to the actual coloring of the bull's-eye in the different countries.

The color symbolization of fear and cowardice seems to waver, so far as we are concerned, between yellow and white, as evidenced by "You're yellow!" as against "showing the white feather" and "white-livered." The "yellow" connection seems to be with jaundice, which saps your vitality and courage (but don't a lot of other ailments?). "Yellow plague" or "yellow sickness" in the sense of "jaundice" appear in the middle of the sixteenth century, but the "cowardly" connotation is not attached until 1896. "Yellow dog" was used literally in the U.S. to describe a type of hound since 1840, but as applied in labor relations ("yellow-dog contract") it does not appear till

1902. "To show the white feather" was in origin a hunting expression; a white feather showing in a game bird's tail was considered a sign of inferior breeding. "White-livered," first appearing around 1600, is based on a superstition that the liver is discolored by a deficiency of bile or "choler," which is supposed to lend vigor, spirit, and courage to its possessor.

To the Spanish speaker, a "white" can be either a coward or a fool, while "yellow" to the French would mean a scoundrel or blackguard, and to the ancient Romans it meant effeminate. The Romans had a special expression for someone born lucky, or "with a silver spoon in his mouth"; they called him "the son of a white hen." Our "white meat," used of fowl in contradistinction to "dark meat," appears in Italian in opposition to "red meat" (beef or pork), and is used collectively for fowl, lamb, and veal. To a Frenchman, "white flag" might mean not the token of truce or surrender, but the old lily ensign on a white field of the Bourbon monarchy.

"Yellow press" is fairly international today. It begins, however, in the U.S. In 1895, the New York *World,* priding itself on sensational news coverage, appeared with a central figure wearing a yellow dress on its front page. It was labeled a "yellow paper" by the day's conservatives, and the term spread to other sensation-mongering sheets. Russian uses "yellow house" for insane asylum, but for this there may be, or have been, a literal justification. The Russians also speak of a "red line" for a new paragraph, and use "red-talking" for "eloquent" (but here they are probably using "red" in its more ancient meaning of "beautiful"). Germans who feel sick or nauseated speak of "getting green and yellow before their eyes," but again this may be literally interpreted.

Red and green are among favorite symbolic colors ("red herring," "red-letter day," "to be caught red-handed," for which French and Italian would say "to be caught with one's hands in the bag"). But the red herring is an actuality, being strong in scent and used to draw hounds away from their true quarry. "Red-letter day" goes back to medieval ecclesiastical calendars, which showed important church festivals in red. The German way of saying "here today and gone tomorrow" is "today red, tomorrow dead."

The Spaniards speak of "giving oneself a green" (*darse un verde*) for "to take time off" or "to have a ball." The French refer to slang as "green language." A "greenhorn" is to the French either a "white beak" or a "blue." Our term appears in 1682 as the equivalent of "raw recruit," but "green" in the sense of inexperienced goes back to the middle of the sixteenth century. "To green" in the sense of "to hoax" or "to take" (someone) was once current.

Two colors that lend themselves to indefiniteness and confusion are purple and pink. For the first, many languages use "violet-colored." The word that directly corresponds to purple in Italian is *porpora,* but getting the *porpora* means becoming a cardinal, not a king, and the cardinal's color is red. "To blush" can in Italian be *imporporarsi,* which would literally mean "to turn purple," something we do when we are angry or drowning. There is, however, an explanation. The original meaning in Greek was "crimson," which was the royal color. But about 1440 a deeper tone was given to the royal purple when the royal family was in mourning. Eventually, the color turned to what we now know as purple. Russian translates "purple" by *lilovy,* which means "lily colored." We have only to think of our "Lily-white" of the South to realize that there is some mix-up in the imagery, due, no doubt, to the fact that lilies can be of different colors. We are fortunate in having a special word for "pink." Most languages get along with "rosy" or "rose colored," and here again the fact is that we have red, white, and yellow as well as pink, roses. To the French and Italians, "brown shoes" are "yellow shoes," but brown shoes were once much lighter in color than they are now.

The word for "ink" causes a few surprises. The Romans called it *atramentum,* "that which produces black." This imagery got into Russian and several other languages, where the word for "ink" comes from the root of "black," even if the ink is red, blue, or green. Spanish, which uses *tinto* (basically the same word as our "tinctured") for red wine, has its feminine form, *tinta,* for "ink."

There is an occasional racial touch in color designations. Outside of *negrero* (Italian *negriero*) for "slave driver," Spanish gives us *boda de negros,* literally "Negro wedding," which has the idiomatic meaning of "noisy revel," and *negra,* "Negress," used affectionately in some Latin-American countries in the sense of "honey" or "sweetheart."

"White" in the sense of "honorable," "square," is a rather recent (1877) American usage. "Speak white!" is a fighting expression in Canada; it is occasionally used by intolerant English speakers to their French-speaking compatriots.

While *colorado* has in Spanish the meaning of "red," not "black," and is never racially applied, "colored" has in South Africa a different meaning from the one we give it, which is synonymous with "Negro." In the land of *apartheid*, Negroes are invariably called "blacks," and "colored" is applied to half-breeds and immigrants from India and other Asian countries. Ancient Latin had a full-blown expression of racial tolerance which was used in the sense of "it makes no difference to me": "I don't care whether he's white or black."

Psychologists have occasionally tried to establish connections for color sequences as they appear in different languages, but with no conclusive results. Why does the English cliché run "black and white," while the Spanish goes in reverse: *blanco y negro*? The simplicistic theory is that the names of colors are ranged in alphabetical order, as would seem to be borne out by Italian *bianco, rosso e verde* ("white, red, and green," though in the Italian flag green is next to the staff, white in the center, red on the outside). That this theory holds little water is shown by English "red, white, and blue," and by French *le rouge et le noir* ("the red and the black"). Until a better theory is evolved, we must assume that these color clichés simply grew, like Topsy.

Another angle that is of interest to psychologists is that of colored hearing. This writer, in his early boyhood, used to envisage the vowel *a* as white, *e* as green, *i* as red, *o* as blue, *u* as black. Don't ask me why. My scheme of colored vowels had at least the merit of jibing with mouth position: the front vowels, *e* and *i*, were associated with the brighter, more garish colors; *a*, the middle vowel, with the blend of all colors; *o* and *u*, the back vowels, with the more sombre colors. Much to my surprise, however, I later ran into a poem by the French writer Rimbaud who describes his own vowel scheme as black for *a*, white for *e*, red for *i*, green for *u*, blue for *o*. Though his poem goes on for fourteen lines, describing *a* as flies swirling around dirty puddles, *e* as glaciers, *i* as a woman's lips, *u* as the green seas, *o* as the ray of God's eye, his imagery still seems to me quite arbitrary.

Far more scientific in scope are studies based on the response to the color spectrum of different language groups. In many languages certain color words are lacking, and have to be replaced by similes. Spanish and Italian have no word for "tan," but tan-colored objects are usually described as "cinnamon colored" or "milk-and-coffee." German distinguishes between dark and light blue by calling one "Oxford color," the other "Cambridge color." Japanese uses "peach colored" for pink, "tea colored" for brown, "mouse colored" for gray (reminiscent of our "taupe," which originally means "mole colored"), "wasp colored" for yellow (here we have the imagery in reverse in "yellow jacket").

Italian and French will use "chestnut" for brown, particularly in speaking of hair color (*castagno, châtain*), but the word that etymologically is related to "brown" for a generally dark complexion (*brun, bruno*). They have two words for "gray" (*gris* or *grigio, bis* or *bigio*); the latter, however, may also betoken "tan," "tawny," and "brown," and French speaks of *pain bis,* or "gray bread," where we would use "brown bread" and German "black bread."

Italian and Russian have a plethora of words for blue, none of which seems fully satisfactory. In Italian *celeste* is definitely associated with the color of the sky, *azzurro* is "azure," *turchino* is Turkish, or rather dark, blue, and *blu,* borrowed from French, is an all-purpose word that runs from the navy blue of a man's suit to Modugno's popular song "I was up in the blue-painted blue." Russian *nebesny* is definitely associated with the sky (*nebo*), *goluboy* literally means "dove colored"; *siniy* is an all-purpose-word, but may have *temno-* prefixed to it, making it a dark blue.

It has been brought out by a good many writers that the ancients had a very poor sense of color, and that Homer was probably color-blind, to judge from the way he describes certain objects (color amnesia is a medically ascertained fact, but it is generally associated with aphasia, which Homer seemingly did not suffer from). At any rate, he uses *glaukos* (the word from which we derive "glaucoma") in senses which have been variously interpreted as "gleaming," "silvery," "bluish-green," "light blue," and "gray." For this there is a striking parallel in Japanese *awo,* which can mean "green" as applied to vegetation, "blue" as applied to the sea, "dark" as applied to clouds; as well as in Welsh *glas,* which can mean "blue," "green," or "gray."

On the other hand, where we see one color, other groups may see many different ones. Lithuanian uses different words for "gray" as applied to wool, horses, cows, or human hair. Latin made a distinction between dead, dull black (*ater*) and shiny black (*niger*); also between dead, dull white (*albus*) and gleaming white (*candidus*); not to mention a snowy white (*niveus*). *Canus,* on the other hand, a favorite term for hair, could be translated by "white," "gray," or "hoary." *Flavus* was a golden yellow, *fulvus* a tawny yellow; their derivatives Flavius and Fulvius were used as proper and family names, indicating original blondness somewhere along the line. *Glaucus,* borrowed from Greek, was used indifferently for "blue," "green," and "gray"; it, too, was used as a first name.

It is a commonplace among anthropologists that different ethnic groups segment the same objective reality in different fashions. Nowhere is this more apparent than in the color spectrum, where all sorts of distinctions and mergers are made. Malay uses *bolong* for both black and dark blue, and *merah* for both red and brown. Navajo, which, like Latin, distinguishes between the black of darkness and the black of coal, merges gray and brown, as well as blue and green; but the Navajo term for "yellow" covers in part what to us would be green. Zulu merges blue and green into a single term, *luhlaza.* Bongo *kamaheke* does duty for both red and yellow. The most extraordinary color segmentation is perhaps that reported by Dr. James Gleason for the Shona of Rhodesia and the Bassa of Liberia. It is best set forth as a graph:

English	purple	blue	green	yellow	orange	red
Shona		cipswuka	citena	cicena	cipswuka	
Bassa		hui		zīza		

Citena may also serve for "black" and *cicena* for "white," while *cipswuka* runs right around the spectrum, treating it as a circle. The final division of colors into two basic classes appearing in Bassa *hui* and *z̃za* corresponds precisely to the distinction made by Western botanists between "cyanic" and "xanthic" coloration. Which goes to prove that the Family of Man, despite infinite diversities, is basically one.

CHAPTER 14

The New Yorker's Languages

A minority group implies the existence of a majority. The term "minority" has of late become the vogue among sociologists and psychologists who wish to find an explanation for juvenile delinquency and slums, and they customarily apply it to what former generations used to call "immigrant groups." This usage is quite legitimate, but it is somewhat at variance with the way the term is used in Europe.

The linguistic minorities of Europe are usually found along the borderlines of countries, and they often, but not always, have affiliations with the countries across the boundaries. The minority areas are seldom simon-pure. There are regions where the language group that constitutes the country's majority appears as a minority, with the national minority constituting the local majority. A political parallel would be the western counties of North Carolina, a strongly Democratic state. In these western counties the Republicans predominate. There are regions of Europe where not one but half a dozen minorities are hopelessly intermingled.

The linguistic minorities of the United States are for the most part composed of immigrant groups that arrived here after the country had been settled, and these regularly accept cultural and linguistic integration as the price they have to pay for the hospitality and opportunities they receive. By historical standards, their absorption is quick. In a century or less, the English-speaking majority absorbed the Huguenot French and the Dutch of New York, the Delaware Swedes, the Florida Spaniards, and vast waves of later arrivals, particularly the Irish, Germans, and Scandinavians of the nineteenth century. By human standards, the process is somewhat slow, since it involves more than one generation and often extends

121

over a period of nearly a century. The process is now largely completed for the Italian, Jewish, and Slavic groups that arrived here between 1880 and 1914. It is being somewhat painfully repeated for the Puerto Ricans, who are American citizens but belong to an altogether different ethnic and linguistic culture. Despite the wishful thinking of certain anthropologists and social scientists, there is no substitute for time.

One favorable element in the absorption of immigrant groups is that they come to a country already settled, where a predominant pattern already exists. Another is that in a very large number of cases there is an active desire to become part of the American, English-speaking culture. Even where this desire does not appear in the first generation, it comes very much to life in the second. A third advantage is the large number of different language-and-culture patterns gathered together in a single American locality, which ordinarily prevents any one of them from becoming a local majority.

New York, probably the most international city in the world, is a good example of this situation. In the early decades of this century it was quite possible to draw a map of the city's various boroughs indicating the mother country of the bulk of the population in each district. Today such a map would be considerably more blurred and less well defined.

Nevertheless, such a map can still be drawn for the borough of Manhattan and a few adjacent areas of Brooklyn. Taking Manhattan from north to south, the map shows, in the vicinity of City College, a rather broad band where Spanish, Greek, and Russian predominate, in haphazard, intermingled fashion, with Spanish gaining the upper hand over its two competitors in recent years. South of 125th Street and east of Fifth Avenue, the Spanish coloring is almost complete, save for a small patch of Finnish in the vicinity of 125th Street and Lexington Avenue, running eastward as far as Third Avenue, where it is replaced by an older layer of Italian that reaches to the East River. Both Spanish and Italian come to an abrupt halt at 96th Street, to be replaced, east of Lexington Avenue, by the German of Yorkville, which merges almost imperceptibly into the Czech, Slovak, Hungarian, and Polish of the East Seventies and Sixties. Between Lexington Avenue and the Park lies an aristocratic, silk-stocking, English-speaking district which is, however, studded with foreign consulates and UN embassies that give it a thoroughly international flavor.

On the west side of Central Park, the area from 110th Street to 72nd Street used to be divided into two distinct zones, with an Irish-German element occupying the long blocks from Central Park West to Broadway, and a mixed population, largely Jewish in origin, holding the territory between Broadway and Riverside Drive. Today only remnants of the older populations are left. The staccato Spanish of the Puerto Ricans now pervades most of this area, particularly in its northern and eastern reaches.

South of 59th Street, on the West Side, there is a considerable French and Italian population, extending southward to 42nd. The East Side, in the same latitudes, presents a mixed picture, with occasional patches of French and Lithuanian.

The next big foreign-language agglomeration comes on the East Side between 34th and 23rd Streets. Here, particularly along Lexington Avenue, are Armenians and other Near Eastern peoples, intermingled with Italians who favor the blocks east of Third Avenue. On the West Side, the most striking midtown linguistic development is the large-scale injection of Puerto Rican Spanish.

South of 14th Street, the East Side shows a predominance of Russian and Polish, followed by Yiddish in the area where Williamsburg Bridge begins; but as you come to the other great bridges that link Manhattan with Brooklyn, it's Italian and Chinese. The latter thrives in a restricted area, centering about Mott and Pell streets. Italian, not content with the upper reaches of Mulberry and Mott, goes on to surround Washington Square and become the predominant foreign language of Greenwich Village. The only other group worthy of note is the Arabic-Syrian concentration on the extreme lower West Side, in the region of the old Washington Street market.

We have failed to mention one numerous Manhattan minority, the Negroes, who used to be concentrated in Harlem, but now, in accordance with more enlightened policies, are to be found in many other districts. Most of them are native Americans, and their language is English, though with a Southern flavor for a good many recent arrivals. But a large number of them are Puerto Ricans who speak Spanish. Julio Camba, a visiting writer from Spain, at one time remarked about the two varieties of Negroes he had found in New York; he labeled them as Anglo-Saxon Negroes and Latin Negroes.

The Irish, too, regularly speak English. So do the very numerous Americans who come to New York from other parts of the United States, bringing with them their soft Southern speech, or New England twang, or strong Midwestern *r*, all of which somehow fuse and blend in the great language melting pot that is New York.

Native New Yorkers? Yes, there are millions of them. A few are descendants of the old Dutch and English settlers, but the overwhelming majority are the result of the blending and fusion of the many races and nationalities that have made New York their home. Have their ancestral tongues influenced their English speech? On this subject opinions vary. Some linguists claim that the characteristic and exquisite diphthong heard in the way some New Yorkers pronounce *bird* ("A little boid sat on the coib and choiped, choipéd, choiped") goes back to the Dutch. Others say that the linking of final *-ng* sounds, as in "getting gout" and "Long Gisland," is something New Yorkers have gotten from Yiddish. There is no definite proof of all this, and it seems more likely that New York English is a purely local development of the general Eastern speech which is one of the three great subdivisions of American English.

However we look at all this, there is little doubt that New York is a linguist's paradise. Here we can find and study practically any language on the globe, from Burmese to Estonian, and from Basque to Mohawk (yes, there is a community of Mohawk-speaking American Indians to be found in a certain block in Brooklyn). We can listen to each and every type of American accent, and to all the English varieties of Britain and the British Commonwealth. We can directly observe and study each and every process of language that we read about in our manuals.

CHAPTER 15

So Spanish Is All
You Need in Latin America!

A party of American businessmen once went on a trip to South America to build up good will and, incidentally, business. Before starting out, they spent hours in the public library finding out about the countries they were going to visit.

At each of the South American capitals where they stopped, one of their number would pull out a predigested piece, composed for them in Spanish by an expert, in which he introduced the group and stated its purpose, and read it off to the best of his ability. It worked wonders in Caracas, Bogotá, and Quito. Then they came to Rio de Janeiro.

They noticed that the welcoming committee looked a bit puzzled as their spokesman read. When he finished, the customary applause was not forthcoming. One of their number whispered an aside to a Brazilian welcomer who had already demonstrated his knowledge of English. "Don't you have that speech in Portuguese?" the Brazilian whispered back. "But we're not going to Portugal!" replied the American. "We're sticking to the Western Hemisphere this trip!"

The books they had consulted in the library had failed them in one important respect. They had not informed them that Portuguese, not Spanish, is spoken in Brazil, South America's largest and most populous country and our leading customer among Latin-American nations.

Seventy-six million South Americans, in nine different countries, speak Spanish. Seventy-eight million, located in Brazil alone, speak Portuguese. The two languages are close, but not close enough to be interchangeable. Besides, Brazilians are touchy about their national tongue. They resent being lumped with their Spanish-speaking neighbors, to the point of preferring to use English rather than Spanish. Yet American tourists, diplomats, businessmen persist in ignoring this fact. They make the same mistake over and over again.

There is a funny story (perhaps it's true) about a great American magazine which, having prepared a Spanish edition, decided to try it first on Brazil, South America's biggest and most important country. They felt pretty good about it, and having sent several thousand copies to Rio, they settled back to wait for the chorus of approbation. Instead, they got a barrage of verbal brickbats. A Portuguese edition was rushed through to repair the blunder, and the Brazilians were ultimately mollified.

A few years ago a nationally known shaving cream plastered our most widely read magazines with a full-page ad showing a beauteous young lady from Rio, who "lawves" to come to New York to visit her rich American uncle whose face is always—oh!—so smooth! She would wind up her pretty little sales talk with an emphatic "Bueno!" which means and sounds "Fine!" in Buenos Aires, but not in Rio, where the word is "Bom!"

A visiting American college professor was once discussing with a Brazilian colleague the difference between the two languages. "Granted," said the American, "that Portuguese and Spanish differ considerably when spoken; they do, however, look very much alike in written form. Surely a man who knows how to read Spanish can read Portuguese!"

"Is that so?" countered the good neighbor. "Come around tomorrow and I'll show you how much alike they are!" The next day, he faced the *Norteamericano* with a written letter he had composed overnight in Portuguese. "You can read Spanish quite well, *senhor*," he said with a twinkle in his eye. "Now just see what you can do with this!" The American scratched his head. Not a single word was familiar to him, outside of a few conjunctions and prepositions.

The Brazilian had gone out of his way to prove his point, no doubt. Still, Portuguese can bob up with the most disconcerting differences. "Window," for instance, which is *ventana* in Spanish, is *janela* in Portuguese. *Ninho* sounds just like the Spanish word for "child," but it means "nest." The Spanish *muchacho* is *rapaz* or *moço*, the Spanish *perro* ("dog") is *cão*, the Spanish *comer* ("to dine") is *jantar*.

Though both languages originated in the Iberian peninsula, Portuguese is in no sense a dialect of Spanish. In fact, Portuguese boasted a lovely, flourishing literature when Castilian was still the rough and ready tongue of the soldiers who were battling the Moors out of Spain.

But Spanish and Portuguese put together are still far from solving all the language problems of what goes under the name of "Latin America." On the Antillean island of Santo Domingo two small nations live side by side. The Dominican Republic, named after the island itself, speaks Spanish, but her sister republic of Haiti has French as its national tongue. This French is spoken by a black population, the descendants of the Negro slaves who rose up in revolt under Toussaint l'Ouverture at the end of the eighteenth century, killed off their French masters, and set up a completely independent nation. In the jungles of Haiti voodoo rites and a pidgin form of French still predominate, but in the cities, particularly Port-au-Prince, good Parisian is spoken by the more educated classes. The lower classes speak a French Creole of which this is a sample: *"Car Bon Dieu té r'aimé créatures-li si tant, que li baille seul Petite-li"* ("For the Good Lord loved His creatures so much, that he gave them His only Son").

French also appears in French Guiana, or Cayenne, noted for its pepper and the now discontinued penal colony of Devil's Island. It appears in the French islands of Martinique and Guadeloupe.

Dutch is the language of Dutch Guiana or Surinam; but the former British Guiana, now the independent country of Guyana, along with British Honduras, the Jamaican Federation, the Bahamas, and the Bermudas, uses English. This, however, is more likely to be a variant of the British King's English than of the American Language.

Side by side with these official tongues, there are curious pidgin languages. Like Melanesian-English and Chinese-English pidgin, they sprang up in areas where speakers of many different languages had to find some means of common intercourse.

Most picturesque among South American pidgins is the "wind-blown language," Papiamento, used by the native population of Curaçao in the Dutch West Indies. Its backbone is a mixture of Portuguese and Spanish, but it has words from many other sources, including English, as proved by *busnan* ("busman") and *trucknan* ("truckman"). A sample of Papiamento is *"Bo ta gusta mi sombré?"* ("Do you like my hat?").

A Negro-English pidgin called Taki-taki ("Talkie-talkie"), interspersed with Dutch and Portuguese words, is spoken in Dutch Guiana. Here is a specimen: *"Lookoo, mi sa meki dem kom an begi na you footoosi"* ("Behold, I will make them come and beg before your feet"). In Guayana and our own Virgin Islands, the tourist will come across a Dutch Creole, but this does not differ too much from Amsterdam Dutch.

Our own American Indian languages are fast dying out, despite the efforts of a few linguistic scholars to revive them. This is not at all the case with the Indian languages of Latin America. There are entire regions in the interior of Mexico where Nahuatl, the ancient language of the Aztecs, still holds its own, and the tourist who wants to buy a *serape* or piece of pottery will find it easier to use his English than his Spanish. The same is true of Guatemala and other Central American republics, where Mayan still lives. In South America, Quichua, the tongue of the Incas, is still used almost exclusively by some six million natives, extending in a broad band from Ecuador, across Peru and Bolivia, to northern Argentina. In Paraguay more people speak Indian languages than Spanish.

The figures on the racial composition of the various Spanish-American nations supply the explanation. In Mexico, Central America, Peru, Ecuador, Bolivia, and Paraguay, people of Indian or mixed blood account for 90 per cent of the population. In Venezuela and Colombia, Indian and mixed blood is 75 per cent of the total. Brazil's racial composition is three almost equal parts, white, Negro, and Indian. The only Latin-American nations where white blood predominates are Cuba (about 70 per cent), Chile, Argentina, and Uruguay (90 to 95 per cent).

When we come to the Spanish language itself, we find that it is official in Mexico, Central America (outside of British Honduras), Puerto Rico, Cuba, and nine countries of South America, with total populations of some 140 million. A six-week Berlitz course, we think, and we have learned enough Spanish to manage to get along with those 140 million. Spanish is supposed to be easy!

Not so fast! There is Spanish and Spanish. To begin with, there are some very noticeable pronunciation differences. We learn Castilian in high school or college, and then wonder why we can't readily understand the Puerto Ricans or Cubans. It is because they speak the same language with a different pronunciation, rhythm, and intonation. This was my own amusing experience: having been hired as private tutor by a very wealthy and aristocratic Cuban family, I went to Havana and discovered that while I could communicate readily with the house servants, I could not understand the masters. The servants were Spaniards imported from northern Spain; and spoke the Castilian I had learned. Cubans disdain domestic work, and prefer the sugar-cane fields; but high or low, they speak their own Antillean brand of Spanish. It did not take me too long to get accustomed to their pronunciation. A name like *Francisco,* pronounced fran-THEES-koh by its Gallego owner, would sound like fran-SEEH-koh in the mouth of the bosses. The final -*s* in forms like *los Cubanos* is practically lost in Cuban speech. Some words change meaning. *Cigarro* is in Cuba not a cigar but a cigarette. *Tabaco* is not tobacco, but cigar. *Manteca* is not lard, but butter.

Similar differences appear in most Spanish-American countries. They are not too radical, but radical enough to throw you off the track, like some of the differences between British and American English. The word for "horse" (*caballo*) will sound ka-VAH-lyoh, ka-VAH-yoh, ka-VAH-zhoh in different Hispanic lands.

A technical lexicographer once drew up for me a striking list of words calling for different translations in the various Spanish-American countries. If you want gasoline for your truck in Britain, you should ask for petrol for your lorry. In Mexico, it's *gasolina,* in Chile *bencina,* in Argentina *nafta,* and in Spain *esencia.* Rubber is generally *caucho,* but *hule* in Mexico and *jebe* in Peru. An automobile spring is *balleste* in Spain, *resorte* in Chile, *elástico* in Argentina, and *muelle* elsewhere.

Fortunately, Spanish speakers are generally tolerant of one another's pronunciations and vocabulary differences, and tend to stress their linguistic unity. Yet the differences exist, and rise to plague the good neighbor from the north who tries to communicate with his Spanish-American friends. Again fortunately, they are tolerant of your mistakes as well as of their own divergences.

CHAPTER 16

The Challenge
of Linguistic Realism

This is the era of Realism and Authenticitism, both spelled with capitals. Books, newspapers, magazines, radio, television, films, along with all other branches of mass education, mass information, and mass entertainment, are, or seem to be, vitally concerned with giving their readers and viewers impressions of authenticity and reality. If a scene is to be depicted, it must be portrayed as it would occur in real life. Conversational interchanges, factual or fictional, must be reported as they actually would take place, with all the errors and improprieties of lower-class speech, with which we are instructed to familiarize ourselves (one book on linguistics, aimed at elementary and high school teachers, urges them to learn the meaning of such phrases as "Cha doon?", which stands for "What are you doing?"; another extols the merits of "Wotchagonnado?", a third says that "Them dogs is us'uns" is good, clear, native-speaker American English). Works like Salinger's *Catcher in the Rye,* composed from beginning to end in the "idiolect," or individual natural speech, of the relator, stand as monuments to linguistic realism in the field of literature and are prescribed reading in some English high school and college classes.

Writers of historical novels and editors of popular magazines spend many weary hours of research to assure themselves and the public that every minor detail is authentic and authenticated. Producers of movie spectaculars put millions of dollars into making sure that they have the correct military posture and salute for Alexander's hoplites or Caesar's legionaries, the right kind of lamps for Marco Polo's

China and Casanova's Venice, the authentic attire for the Cid's Spain, Elizabeth I's England, and Mme de Pompadour's France.

But how does the world of fictional writing, of stage and screen and television, react to the problem of language diversity and language difficulties, which is a very real problem in real life? Here an illusion must be created for the benefit of readers and audience. One hundred per cent realism, the sort of thing authors and producers strive for in architecture, attire, customs and costumes, even gestures and mental attitudes, obviously won't do. If the scene of the action departs from the English-speaking world (and it has to be a fairly up-to-date English-speaking world, certainly no farther removed from us than the days of Shakespeare and King James), then realism must be faked, under penalty of throwing your present-day audience into utter confusion.

One might say in passing that the perfectionism of authenticity so manfully striven for in the historical field, where there is the ever-present danger that some carping critic will remind the writer or producer that the type of beard or the style of dueling he portrays is either anachronistic or two centuries ahead of its purported period, is all too often thrown into the discard where perfectly modern scenes are concerned. What man ever completed the operation of shaving in the six strokes and ten seconds flat devoted to it by so many of our movie and TV male stars? When did anyone ever see a starving man sit down to a meal, consume three forkfuls of whatever is spread out before him, then lay down his knife and fork and pass on to other types of action, his appetite seemingly sated? These inconsistencies are harmless. What is not so harmless, perhaps, is the type of slugging and other assorted forms of mayhem displayed on our screens with no seeming permanent harm to the recipients, who get up, rub their chins and stomachs, and move on to further action after undergoing punishment that in real life would send its victim to a permanent niche in a cemetery or, at the very least, consign him to a hospital ward for a month. It has also been suggested that viewing this type of action scene by the immature may be partly responsible for our juvenile crime waves, not only because it glorifies violence, but even more because it minimizes the physical effects of violence.

But the item that directly concerns the man interested in language is the problem of linguistic realism and its handling. Here illusion is not merely justified, but necessary. What are the devices or conventions by which the producer conveys to his audience these various linguistic realities: (1) when the characters he is watching are speaking a language other than the viewer's own; (2) when different characters are speaking different languages, each in his own environment and to his own fellow speakers; (3) when the characters speak different languages, and are having trouble understanding one another?

The problem of linguistic realism arose in literature before it came up on stage or screen. It has been handled differently in fictional and non-fictional writing. Homer's characters are Greeks and Trojans. The latter, presumably, spoke Phrygian, a language quite different from Greek, and thought to be of Illyrian stock. Yet in the *Iliad* there is at all times perfect communication between the two groups, with no hint of a language difference or difficulty. This situation is repeated in Virgil's *Aeneid,* with the added embellishment that Aeneas, a refugee from Troy, has no trouble whatsoever in giving a detailed account of his vicissitudes to Queen Dido of Carthage, who presumably spoke Punic. In contrast, non-fiction writers generally display their awareness of the language problem. Livy, Pliny, Cicero, and Caesar, to name a few, mention the need for interpreters in dealing with non-speakers of Latin. The third-century A.D. Ulpian Code makes it legal to draw up a will not only in Latin or Greek but also in Gaulish, Punic, or any other language whatsoever. St. Augustine and St. Jerome both show in their writings that language diversity exists, and must be reckoned with.

This interesting dichotomy between the chronicler of fact and the creative writer continues into the Middle Ages. While Christian missionaries were busy translating the Bible into many languages for the use of their converts, and Charlemagne prescribed specifically at the Council of Tours in 813 that church sermons henceforth were to be given not in Latin, but in the Teutonic or "Rustic Roman" (early Romance) tongues of the congregations, literary writers continued merrily to ignore the language problem. In the eleventh-century *Chanson de Roland,* Arabic-speaking Moors and French-speaking Franks communicate with the greatest of ease and with never a reference to a misunderstanding or an interpreter. It is only a century later, in the bilingual *contrasto* of Rambaut de Vaqueiras, that we find the Genoese heroine complaining that she does not understand her Provençal swain any more than if he were a German, a Sardinian, or an inhabitant of the Barbary Coast. Chaucer's prioress, who could speak the French of Stratford but not that of Paris, is further evidence of the growth of linguistic realism in literature.

In modern times, there is one feature of linguistic "realism" appearing in literature which is not realism at all, and is constantly deplored by linguists. This is the so-called "eye-dialect," that written form of a spoken dialect which purports to represent dialectal features or substandard language. This erroneous cleavage to realism leads some writers to put such spellings as "wuz," "sez," "likker," "kernel" into the mouths of their characters, largely for the sake of local color. Recently, Walter Winchell in creating a Damon Runyon character put the word "kidnapt" in the mouth of a speaker. Actually these spellings represent a quasi-phonetic transcription of perfectly good, normal pronunciations of such written forms as *was, says, liquor, colonel* and *kidnaped*. Here we might say that it is the cultivated written language that has strayed from reality.

But literature is only a symbolization of reality. The writer can conjure up for his readers any scene he wishes, merely by the judicious use of a few words. By the same token, he can take care of any linguistic situations by injecting a phrase or two into his narrative: "He spoke with a heavy German accent"; "John could barely understand what the *agent de police* was saying to him in French"; "Where language failed, they helped themselves out with gestures."

With stage and screen it is different. The entire action unfolds under your very eyes, as though it were real. The participants are alive, or endowed with life-like qualities. What to do?

The simplest thing, of course, is to ignore the problem altogether. Shakespeare's actors could, and still can, pretend that their clipped British English is the Venetian form of Italian in *The Merchant of Venice* or Copenhagen Danish in *Hamlet*. The audiences go along beautifully with the unspoken convention, and no one dreams of objecting. This is fine so long as the characters are all of one unified language background, whatever it may be. In the earlier days of the screen, and in the later days of television, it is quite all right for everyone to pretend that Chekhov's or Tolstoi's characters are all speaking Russian, which is somehow miraculously transformed into the English of an American audience, without even the benefit of the simultaneous translators and earphones of the UN.

The real trouble starts when the characters are of different ethnic backgrounds and speak different languages, as happens so often in modern movies and TV sketches. Here at least half a dozen devices are employed, some more ingenious than others. They have never, to my knowledge, been fully described and discussed.

I recall seeing, not too long ago, a TV-reproduced picture of the vintage of 1950 or thereabouts, dealing with a love affair, in occupied Budapest, between a Hungarian girl and a Russian officer. They, and all subsidiary characters with them, spoke perfect American English. This blissful ignoring of the language problem is on a par with the *Iliad* and the *Chanson de Roland*. It flavors the proceedings with a touch of unreality which may not strike all people, but is bound to strike some. "What are they supposed to be using for language?" is the question that arises in the mind of anyone who knows that language differences exist.

But some of our TV realists rise to the occasion. When the heroes of "I Spy" go after a ring of wicked Chinese Communist agents, the latter, every time they communicate among themselves, use good Peking Mandarin. The subsequent action clarifies the general meaning of their words, even if it does not translate them. The sense of linguistic logic of people like me is satisfied.

It is not at all satisfied, on the other hand, in other movies or sketches, where a group of Hungarian refugees use broken English among themselves, in the privacy of their own meeting place, as well as to the American detectives who are investigating them. It stands to reason that Carrol Naish would not be using synthetic broken English to a fellow Italian. Worse even than ignoring the problem of different languages is the attempt to solve it by having the characters use English flavored with a heavy accent, not merely when addressing Americans who do not know their language, but among themselves. Logic demands that if we are going to conventionalize their utterances, we do so in an English as perfect as their own native tongue would be.

Another somewhat more successful attempt at linguistic realism is typified by a series like "Combat." Here the GIs speak American English. The Germans speak German among themselves, as they should, and the French civilians speak French. The action usually takes care of the meanings. This is fine up to a point, and the point is where French, German, and American speakers have to intercommunicate. One of the GIs in Sarge Saunders' group is a French Canadian, and he does a fine job of translating from and into French whenever he's around. All the German officers, and occasionally some of the privates, speak English. This is realistic. They could have learned it in school. But their English is a trifle too perfect, as is that of too many French peasants and workers who must make themselves understood when our French Canadian friend is not in evidence. In less well-done pictures of the same type, one gets the impression that every inhabitant of an Italian or Japanese village speaks passable English, and this goes beyond the bounds of credibility.

An interesting if not too plausible variant of this attribution of high linguistic ability to everyone we come in contact with but ourselves is displayed in science fiction offerings of the "Outer Limits" or "Twilight Zone" type, where all sorts of visitors from outer space have taken the precaution to learn our language before setting out on their interplanetary wanderings. How did the boys from Mars know that they were going to come down on English-speaking territory? Don't any of them ever learn Russian, or Spanish, or Chinese by mistake? A highly ingenious creation in this division is *Star Trek*'s Universal Translating Computer, which handles all sorts of interplanetary communications, even when they are not in the form of speech. This is fine for actions that take place some centuries in the future, but would not be realistic for science fiction where the action occurs in the present.

One of the most effective devices, combining convention with realism, appeared in *The Last Bridge*. Here the action involves Yugoslav partisans and German occupation forces. By unspoken convention, the Germans are equated, for purposes of an English-speaking audience, to American GIs, and speak among themselves a straight GI English. The Yugoslavs, on the other hand, invariably talk among themselves and even sing in Serbo-Croatian, which does not interfere with the action. The personal plot revolves around the partisan leader and a German woman medical officer whom his men have captured, and whose professional services are needed. They use the English which is conventionally the equivalent of German. It is not unreasonable for the partisan leader, evidently a man of fair education, to know German, which in any event is fairly widespread in Yugoslavia. The picture does not jar.

The cover-up and fade-out device is seldom used. This is unfortunate, because it is altogether effective in creating the illusion of reality and easing acceptance of the convention. In one picture dealing with the invasion of the Roman Empire by the barbarians, which I saw many years ago, the voice of the Roman historian Tacitus is heard, describing the Germanic tribes in his own original Latin. It quickly fades out and is replaced by an English translation, but the audience is properly alerted to the fact that what they are going to hear subsequently is supposed to be Latin. Curiously, this method, so seldom employed in anything fictional, is, if anything, overused in news reports, where we are barely allowed to hear the very first words uttered by Kosygin in Russian or de Gaulle in French before the speaker's voice is covered by the translator's. This jars one person out of a hundred, and it is my luck that I am that one. The other ninety-nine would be far more grievously jarred if the translator did not quickly come to their rescue. In certain programs of a semi-educational nature, the cover-up is even more effectively used. In "The Signing of the Magna Charta" on Walter Cronkite's "You Are There," I, disguised as the court clerk, read off the original Latin version of the document, being covered up most of the time by the translator, but coming to the fore again and again in the course of the reading, so that a perfect illusion could be sustained.

The issue of linguistic realism hardly comes into play in the case of foreign films, spoken in their original tongues, with or without English subtitles. The criticism is often voiced that the written subtitle flashed across the bottom of the screen translates less than half of the utterances, and poorly at that. For this there is not much help, since the spoken word far outdistances writing in speed.

Realism again comes into play in the widespread advertising on radio and TV carried out wholly or partly in foreign languages. Here it is a moot question whether the basic idea in the back of the Madison Avenue mind is snob appeal, appeal to foreign groups in our midst, or a blend of both. What must be cheerfully admitted is that such advertising is generally done not only with intelligence and good taste, but with remarkable accuracy. Toothpaste commercials featuring French, Spanish, Italian, and Hawaiian scenes, complete with native speakers, macaroni commercials displaying pasta products being cooked in the interior of Florentine palaces, beer commercials showing Poles and Germans, Italians and Puerto Ricans, Swedes and French Canadians disporting themselves in native dances and songs as they imbibe their supposedly favorite beverage, are all done with a maximum of skill and precision, even to the voice of the English-speaking announcer who informs you that in New York there are more Hungarians than in Mohács and Eger combined, and pronounces both place names with absolute accuracy.

One last facet of linguistic realism applies to our own language, and forms part of a much broader picture. Should Shakespeare be put into modern dress for what concerns language? Should the language of the King James Bible be brought down to date? In like manner, if a producer is doing a spectacular that deals with Richard the Lion-Heart, King John, or Robin Hood, should an antiquated, stilted language be used, or are we justified in expecting twentieth-century locutions? The argument in favor of modernization is that since the characters in *Falstaff* and *Robin Hood* are supposed to be speaking the colloquial, even the slang, of their period, the proper way to achieve realism is to use the colloquial and slang of ours, thus rendering the spirit rather than the letter. The counter-argument runs that there is something highly incongruous about a Little John attired in Lincoln green yelling out to his comrades: "Hey, you guys, get a load of this!" even though this may be the present-day semantic equivalent of the "Look ye hither, my lads!" of the late twelfth century.

Combine time spread with language differences, as when Richard and Saladin meet in *The Crusades* and give each other samples of their prowess as swordsmen while they converse freely and easily in twentieth-century Hollywoodese, and you have a real problem.

It is perhaps fortunate, on the whole, that the average man worries as little as he does about language and its far-flung implications.

PART THREE

Language, Books, and Education

Language, Books, and Education

The process of education covers many different areas. One of the most important is language, which is the medium by which practically all education is imparted. But language comes in many forms—spoken, written, printed, recorded, taped, televised, telephoned. It comes in many varieties—native, foreign, local, nationwide, cultured, uncultured. It gives rise to many queries and problems.

Can language be bypassed in the educational and informational process? Can it be replaced by other media? Are medium and message (or "massage," if you prefer) synonymous? Which is more important, speech or writing? Can we successfully dispense with either? Is Marshall McLuhan justified in viewing the "linear," written language as on its way out?

In our ultra-modern civilization, what is the educational function of books, hardcover or paperback? Does one favor the educational process more than the other? Can we go back to a purely oral tradition, even if it is embodied in such modern devices as tapes, discs, and TV screens? Can we skip grammar in handling language?

What is the role of foreign languages in American life? Are we justified in regarding them as superfluous in the educational process, or, at the most, as an expensive and non-essential luxury?

How can foreign languages best be imparted, and at what age? Is there a hierarchy in the world of languages? What is its base? Are there valuable by-products that accompany language learning?

We can only attempt to answer some of these questions.

CHAPTER 17

Books and Language

Books represent the accumulated wisdom of the human race. They are the repositories of mankind's experience, in the six thousand and more years that have elapsed since it first occurred to man to record that experience in permanent form.

Ever since its inception, man has considered his gift of writing so precious and unique that many of the nations of antiquity created legends to the effect that it had been bestowed upon them by the gods. The name of the Sanskrit alphabet, still used today by Hindi, Bengali, and most of the other languages of India, is *Devanagari,* which literally means "pertaining to the city of the gods." The hieroglyphic system used by the ancient Egyptians means, in Greek, "sacred stone writing"; the Egyptians believed that the art of writing had been devised by Thoth, god of wisdom; their own expression for writing, literally translated, is "the speech of the gods." The Assyrians and Babylonians thought their cuneiform characters had been given to man by the god Nebo, who held sway over human destiny. The Mayas attributed their writing system to their most important deity, Itzamna. The lost prehistoric writing of Japan, replaced about A.D. 300 by the Chinese characters, was styled *kami no moji,* "divine characters." Even today, backward groups that receive from missionaries their new code of belief and behavior receive from them also the gift of literacy. To many of these groups, writing and religion are inextricably intertwined.

While the ancients immortalized their thoughts on stone and bricks of clay, wax tablets and rolls of papyrus, our own most important and permanent form of writing is books. It is books that give us access to all the varied forms of thought of the past and present—

religious, philosophical, artistic, poetic, fictional, scientific. The burning of books is a favorite practice of those totalitarian regimes that wish to stifle free thought. Destroying books goes hand in hand with slaughtering human beings, because the book is capable of pointing an accusing finger at a wrongdoer with the same precision with which a man says: "I accuse!"

This writer can still recall the days when there was neither radio nor television. There were fewer books then than there are now, but more were read. Books were a precious possession. I can still remember how I treasured the few books I brought with me, at the age of seven, from my native land, and how until I had mastered my new language I read those books over and over and over again. They were more than friends. They were guides and counselors. They were signposts, pointing the way to self-improvement and achievement.

The written language, the spoken language, and thought stand in the same relation to one another as the check, the dollar bill, and purchasing power. The relationship is based on symbolism. Language is in itself only a symbol of thought. Writing is then a symbol of a symbol. It portrays the spoken language, which in turn portrays the thought. This is what happens in the majority of written languages today. There are, however, some exceptions, as will be seen later.

At first, writing was probably merely a series of pictures, similar to a comic strip. The writer would portray in pictorial form, and in sequence, the episodes he wished to describe. Eventually he would come out with a complete story in pictures of all the episodes he wanted to depict to his "readers." This was often done by the American Indians, who carved on trees records of their hunting and fishing trips or war expeditions.

However, this system began to give way early in history to a pictographic system whereby the written symbol would portray an object that could be pictured. As time went on, this system was modified into an ideographic one. To portray concepts which were not picturable, two or more pictographic symbols would be ingeniously combined. The Chinese, for example, combined into a single ideograph the two pictographs for "tree" and "sun." The sun rising over the tree would then ideally stand for the concept of "east." In this sort of system, the symbolization is of thought, not of spoken language. There is a direct line between the thought and the written symbol, and the spoken language is bypassed. Or we might say that the line runs in two different directions from the thought concept: on the one side to the spoken symbol, on the other to the written symbol. The spoken and the written symbol are independent of each other.

But there came a time when some of the races that used these pictographic and ideographic systems turned them into picturizations of the language sounds, rather than of either objects or thought concepts. This seems to have happened for the first time with the ancient Phoenicians. They had a system of pictographs and ideographs whereby, for instance, the head of an ox stood for the spoken word *aleph,* which meant "ox." As they began to develop their new system, the symbol of the oxhead was used instead to portray the initial consonant sound of the word *aleph,* a glottal stop which in Semitic precedes the *a.* In like manner, they had a symbol that portrayed a house, and this stood originally for the spoken word *beth,* "house." When they shifted over, they began to use the same written symbol with the value of the initial *b* in *beth.* At this point, we have a shift from a pictographic-ideographic system to a phonetic system.

The phonetic system became generalized throughout the West, whereas in the East, in countries like China and Japan, they continued to use the old pictographic-ideographic system, so that even today, in spoken Chinese, there is next to no link between the sounds and the written representations. The link is between the written representation and the thought concept on the one side, between the thought concept and the spoken word on the other, and the two are independent of each other.

More people throughout the world use phonetic than pictographic-ideographic systems. But considering that in China there is a population of between 600 and 700 million, it can readily be seen that the old system still survives to a considerable degree. Both systems have their peculiar advantages and disadvantages. The main advantage of the older system lies in the fact that it can be used internationally. We can use our written symbol "$10" internationally. The $ symbol and the written figure 10 will be understood no matter what the spoken representation is: *ten dollars,* as in English; *dix dollars,* as in

French; *diez dólares,* as in Spanish; or in any other form the language may prescribe. In a country like China, where there are mutually unintelligible dialects, the same written language can be used throughout the entire country, and everyone who is literate understands it with little or no difficulty. At the same time, there is some mutual comprehension between Chinese and Japanese in written form, though the two spoken languages differ radically.

But the pictographic-ideographic system has the disadvantage that it does not represent sound, and cannot be referred to the sounds of the spoken tongue. This means that knowledge of spoken Chinese will in no way aid you to read its written form, while knowledge of the written form will be of no help whatsoever in speaking or understanding the spoken language.

The great disadvantage of the phonetic system of writing, used in most Western countries, is that it very often reflects a past, not a present, state of spoken-language affairs. This is particularly noticeable in English, where written words are couched in a spelling that often represents the sounds of ten centuries ago, not those of today. In a word like "knight," there is little if any coincidence between sounds and spelling; but if we take the spoken language back ten centuries to the time when they said *cniht,* we have a fairly close approximation to that sound with the present-day spelling. In addition, there are languages that are not fully standardized, where there are different dialect forms. Then the spelling system tries to conform to one or another of those forms, but cannot conform to all of them. The spellings "marry," "Mary," "merry" reflect the different pronunciations for those three words that prevail in the East of the U.S., not the uniform pronunciation for all three that is characteristic of the Midwest.

The phonetic system is further subdivided into syllabic and alphabetic. There are languages that represent by their written symbols not individual sounds, but combinations of sounds, usually in the form of a full syllable. The Japanese have done this to a certain degree, using their syllabic characters side by side with the pictographs and ideographs they borrowed from Chinese.

A fully alphabetic form would have the ideal relationship of one sound for one symbol, but while this was approximated at the outset, it seldom works out in practice today because of the historical factor of change in the spoken tongue unaccompanied by a corresponding change in spelling.

Practically all alphabetic systems in use today stem directly or indirectly from the ancient Phoenician, which gave rise to the Hebrew characters, those of Arabic and Greek, the Roman characters used in most Western countries, and the Cyrillic used by the Russians and other Slavic groups. Alphabetic writing has been applied to both ancient and modern languages. Generally, so far as sound is concerned, it is much more faithful in the ancient than in the modern tongues. Spoken language is in a continual state of change, while written language tends to lag behind. In languages like Greek and Latin, the alphabetic notation coincides reasonably well with what we know were the early spoken forms. But as the languages evolved, the spoken tongue tended to outstrip the written, so that discrepancies between the two arose and grew. Ancient Greek was quite faithful to its written representation; modern Greek is not. Classical Latin is quite well represented by the letters of the Roman alphabet, but the modern Romance languages that stemmed from Latin have had to make use of all manners of spelling devices to represent sounds that are innovations in those languages and did not exist in Latin. The Anglo-Saxon alphabet served the purpose of representing the tongue of the Anglo-Saxons rather well, but our present-day Roman alphabet as used in modern English presents wide and illogical discrepancies and divergences.

There are other alphabetic forms where the spread between speech and writing is greater or almost as great. Spanish, Italian, and German are reasonably faithful to their written representations. French is almost as bad as English, while the modern Gaelic of Ireland is worse (though a spelling reform is in progress designed to narrow the gap). In Finnish, on the other hand, there is almost complete coincidence of spoken sound and written symbol. This generally happens when the language is of recent recording (not of recent origin, because languages were generally spoken long before they were written). Accordingly, we find that other languages, such as Hungarian and Albanian, where the written form was developed in relatively recent times, are fairly faithful to their spoken system. Turkish, which came over to the Roman alphabet within the last fifty years, has practically sound-for-symbol correspondence. But languages that have been around in written form for a long time, like French and English, tend to show a large spread.

This means that in the schools of the various countries different provisions have to be made for the learning of the written form. Where the spoken language is fairly well represented by its written counterpart, relatively little time has to be devoted to the spelling problem. The alphabet is presented, then the students are instructed to use it logically, to put their words together, and when they hear a certain sound to use a certain letter. This becomes impossible in languages like English and French, where the same sound may be denoted by as many as ten or more different written combinations. This means that in countries where the big spread exists, people are compelled to go through a long, troublesome, time-wasting process of learning how to spell, read, and write. This means in turn that all the time that is devoted to learning to read and write has to be taken away from other, more factual, subjects. It has been suggested that one of the reasons why English speakers run somewhat behind those of other countries in their acquisition of factual subjects is that they have to devote so much time to the study of their alphabetic system and the correlation between speech and writing.

In a country like Italy, for instance, learning to read and write is a rather simple process. The alphabet is set up on the board, and various syllabic combinations are presented (*a, e, i, o, u; ba, be, bi, bo, bu; ca, che, chi, co, cu,* etc.). Each of these is gone through, and then all the student has to do is put these combinations together to represent whatever sounds he happens to hear. All this can be done easily in the course of two or three years. Beyond that, there may be some confusion once in a while as to how to spell a word, but such confusion is rare. In English, on the other hand, the process of learning to spell individual words goes on through elementary school, continues in high school, even in college, and eventually people emerge with a Ph.D. degree, but still have to look up words in Webster's.

In countries that have more complicated systems of writing, the problem of literacy becomes even more complex. In most languages of India there is not an alphabetic system indicating individual sounds, but a syllabic system where the symbols stand for certain syllables. This means that the symbols are multiplied. Instead of having twenty-six or thirty-two letters of the alphabet, there are perhaps a hundred written syllabic symbols. This puts a strain on the memory. Each of these symbols has to be learned and assimilated. Even when people become literate, there is a good deal of backsliding. If they stay away from school for a time, when they try to read and write again they find they have forgotten how to do so, and have to make a fresh start.

In languages like Chinese and Japanese there are written symbols that stand neither for individual sounds nor for syllables, but betoken thought concepts. While they have the advantage of being international in scope, their number is multiplied beyond all reason. A true Chinese scholar has to know at least ten thousand of these symbols, and even the ordinary person has to know about four thousand before he can read an ordinary newspaper. The strain upon the memory of learning four thousand characters to the point of recognizing them in reading and forming them in writing constitutes a large chore for the school system, and takes time away from chemistry, biology, mathematics, history, and other school topics.

All languages are equally easy, in spoken form, to their own speakers. A Chinese child finds spoken Chinese no more difficult than an American child finds English. But this emphatically does not apply to the written language, where there are definite inherent standards of ease or difficulty. A language may be said to have an easy written system when the latter is completely or almost completely phonetic, and there is what the linguists call "fit" between the spoken word and its written symbolization. Other languages have an inherently difficult written system when they get away from sound-for-symbol fit, having either irrational spellings, like English or French, or a symbolization of concepts rather than of sounds, like Chinese or Japanese.

The problem of making people literate therefore differs from country to country. It can, of course, be overcome in all countries by the process of education. There is no question that, given enough time and effort, a speaker of English can be made as literate as a speaker of Spanish or Italian, and that this process of education for literacy can be extended to all the people of China and India, but the problems are going to be different in each country, both in kind and in magnitude. To a considerable degree, the differences in literacy levels we find in the various countries of the world are due to the extent of divergence between the spoken and the written form they happen to use. It is perhaps no accident that in India there are at present still something like 70 per cent illiterates, while in Germany or Finland literacy is practically 100 per cent. On the other hand, the proof that the literacy problem can be licked anywhere through education, regardless of the "fit" between speech and writing, is offered by Japan, where the percentage of literates is higher than our own, despite the fact that the Japanese have to use the same system of pictographs and ideographs used by the Chinese. They all go to school for a long enough period, are properly trained and taught, and all learn to read and write. But there is no question that it might be worth while for some countries to revise their writing systems in order to achieve greater ease of learning and a better balance of educational standards. Therefore, in various countries, the problem of reform of the written language comes to the fore.

It is not only in English-speaking countries that people have suggested that spelling be changed. The same idea has occurred in many countries, and in some it has been put into operation. For languages like Chinese and Japanese, the suggestion has been made and favorably received by many that it would be better to use a phonetic alphabet instead of pictographs, ideographs, or even the syllabaries in partial use in Japan. In both countries there are large and strong movements for Romanization, with a phonetic form of the Roman alphabet, so that the link will be between the language sound and the written symbol.

Interesting orthographic reforms have taken and are taking place in several countries. One was conducted in the Soviet Union not long after the Soviets came to power in 1917. There it was mainly a question of discarding some alphabetic symbols that were no longer needed and caused confusion by reason of duplication of symbols for the same sound. But this did not go very far, and was not a true reform. While Russian is more phonetically spelled than English, there are still considerable divergences between sound and spelling.

A very radical reform took place in Turkey. It was the work of Mustapha Kemal Atatürk, who decided that the Turks should shift from the Arabic alphabet they had been using, which did not represent Turkish sounds very well, to a Roman alphabet so constructed and adjusted as to represent those sounds precisely. Kemal's reform was made easier by the fact that Turkey's illiteracy percentage was very high, with no more than 20 per cent of the population able to read and write. Many people were able to start from scratch, learning the new system without being handicapped by knowing the old one. Today Turkish is universally written in Roman characters, properly adjusted to the sounds of the language, and Turkish is one of the most phonetically written languages in the world. The result has been that literacy immediately began to spread, and now at least half the population can read and write.

Something similar took place in Indonesia, which had been using a mixture of different scripts while it was still the Dutch East Indies. Certain native Javanese alphabets were used in Java, many of the Moslem population used Arabic characters, and wherever Dutch or English influence extended the Roman alphabet was used to represent the sounds of Indonesia's many languages. When the Republic of Indonesia was created, it was decided to create a standardized national language which was given the name of Bahasa Indonesia ("language of Indonesia"). It was also decided to shift over completely to Roman script, using it in its so-called English version rather than its Dutch version. (This meant that a place name like Bandung gave up its Dutch-version spelling form *Bandoeng*.) Today the Indonesian language is one of the most phonetically spelled in the world, and can be read easily once one has learned the sounds of the letters of the alphabet.

Very interesting experiments are being tried all the time in constructing alphabetic forms for backward groups that have never had a system of writing. Missionaries who go to Africa or South America to convert the natives generally also undertake to give them a written form of their language. To do this, they have to adapt an alphabet (usually the Roman) to the sounds of whatever African or American

Indian language they are dealing with. There are at least a thousand languages of backward groups spread throughout the world that have received a written form within the last fifty years through the efforts of the missionaries.

In the case of our great Western languages, such as English and French, various questions arise: Is spelling reform desirable? Is it feasible? If it is both desirable and feasible, how to go about it?

There has existed for many years a group called the Simplified Spelling Association, with branches in both Britain and America, that has been advocating some sort of phonetization and modernization of English spelling. They have not progressed too far because people are traditionally minded and don't care to be disturbed in their ways and habits.

But there is a deeper underlying reason for the lack of spelling reform in English. English is not only a language of conflicting spelling and pronunciation, but also a language of conflicting pronunciations. It has no set standard. There are dialects in English, and none is official. There is no acceptance in America of the British "King's English" (or "Queen's English," depending on who sits on the British throne; this semi-official type of British English is based on the usage of cultivated Londoners and is regularly used in BBC broadcasts). There can be no acceptance in Britain of an American standard that doesn't even exist, as can be seen by glancing at Webster's dictionary, where plenty of alternative pronunciations appear, based on regional usage even of the more educated classes.

If we undertook to give English a phonetic spelling, the question would come up: "Phonetic of what?" Which form of pronunciation would be standard, and be reflected in the new orthography? We would have to classify and label certain sounds and pronunciations as "correct" or "incorrect," something that American linguists are quite averse to doing. But if it is not done, we shall have, embedded in any revised spelling, the same difficulties we have now: primarily, a spelling that does not fully reflect pronunciation.

Many spelling reformers are compromise-minded, and willing to settle for partial reform, something less than full phonetization, as illustrated by such spellings as *nite* for "night." But this would lead to even greater confusion.

The question also arises whether we want to retain our present Roman alphabet of twenty-six letters. If we do, we shall not have enough characters to cover all the phonemes (or significant sounds) in the language. The number of these varies with different dialects, but forty is the average. What to do with the phonemes for which we don't have symbols? If we use combinations of symbols, like the *th* of "through," which represents a single spoken sound (but *th* can also represent two separate sounds, as in "outhouse"), we lose the principle of sound-for-symbol.

If we use a true phonetic alphabet, such as the IPA (International Phonetic Alphabet), we shall have precise correspondence of symbol for sound.*

The following, for instance, is how a Shakespearean quote would look using the IPA:

> All the world's a stage,
> ɔːl ðə wɜːrldz ə stejdʒ
>
> And all the men and women merely players:
> ænd ɔːl ðə mɛn ænd wɪmɪn miːrlɪ plejərz
>
> They have their exits and their entrances,
> ðej hæːv ðeːr ɛgzɪts ænd ðeːr ɛntrənsəz

---

* The following is a sample of an IPA transcription, using the author's Eastern American pronunciation:

> ɔː = *all*
> ð = *the*
> ə = the
> ɛ = *met*
> ʒ = ple*s*ure
> æ = *a*nd
> ɪ = *it*
> eː = th*ere*
> ŋ = si*ng*
> j = bo*y*
> ej = st*age*

And one man in his time plays many parts,
ænd wɔn mæn ɪn hɪz tajm plejz mænɪ pɑːrts

His acts being seven ages.
hɪz ækts biːɪŋ sɛvən ejdʒəz.

But such an alphabet, for the adult generation, would mean learning to read and write all over again, unlearning what they already know, having acquired it at the cost of great effort in their youth. This would not apply to children, who would learn the new system by a natural and simple process that would take relatively little time. But then the problem of overlapping generations comes up. Since we cannot scrap and reprint overnight all of our books and written records, the young generation will have to learn the old spelling anyway, if it wants access to those still current books and records.

Last, but not least, comes the question of political complications. In most countries, education is a function of the central government, which is in a position to implement nationwide reforms. In America and Britain, education is a function of state or local government, so that spelling reform would have to go state by state, or school district by school district.

One final aspect of the question of the written language has distressing overtones. Several writers have been insistently, and even somewhat gleefully, hinting at the eventual disappearance of the written language.

This hypothesis is startling, yet it has some foundation. The written language used to have two great advantages over speech. It permitted communication across time and across space. Today, it is losing both of those advantages. We transmit speech directly, across space, by radio waves and telephone. We can tape a record, and keep a spoken instead of a written record. Should we look forward to a time when speech will universally take over, and writing, after having served mankind for so many centuries, will wither away and disappear, much as the horse, or even the railroad, are disappearing as means of transportation before the inroads of the automobile and the airplane?

If this were to happen, it would be highly ironic that at the very time when we are finally succeeding in making everyone literate, the object of literacy should vanish. The countries of the West have achieved, to be modest, at least 90 per cent literacy. The same applies to the Soviet Union and other European Communist countries. China has been making great strides, and Japan outstrips us in literacy. Literacy campaigns are being successfully waged in Latin America, in Africa, in southern Asia. By the end of this century, we confidently look forward to literacy so widespread as to be practically universal. And precisely at that time, according to some, there will be no further need for literacy, because all people will transmit their thoughts through speech, either directly or in "canned" form, across both time and space!

But there are other considerations. The written language has æsthetic as well as practical functions. Can one get from a recording, or even from a play spoken on the stage, precisely the same values he gets from reading that play? In the written language, there is the possibility of slowing down or speeding up to suit yourself. If there is a passage that particularly strikes you, that you really want to sink in, you may read it word by word; if it is not particularly important, you may skim over it. This cannot quite be done with a phonograph recording, and even less with a live voice. To a certain extent, it is still true that *Verba volant, scripta manent,* "Words fly away, but writing remains."

Even from a material standpoint, is it quite true that everything can be portrayed by means of the spoken voice? There are many things that normally appear in writing and not in speech. You call for the menu in a restaurant, run your eye over it, and out of a hundred possible items pick out three or four. How could that menu be properly presented in spoken form?

In spite of Marshall McLuhan and all his omens, it is likely that the written language will endure. This is desirable on practical grounds, because some things are better said in writing than in speech. It is desirable on æsthetic grounds, because certain values and certain pictures that are aroused in the mind by the written word cannot be aroused by speech, or even by picturization of the episode. Some things we would rather read than hear. Others we would rather read than see. There are works of literature which to be properly appreciated must be read. How can a beautiful piece of poetry by Shelley or Keats be put on the screen? How can it be recited in such a way that it is suited to the tempo and temperament of each individual? Screen and speech have their own value, but the written and printed word has a certain power that cannot be rivaled or replaced.

CHAPTER 18

The Medium Is
Not *the Massage*

I may describe myself as one of the early discoverers of Marshall McLuhan. In 1952, I wrote in my *Story of English**:

"H. M. McLuhan, Professor of English at the University of Toronto, in a discussion of the increasing emphasis on picture books, states that 'literary culture is through, at least temporarily,' and that 'we are in for auditory and visual media,' something he does not regret, since 'the great periods of history have not been literary.' Children, he goes on, should not be dragged through a literary education, and 'only the highbrows hold the line against the popular arts.' "

The views expressed at that time by McLuhan have since been systematized and expanded into a philosophy of life and a blueprint for the present and the future. It is far more than the written language that McLuhan consigns to oblivion in his most recent works.

The media by which men communicate are of far greater importance in shaping societies than the content of the communications, says McLuhan in his *The Medium Is the Massage*. To a linguist, this is highly reminiscent of Benjamin Lee Whorf and Stuart Chase, who claim that the type of language used by various groups influences and dictates the thought processes, behavior, and attitude toward life of those groups. Perhaps McLuhan does not consider any type of civilization outside of our own Western one worth discussing, or perhaps he figures that our type of civilization is destined to be

---

* J. B. Lippincott, p. 278.

the universal civilization of all mankind. At any rate, he generalizes the situation, and his generalization has apocalyptic overtones.

McLuhan's theory in a nutshell is this: Our new media (movies, Telstar, flight, etc.) supply us with a mass of information that far transcends anything known before. This information can no longer be absorbed, digested, and assimilated on a linear basis (that is, by the traditional "learning" process). It must be sensed and grasped all at once. What you miss, you miss. What you misinterpret stays misinterpreted. There is no time for study, no leisure for introspection. The learning of the future comes through the senses and by-passes the conscious brain.

Unfortunately, a good deal of this is true. McLuhan points to the disappearance of the conscious, critical individual, with a mind and viewpoint of his own, to the mass public and the packages of passive entertainment ("education" if you will) fed to it. He describes mass participation, through the viewing screen, in what goes on in the outside world. The family circle as a means of education and training is largely dead. So is the religious circle (after all, "God is dead"). All that remains is the impression, the "massage," conveyed by the new media.

One by-product of all this is the doctrine of collective responsibility and collective guilt, as apart from the freedom of conscience and the discrimination between right and wrong of the responsible individual. Since we all "participate," are we not all guilty? Perhaps McLuhan forgets that we don't all necessarily participate, and that media can be so manipulated as to bring us misinformation, which in turn means that we respond to the wrong "massage." "Precision" McLuhan admits, "is sacrificed for a greater degree of suggestion," and the result is the creation of a myth. Real, total war becomes information war. The hydrogen bomb is "history's final exclamation point, ending an age-long sentence of manifest violence."

All this is at least partly true. The question is, how do we react to it? McLuhan seems to view the process he describes with tacit approval, investing it with an aura of inevitability that has a tinge of Marxian determinism. "This is the way history is heading. Within a century, we shall all be robots, manipulated (or 'massaged') like computers," he seems to say. Who will do the massaging? Presumably the same combination of political, military, and commercial propagandists who are doing it now. But they, being conditioned by the same media and circumstances, will themselves be robots. The world machine will ultimately run by its own momentum, without conscious direction.

Yet history is there to show us that man has seldom bowed to the "inevitable." Hitler wanted us to believe that the next thousand years would "inevitably" be dominated by a race of supermen; he was proved wrong. The Marxist-Leninist-Maoist theorists want us to believe that we must all "inevitably" submit to a Red bureaucracy, running an all-powerful world state machine in which all individuals will be cogs. The struggle is still in progress, but so far the Communist wave has been turned back in a considerable number of places. All that is needed is the will not to submit to the "inevitable," meeting ideas with better ideas, and force with greater force, if necessary.

McLuhan's prophecy of a universe dominated by media without content—or with a made-to-order content, which is closer to the truth —is still an unwarranted assumption. There is widespread revolt right now against films of violence and sex, against tasteless, graceless, greedy commercials on radio and TV, against what goes on in some highly publicized circles under the name of modern literature, modern art, modern music. By and large, man is still a thinking, rational, critical animal, and wants to remain one.

The mere fact that man accepts and utilizes the comfort and convenience of modern devices (communication media among them) does not mean that he is discarding his basic faculties and points of view. For a certain number of morons who allow themselves to be influenced by violence and sex or by vapid commercials on the TV screen, there are far more people who take both in their stride, and continue to lead their own individual lives and think their own individual thoughts in their own individual fashions.

McLuhan is wrong even on a purely material plane. Let us take one aspect of his gospel, the one with which this writer is most familiar. Writing, says McLuhan, is dying. "The alphabetic and printed technology fostered and encouraged a fragmenting, individualistic process of specialism and detachment, while electric technology fosters unification and involvement."

Were this really so, we should expect to see manifestations of the written and printed word diminishing. Actually, at no period in history has literacy been so widespread. Books, magazines, newspapers, written material of all kinds are multiplying at the fastest rate in history. More information is being spread through the printed page than ever before. True, this written information is flanked by audio-visual auxiliaries, by recordings, tapes, radio, TV, telephoned messages. Let us say that the sum total of available information has multiplied a thousandfold, and that its channels of distribution are far more numerous than they were in the past. But the printed word remains and expands. Even those cultures which should be most sympathetic to McLuhan's basic theory of the identity of medium and massage, with minimal or severely restricted content, make use of the written language to an unprecedented degree. The Soviet output of books (good, serious, scientific and literary works, shorn of all propagandistic content) is astounding. And does not every Red Guard in Red China have to possess at least one copy of Chairman Mao's *printed* thoughts, and flash it like a Lark pack to all and sundry, on every occasion? And what of the *written* posters that festoon every Chinese mainland city?

Newtonian physics, which McLuhan deprecates, is not dead merely because we have added a new Einsteinian dimension. The linear, reflective, individualistic type of thought betokened by the written, printed word is not dead because we have added an audio-visual dimension. What may be in store one thousand years from now is not yet clear (even McLuhan seems to have his doubts when he mentions the hydrogen bomb). But, as of today, the medium is not yet the total massage. In fact, even in its vastly expanded and variegated form, it is still largely what it always has been—a medium!

CHAPTER 19

The Case for
Prescriptive Grammar

The doctrine of usage pushed to its outer limits implies that everyone may and should talk, write, and spell as he pleases. In the final analysis, this is perhaps precisely what happens. If I speak and write "correctly" (that is, in accordance with traditional standards) it is because it pleases me to do so.

Does this individual preference give me the right to interfere with someone else's preference, or attempt to force him to subscribe to the same standards? Basically, no. Does it give me the right to formulate value judgments concerning the other person's intelligence, educational background, or ability to perform certain tasks? Basically, yes. My right to formulate an honest opinion is as basic as the other person's right to speak and write as he pleases. Note, by the way, that he is equally free to formulate his own judgment about me.

Above all, he is free to question the grounds on which I formulate my judgment about him. When he does this, I had better have the right answers. It emphatically will not do to reply "Because we've always done it this way." Traditionalism *per se* is no satisfactory explanation.

The fact that language changes is too well known to call for repetition or examples. Innovations lead to change. If one person starts an innovation, and a sufficient number of people accept it, we have a language change, and the innovation thereafter becomes part of the standard language. This means that the NBC executive who decided to label a certain documentary "Khrushchev in Exile," and justifies his use of *exile* on the ground that Khrushchev is "exiled" from his former post of power (surely not from his native land, or familiar surroundings, or privileged economic state, as the picture makes abundantly clear) must rely on enough people accepting his definition of *exile,* which is not supported by any of the existing dictionaries.

When commercial advertisers use forms like "Us Tareyton smokers" and "like a cigarette should," they are actually relying on a considerable body of speakers who already accept and use those constructions. When they go on to *macaroniest, peanuttiest,* and *coffee-er coffee,* they stand on weaker ground; but they may be building up support, since Barry Goldwater recently described Lyndon Johnson as one of the "throat-cuttingest" politicians on record, and a university president stated orally that he intended to be the "buildingest" president his institution ever had.

Prescriptive grammar, like the traditional dictionary, aims at giving a cross section of cultivated usage. Why cultivated? Is it merely a matter of snob appeal? Are we setting up an aristocracy of language? Perhaps so; but the aristocratic feature is solidly based. For one thing, the aristocracy is one of education, which in the final analysis means ability and power to use words and forms meaningfully and effectively, through a precise knowledge of their origin, history, and generally accepted meaning. It stands to reason that if we are using a long word of Latin origin, the man who knows the original form and composition of the word will be able to use it more precisely than the man who knows it only from hearsay.

But there is a deeper reason for preferring the cultivated language. The cultivated language is generally more standardized throughout the speaking area than the untutored language. This means that the same word or form will carry the same meaning to all who use it. Uncultivated language is fraught with localisms which are incomprehensible to speakers from other parts of the area. This community of meaning leads to a community of understanding, and a better possibility of effective collaboration. Speakers of local dialects who do not possess a common cultivated language are often as much at a loss to grasp one another's meaning as are speakers of different languages. This gives prescriptive grammar and the prescriptive dictionary a utilitarian, practical advantage over uncritical descriptive grammar and the dictionary that records all usage without stating what is standard language and what is slang, vulgarism, or localism.

Lastly, the prescriptive grammar has the effect of slowing up language change. Language change can never be halted, nor would it be desirable to halt it. But when it progresses at too fast a rate, it can lead to the same type of confusion and misunderstanding as local dialects. Orderly progress is superior to anarchical, haphazard change, which makes the language of one area, class, or generation incomprehensible to another.

Besides, there is the matter of worth-while distinctions of meaning. The prescriptive grammar will tell you to use *disinterested* and *uninterested* in two different connections rather than advise you to jumble them up on the ground that many people do it. It will establish a distinction between *bi-monthly* and *semi-monthly*, between *imply* and *infer*, between *principle* and *principal*. All of which is worth while.

What may not be worth while in a prescriptive grammar are certain pettifogging points of usage that serve no useful purpose (the absurd distinctions between *shall* and *will*, or between *that* and *which* as a relative pronoun, so dear to the hearts of Fowler and Follett, for instance). Here it is up to the speaker to make his own choice and decide what he will use.

It is sometimes charged that prescriptive grammar is bad because it is based on the structure of older languages (Latin and Greek) rather than on the structure of modern spoken English. To find the slavish imitations of classical models described and condemned by some modern linguists we have to go rather far back in history; the works they condemn have been out of print for decades and centuries. What they really object to is not structural models, but judicial, discriminating states of mind—the labeling of certain forms and uses as "good" or "bad," "correct" or "incorrect," "right" or "wrong." For these expressions, they often substitute "standard" and "substandard," or "acceptable" and "unacceptable in certain milieus." Basically, this is quibbling. It is an interesting fact that the critics of prescriptive grammar are its most faithful followers. They may advocate extending equality to substandard usages in theory, but they actively discriminate against them in practice.

There is room in the scholarly world for both approaches. Descriptive grammar, recording all substandard usages, improprieties, even scatologies, is legitimate and desirable for purposes of scientific research. We want to know what people say, whether we use it ourselves or not. Prescriptive (not dictatorial) grammar serves the purpose of telling us what goes on in the upper echelons which most of us are striving to enter. There is no inherent contradiction between scholarly objectivity and social desirability. Hierarchies are basic and universal in all human societies, even the most equalitarian, and language is the most human of man's pursuits.

CHAPTER 20

Languages in Paperback

The paperback, once a book form restricted for the most part to fiction with lurid covers and occasionally lurid contents, is now a mighty instrument of mass culture at low prices. More than that, it has entered highly specialized fields where hardcover publishers hesitated to venture because of low commercial yield, and fields which were once reserved exclusively for the university presses.

Even a cursory glance at *Paperbound Books in Print* brings to light the fact that we now have available, at prices ranging from 50 cents to $2, works that sell in hardcover for $3 to $12. And there are ever-growing lines of specialized books originally and solely published in paperback. There are serious non-fiction works by the thousands to broaden the outlook of the population at large and speed the educational process.

The paperback has made it possible for the serious student to acquire and own not only some necessary textbooks, but also large blocks of works prescribed for outside reading. Only one who went through the educational mill before the evolution of paperbacks can fully appreciate what this means—the vast saving in money, time, and mental strain to the student, who can now buy a fresh, unused book instead of having to bargain for a pencil-marked secondhand copy; who can have his collateral reading at his own disposal for use at home or on a bus, instead of having to do it in the library reading room with copies that are on reserve; and who can carry his books around with him easily and comfortably, instead of having to transport ponderous tomes to and from school. The paperback eases the work of the teacher, who can prescribe all the books he deems necessary without fear that they will break his students' backs, both physically and financially. The paperback makes it possible for a man of modest means to acquire a whole library in the field that interests him.

Nowhere is this development more in evidence than in the field of language-teaching and language-learning, which has undergone tremendous expansion and drastic changes since 1940. The Second World War took up to twelve million young Americans of both sexes out of their English-speaking environments and scattered them to the far corners of the earth. There they came in contact, willy-nilly, with millions who knew no English. This experience proved conclusively, even to confirmed isolationists, the living reality of foreign languages and the fact that they were actual spoken tongues, not merely cultural tools. The emphasis in languages shifted, suddenly and dramatically, from the reading-writing to the speaking-understanding objective. Native speakers for imitation and language laboratories became the vogue. But even purely conversational courses have to be based on written materials—manuals and grammatical outlines, readers, dictionaries.

At the same time, the arts of peace call for the study of a language's literary output, either in the foreign language or in translation or both. The cultural angle of a language appears mainly in printed form, and this is where the nascent paperback industry came into the picture.

The increase in language enrollments in high schools, colleges, and universities has been startling—a jump of more than 100 per cent since 1940. But this tells only a minor part of the story. Languages are being studied privately, either in specialized schools of the Berlitz type or at home, by means of courses on records. More and more publishing houses are crowding into the language-records field. But even a recorded course needs a text, and the text is usually supplied in paperback form.

Along with this, there is the vast and growing popular interest in languages that were formerly considered rare and exotic—not merely the Russian, Chinese, Korean, and Vietnamese forced upon us by international developments, but the little-known tongues of Africa and Asia. Today there are available in many colleges, and in numerous recordings and books, paperbacks and others, courses in Arabic and Swahili, Hindi and Tamil, Indonesian and Japanese, Fanti and

Thai. America's linguistic isolationism is definitely a thing of the past.

Language learning has turned from a basically aristocratic pursuit, reserved for a few fortunate individuals with money, leisure, and literary tastes, to a mass activity. The means of instruction must be made economically available to this new mass market, and the paperback industry, based as it is on mass markets, has seen the point in this as well as in other educational fields.

How does the paperback fit into the educational machinery for language study? A good many prescribed textbooks appear in paperback; they are not as numerous as they should be, however. Next we have books not used as texts, but prescribed for reading and classroom reports; the proportion of these in paperback is far higher. Third, we have the work tools, such as foreign-language or bilingual dictionaries; here again the paperback situation, while promising, is not as satisfactory as it might be.

Then there are intriguing innovations devised by the paperback publishers themselves, and accepted only in part and with reservations by the educational world. One such device is the bilingual reader, in which an unabridged short story (or even a novel) by a great foreign author appears in its precise original text on the left-hand pages and in an excellent English translation on the right-hand pages. Old-style classroom readers presented the same material without translation, but in a cut-down, watered-down text, to minimize the trips to the back of the book that the student would have to make when stumped by a vocabulary or construction item. Now the advanced student who wants to read his original text straight through can do so. Whenever he gets stuck, he looks at the opposite page, and the English translation unsticks him and give him the word or construction he needs with a minimum of time and strain.*

In addition, the paperback industry has brought out, in economical and easily transportable form, numerous works by foreign authors, both in the original language and in English translations. Voltaire

---

* Naturally, some old-line teachers object to this procedure. They believe that looking up a word or construction the hard way is a valuable mental discipline, and that lazy students may read their material straight through in English and never glance at the original.

and Diderot may be read in French or in English; you can go as far
back as Villon and the *Chanson de Roland* in either language.
Whether your need is for the original version of *El Cid* or an English
translation of Dostoievsky, Dante's *Inferno* in English or Italian,
Goethe's *Werther* in German or English, there is a paperback for
about $1 to accommodate you.

It is quite true that a great deal remains to be done in this field.
There are thousands, perhaps hundreds of thousands, of works that
mankind's great minds have contributed to the world's culture during
the last three thousand years, and not even the mighty American
paperback industry has been able to supply us with all of them in the
course of a few brief years. But the beginning is there.

There are ingenious educational combinations into which the paperback enters. A newly formed company is at present engaged in producing recorded courses for smaller colleges which cannot afford a
full language-teaching staff. These courses are complete, with a comprehensive series of lectures given by prominent men in the field,
prescribed readings, weekly quizzes, and final examinations which are
impartially and objectively graded by the firm itself. The college acquires the recorded course, presents the lectures in a classroom under
tutorial supervision, administers the quizzes and exams in the same
fashion, sends in the papers to the firm's headquarters, receives the
grades, and grants full credit for the course, just as though it were
given by a faculty member. The textbooks and required readings for
these courses include only such works as have appeared in paperback, and they can be acquired by the individual student for a total
cost of $25 or less. Were these books to be prescribed in hardcover,
they would either cost the student between $100 and $200, or they
would have to be borrowed from or read in the college library. In
paperback, they are in the student's possession at all times, for reading on the subway or on a streetcar, if he is so minded.

College bookstores are becoming increasingly paperback-minded,
having found that there are plenty of profits in paperbacks. The huge
Book Center at the University of Pittsburgh, where I was recently
stationed, is fully stocked with paperbacks on all topics, and these
receive the most prominent display. Hardcover books are available,
but are mostly in the basement. The browsing student or professor

will often succumb to the temptation of buying for $1 or less a book which he would not buy at $5.

The situation is encouraging, but not yet ideal. For specific criticisms, I, who happen to have more of my books in paperback than any other specialist in the field of languages and linguistics, must draw on my own experience and that of my close associates.

To begin with, the paperback industry has not yet sufficiently explored and exploited the pure textbook field, as distinguished from the field of books for assigned reading. It is standard practice for textbook publishers to call upon their authors to revise their works every few years, whether they really need revision or not. This is done for one primary reason. Both the bookstores and the students themselves carry on an extensive trade in secondhand copies of textbooks, and the same copy passes from hand to hand and from class to class until it is so thoroughly worn out that it is no longer usable. The only way for the publisher to check this practice is to bring out a new edition that diverges from the old, even though it be in unimportant particulars. Were these textbooks to be made universally available in paperback, the secondhand trade would diminish radically, both because every student could afford a clean, fresh, unmarked, brand-new copy of the required text and because a paperback is not as durable as a hardcover work.

Many hardcover publishers refuse to have their good, permanent non-fiction sellers published in paperback, because of the erroneous idea that a paperback edition kills the sales of the hardcover. It took me ten years and a comprehensive set of sales figures to convince one of my publishers that this was an error. What actually happens is that hardcover sales increase with the appearance of a paperback, by reason of the paperback's tremendous mass publicity value and the fact that many people, having casually picked up a work in paperback, later decide they want it for their permanent library and buy it in hardcover. Here it is up to the paperback industry to conduct an educational campaign among the hardcover diehards.

However, paperback publishers are just as human and fallible as their hardcover confreres in the matter of what shall and shall not be published. I have in my possession one paperback in my field of which the publisher assured me only 300 copies were sold. Why had he published it? The author had made a big name for himself in another, unrelated field. Had the publisher consulted any experts in the field before signing the contract? He had not.

By reason of such experiences, some paperback houses will turn down any book in this field, whether promising or not. A work that has sold more than three thousand copies in hardcover at $5 a throw, whose subject matter never fails to draw large and enthusiastic audiences at lectures, is turned down because "we sold only three hundred copies of the other book."

This same pusillanimous spirit appears in other connections. There is a novel with profound historical, literary, and educational overtones, which had rave reviews and sold five thousand copies in hardcover and a quarter of a million copies in paperback before the paperback firm that had it was forced out of business. The author had to watch the copies of his paperback disappear from the stands. Despite a lapse of ten years, it is still impossible to find a new paperback publisher for the book, on the ground that "the cream has been skimmed off." It does not seem to occur to the publishers that a new crop of potential readers grows up in ten years, particularly in connection with a book that has educational features.

There is a series of six language manuals for tourists, five of which have been put out in paperback and are selling extremely well. The sixth, dealing with a language not quite so popular as the others, is consistently rejected by the paperback publisher, despite pleas from foreign bookstores and from consular and USIA officials, who would be pleased to see the book on the foreign stands both as a good-will gesture and as an aid for American tourists.

There is a type of book which is almost desperately needed at the present time for the use of foreign tourists in America, who numbered well over one million last year. A paperback original would be a natural.

In spite of such shortcomings, the paperback industry is doing the language field, and education in general, a genuine service. The shortcomings are mainly in the nature of growing pains. As time goes on, they will doubtless be rectified. The educational world acknowledges its deep debt of gratitude to the paperback. At the same time, it expresses its desire to cooperate with its benefactor, mainly by acting in an advisory capacity for what concerns its own needs and markets.

CHAPTER 21

Languages for Scientists

Over twenty years ago, a well-known technical translator and lexicographer, who has since died, Lewis L. Sell, published two very brief works. In these he advocated the creation of an institute for the training of technical lexicographers, translators, and interpreters, and even planned the curriculum that would lead to the degrees of Bachelor, Master, and Doctor of Technical Lexicography. His premise was that as international communications multiplied, and distances were radically reduced by advances in the field of transportation, the man who was a specialist both in technology and in languages, or at least in one branch of science and one foreign tongue, would no longer be an expensive luxury, but an outright necessity.

No one paid much attention to Sell at the time. Although his two works appeared while the Second World War was still in progress, America still held an absolutely predominant position in science and technology. The war-torn nations of the world, including the Soviet Union, were almost altogether dependent on us. The response, therefore, took the familiar form: "Aw, let them learn English!"

It was not until 1957 that America was startled out of its complacency by the placing in orbit of Sputnik I. This revealed that our international rivals had been making giant strides in the field of science, to the point of outstripping us in certain sectors. With Sputnik, we did not even have the poor excuse, offered at the time when the Soviets developed atom and hydrogen bombs of their own, that their spies had stolen our secrets.

The depth of confusion and shame was reached when Prof. A. I. Mikhailov, Director of the Institute of Scientific and Technical Information of the U.S.S.R. Academy of Sciences, informed a group of

American scientists at a news conference in Washington that the Russians had given in their scientific journals plenty of advance notice of their intention to place a satellite in orbit at least a year before it happened. But since none of the American scientists apparently could read Russian, and none of the American scholars in Russian were competent or interested in science, this vital piece of information had gone unnoticed and unrecorded in American scientific and government circles.

It is quite likely that by the time Professor Mikhailov spoke the facts were known, because the launching of Sputnik I had sent both scientists and government men scurrying to the library shelves on which Russian scientific periodicals had been gathering dust between 1947 and 1957.

Should we, as a nation, do something about a situation in which scientists generally know no foreign languages and foreign language specialists generally know no science?

A glance at the Soviet system of higher education shows in what respect we are weak. Soviet university students who specialize in any branch of science (and these constitute a majority of all university students in the U.S.S.R.) are also compelled to specialize in at least one modern foreign language, preferably English, German, or French. By specializing in such a language, the Soviet educational authorities do not mean the two-year course in college or "scientific" German to which some (not all) of our science majors are reluctantly exposed, and which many consider a mere waste of time and distraction from the "real" substance of their scientific preparation. They mean an eight or ten or twelve-year sequence in the foreign language of the student's choice, which begins at the outset of the high school course (in many instances even earlier), and continues without interruption until the university student emerges with his scientific degree. It is certain that even the science student who is poor or "ungifted" in languages will have acquired enough English, French, or German by the end of this kind of course to be able to converse, even though with a foreign accent, perhaps write, but above all read the essential periodicals and reports in his scientific specialty.

This in turn means that the Soviet scientific world is never unaware of what goes on in other lands. Everything reported in the thirteen thousand technical periodicals received from other lands (about fourteen hundred from ours) is duly read, noted, digested, and reported to the proper authorities for appropriate action, or at least for their information. There is not the slightest chance that an announcement of any importance, in any field of science or technology, made in any country outside the Soviet Union, will slip past the language-trained Soviet technicians and scientists.

In recent times both our government and our educational institutions have begun to take a new interest in foreign languages. The number of our language students is increasing, and will probably increase still further. The needs of the moment, however, call for something more than a mere interest in languages.

The fact that you have acquired a foreign tongue, speak it to perfection, write it flawlessly, and read it as your own still does not automatically qualify you to understand or translate a document in a scientific field. You must also know the field the document deals with. A literary or diplomatic translator who can render Françoise Sagan from the French original, or *Doctor Zhivago* from the Russian, or even interpret simultaneously at a UN session, is just as helpless as the man in the street when he is faced with material dealing with higher mathematics, electronics, nuclear energy, astronautics, or biochemistry. He does not know the essential terminology in either language, and each scientific field has its own precise terminology, which is so much Choctaw to the uninitiated.

Try opening a book in English dealing with a scientific field you have not studied, and you will quickly find that you are as much at sea as though you were reading an unlearned foreign tongue. This, by the way, is largely true even of fields that are not primarily scientific—the law, business, banking, art, music, philosophy. Modern civilization is compartmentalized, and while all the speakers of a language may hold in common an everyday working vocabulary and grammar, they emphatically do not hold in common the vocabularies of their specialized work or interests.

All this adds up to two conclusions. If we want to hold our somewhat shaky current lead in the field of science and technology, we must realize that other countries, some friendly, some indifferent, some distinctly hostile to us, are making great strides in those fields. It behooves us to keep abreast of what they are doing. Their findings are published (unless they are security secrets) in their own journals, which normally appear in their own languages. Our scientists must have access to these journals, as their scientists have access to ours. Each of our science majors should be thoroughly trained in one foreign language, so that he can read the periodicals in that language as easily as he reads his professional journals in English. Beyond that, it is merely a matter of our scientists swapping the information they have gathered in their reading. The rocket specialist who reads the Russian journals will tell the man who reads the German journals what the Russians are doing, and will in turn be informed as to German progress in the common field.

This does not mean that every science major must learn Russian. It does not even mean that he must learn either Russian, French, or German. Plenty goes on in the field of scientific publication in Italian, Spanish, Portuguese, Dutch, the Scandinavian languages, Japanese, and Chinese. Give the budding scientist his choice of a language, then hold him to it. Let him not take two years of high school Spanish, then switch to three years of college German plus one year of college French. Let him have at least eight years of the one language of his choice. But let him be qualified, by the time he graduates, to read with ease, and possibly also speak and understand, one foreign tongue, be it even Finnish or Tamil, for possible future advances in countries speaking those languages.

Secondly, it is high time the forgotten suggestions of Dr. Sell go into operation. Modern science and technology, even modern business and finance, are matters of high precision, in which haphazard, incorrect, misleading translation won't do. We should have, in addition to our language-trained scientists, also a body of thoroughly trained technical and scientific lexicographers, people who are able to construct, with speed and accuracy, specialized lexicons, dictionaries, glossaries, and phrase books in the various and very numerous fields. At present, anyone who has a conversational knowledge of two languages is qualified to set himself up as a translator. The situation parallels what went on in seventeenth-century medicine, when anyone who felt the urge or inclination to practice could do so by simply hanging up his shingle.

An institute of technical and scientific lexicography, with established admission requirements, curricula, examinations, and degrees, would begin to provide that guarantee which our free-and-easy American world so sorely lacks—the guarantee that the man called upon to do a piece of translation in any but the purely literary field will have a thorough grasp of the essential terminology in both languages, and not cause the wrecking of a piece of machinery, the death of a hospital patient, or the costly misinterpretation of a business or financial letter by reason of the fact that while he "knows" both languages, he does not know the field.

CHAPTER 22

An Experiment
in Conversation

During the Second World War, I found myself suddenly faced with a request to take on, in addition to my regular graduate courses in Romance Linguistics, at Columbia University, an orphaned undergraduate French class whose instructor had been called away on war service. The end of the school year was only a month and a half away; another instructor could not be conveniently found for that short period; and I had to my credit, in the dim past, an experience of some sixteen years of high school and undergraduate language teaching. I was elected.

It felt a bit strange, after six years of strictly graduate work, devoted to very specialized lecturing, research, and thesis direction, to go back to the recitation, translation, reading, and conversation of my younger years. Yet the work held a strange fascination and, to use an overworked term, a challenge. I had been (at least so I flattered myself) a good high school and undergraduate language teacher at one time; could I still be good at elementary language teaching, or had I lost the knack?

The class was small—about ten students. It was not particularly select, as undergraduate classes go. All that the students were trying to do was to pass the college two-year reading requirement. None of them was specializing in French, or in any other language. Their work had started before the advent of the Intensive Language era, and both method and textbooks were grounded on the old and now greatly deprecated reading objective. The set-up was ideal for dozing through the remaining six weeks, with a little *"Lisez"* here and a

176

little *"Traduisez"* there. But the speaking objective was in the air. My little undergraduates were just about to come of draft age. In a few months they would be in the Army. French (two years, three hours a week, reading objective) was their only, or at any rate, their most extensive foreign language. Within the limitations of time and method, they had been doing quite well under my predecessor. They had a fairly firm hold of grammatical principles and a not too limited vocabulary which had been materially helped, from the military standpoint, by the use of an excellent, up-to-date military reader. Could they be made to speak and understand French?

The new "talkie-talkie" school of linguistics assures us that "reading and writing come very easily, naturally, gracefully," etc., to those who have "learned to speak and understand." My own personal experience has shown me that the converse is true; that if there is a good grammatical background, a fair vocabulary range, and a good reading knowledge, conversational ability comes rather easily once we find ourselves in the environment where the foreign language *must* be used. The fact that the environment and the incentive were almost invariably lacking in prewar days was probably largely responsible for the lack of conversational achievement on the part of American foreign language students.

But now the war was supplying, if not direct environment, at least the incentive for realism. And so I decided on an experiment. The program of the class, as it had been handed to me, called for rather strict adherence to a day-by-day schedule of reading, grammar, and translation. Deliberately disobeying orders, I assigned one day a week to conversational practice. This was sprung on the students without warning during the second week of my regime, after I had gotten my bearings. They had come in with a carefully prepared reading assignment. They were told to put it away. Then came a "pep" talk, delivered in true preinduction fashion. *"Mes enfants,* you know that soon, very soon, you will be soldiers." They nodded expectantly. "As soldiers, you may be called upon to use even your French. But not on the blackboard. Can you visualize yourselves in a situation where French is a living, spoken language, and *has* to be used? For the next half hour, you're a detachment of paratroopers, under the command of Fisher. You have come down from a plane somewhere in southern France." (Little did I know then how prophetic I was.) "Your objective is to cut German telephone and telegraph communications between Toulon and Marseille. You all know some French. I'm the first French native you meet. I'm sympathetic to your cause, ready and anxious to help you and tell you all I know. But I don't know a word of English. You can all collaborate in questioning me. If one of you doesn't know a certain word, anyone else can chip in. You can even use your pocket dictionaries. You can talk English among yourselves all you want. But remember, I'm your main source of information, and I know no English. I'll start you off. *Messieurs, vous êtes vraiment des Américains? Alors, ça veut dire que l'invasion commence! Est-ce que je peux vous aider, vous offrir des renseignements? Je suis à votre disposition!"*

The questions began to come thick and fast. Completely free of inhibitions because (1) they were not being corrected or marked; (2) they could use English among themselves; (3) their goal was comprehensibility, not grammatical correctness, the boys (who, incidentally, knew infinitely more about military tactics and terminology than did their over-age instructor) went at it with gusto. Fisher took his commanding post quite seriously; I had purposely picked him out as *not* being the best French student in the group, so that he would have to call on the others for help. And he did. The questions were intelligent and realistic. In which direction was Toulon? Marseille? How many kilometers away? Where were the telephone lines? Were they guarded? Were there many Germans in the vicinity? How well were they armed? Had I talked to some lately?

The question and answer process went on for nearly half an hour, with no holds barred, no corrections save blank stares and shoulder shrugs when I judged their French incomprehensible, free use of English and pocket dictionaries among the imaginary paratroopers, and complete, baffling discouragement whenever they tried to address me in English. Sometimes I was made to repeat what I had said *"plus lentement, beaucoup plus lentement."* I was amazed at the amount of tactical knowledge possessed by my boys. Their questions were significant, relevant, connected, never rambling. It may be that some of them had had some premilitary training. At the end of half an hour they had a pretty good picture of what they wanted to know

—the terrain, the enemy, the inhabited localities, their own stated objective. The bell rang as they thanked me and I wished them success.

They liked it. "Are we going to have this again?" "Yes, a week from today." What would the topic be? That I refused to disclose. I wanted no advance preparation or set phrases of the type found in conversation manuals. Everything impromptu, *au naturel*. The following week my expectant students found themselves in a French inn, with an innkeeper that was friendly, sympathetic, but knew absolutely no English. They were hungry and thirsty, after a long march. It was up to them to inquire as to the food and drink possibilities and catch the answers. They didn't do badly.

The following week they found themselves occupying a French village and talking to Monsieur le Maire (again a friendly soul who knew no English) about the town, the Germans who had lately occupied it, the inhabitants, the collaborationists, the town records, etc. One week later they were in a Paris bazaar, buying souvenirs, toilet and writing accessories, and a hundred other things. There was one more experience, when they found themselves billeted in a medium-sized town hotel, of which I was the manager. Then came examination week (it may be remarked at this point that despite my "neglect of duty" in skipping reading assignments in favor of conversational practice, they all got through). It seemed to me that they had gained a familiarity with rough-and-ready conversational situations which would stand them in good stead if they ever had to use their reading French colloquially. At least their inhibitions were broken. They knew that incorrect, ungrammatical, halting French was better than none, that there was some practical application for what they had theoretically learned, that a few French phrases in the mouth are on occasion more useful than entire works of French literature in the head.

I passed the idea on to one of our lady professors in charge of navy cadets. She tried it out, and later reported that the impromptu realistic situation was a splendid pedagogical device. In fact, she gave me the impression that the device worked even better in her classes than it had in mine, due, possibly, to the fact that as a young and attractive woman she had situation-possibilities which were beyond the reach of a mere man teacher.

I am passing all this on for what it may be worth. It is unlikely that the impromptu realistic situation will work in a class of forty, or among beginning high school students. On the other hand, it seems to me to have definite possibilities when the students are somewhat advanced, and not too numerous. It places the students on their toes, and they like it. It places the instructor on his toes, and he may not like it so well. I picked out just five fairly obvious, rather simple situations with a war background, calling for no particular preparation on my part. In a postwar full-length course, it is likely that a good deal of preparation would have to go into the devising of a sufficient number of sufficiently interesting and life-like situations. The basis of the idea lies in the theory that languages are primarily for spoken use rather than for literary introspection, and that if we can break down the students' inhibitions, built up by marks, corrections, and insistence upon absolute perfection, we shall have gone a long way toward making language study effective and popular.*

---

* Of course, the real-life situation method is very much in use now, in 1968. It was *not* in use in 1944, when this article was written.

CHAPTER 23

Languages
for the Very Young

A friend of mine who is a well-known surgeon called me up. "I want to consult you about my children's education," he said. Knowing that Norma is four and Eddie, Jr., three, I was a bit nonplussed. After all, I'm a university professor of languages, not a kindergarten expert. But the tie-up came to light when I saw him.

"I could easily endow my children with ten thousand dollars each," he said; "but I would much rather endow them with an art, a skill, a second string to their bow—something that will stick with them and do them some good in their future careers, whatever these may be. I have thought of endowing them with languages—not languages as they are learned in high school and college, but languages as they used to be learned by so many people in Europe, from childhood, so that the recipient grows up with them, easily, naturally, spontaneously, and, above all, conversationally. I'm thinking of taking on three governesses, each of whom will speak a different language to them for a certain part of their day. You are an expert on language-learning. What do you think about it?"

Needless to say, I thought very highly of his scheme.

"Will they *really* learn the languages that way?"

"Yes, they'll learn to speak them like natives."

"Will it interfere with their English?"

"Not in the slightest. At their age, they can pick up any number of languages, and speak them all like natives, without the mutual interference you get later on."

"Will they stick?"

Here was the poser. Yes, they would stick, *provided* they were constantly practiced in later years. Like every other kind of skill, languages grow stale if you do not use them. It is a commonplace to hear a man say, "I was born in Germany, and spoke nothing but German for the first six years of my life. Then my parents brought me to America. I learned English, didn't use my German, and now I've forgotten it."

This was the rub, but my friend decided to take the chance that in later years, after the governesses were gone, his children would get or make conversational opportunities. Today Norma and Eddie, Jr., are learning Russian, French, and German, by the direct conversational method, from three different governesses. They will grow up, like the children of many European families, not merely bilingual but quadrilingual. And with no apparent effort on their part.

Not everybody can find or afford three foreign governesses, or even one. But what can be done by an individual with hundreds of dollars for his own children can certainly be duplicated by State Education Departments, with millions of dollars, for everybody's children.

The desirability of people really learning languages at the child stage is hardly likely to be questioned. In the days of isolation, languages used to be a matter of "culture." Today, as we move hopefully into a new internationalism, they are becoming a matter of necessity. A recent Gallup Poll indicates that the people realize this. To the question: "Should the school children in all countries be required to learn, in addition to their own language, some one language that would be understood in all countries, so that people of every nation could understand one another better?" 76 per cent of those polled said "yes," and only 15 per cent "no," with 9 per cent undecided.

From the standpoint of the children and their receptiveness, there is no doubt that it can be done. It is being done all the time. A French colleague of mine and his wife, whose English is somewhat sketchy but whose French leaves absolutely nothing to be desired, have four children whose present ages range from twelve to thirty-five. All four were brought up by the same method. Nothing but French was used with them till they began going to school. In school and at play they quickly picked up English. Today, their French and their English are both impeccable. The eldest makes his living teaching French to naval cadets. The other three, including little twelve-year-old Babette, are or will be amply qualified to teach, interpret, translate, and, above all, converse. And note this: Their English bears absolutely no trace of their parents' French accent; neither does their French have the slightest sign of the "esker vooz avay" quality of our high school students of French.

By way of contrast, I have a woman friend born and educated in Italy and married to an Italian-born husband. "Speak Italian to your children from the minute they are born!" was my advice to them when they got married. "Of course we will! What else should we speak to them? We both know Italian better than English." But they did not keep their promise. They chose the path of least resistance, which was to use the English they themselves were learning, and which the children brought home from their first outside contacts. Result: Daniel and Flora took up Italian in high school later as a foreign language, and today they can stumble through a few phrases, spoken with a Brooklyn accent.

All this brings up a problem for our education experts. Do we want our children *really* to learn foreign languages? And if so, what is the best method?

A recent poll conducted by a woman's magazine indicated that 78 per cent of those polled were in favor of the study of foreign languages. Small wonder, with the earth getting steadily smaller and more crowded, and jet-propelled planes threatening to cut travel time between New York and Paris to a couple of hours. The people of the United States are language-conscious as they never were before. In New York City's adult education project, the first thing done was to poll library visitors to find what subjects they wanted. Foreign languages got more votes than all other subjects combined. The GI education program in Europe showed our soldiers interested, first of all, in French, partly due to their being stationed in western Europe, where French is the most current language, no doubt; but the GIs were looking sharply to the future, too; many expected to go back to Europe as salesmen, reconstruction experts, and tourists.

But how to do it in the most effective way? The same poll that showed 78 per cent in favor of languages also showed 50 per cent in favor of beginning languages *before* high school. In this, the good people of America show their sound common sense, which so often outstrips the vagaries of the scholars. The Harvard Committee says: "No languages in high school. Wait till they go to college." But the plain citizens know that all their children will ever get in college will be a reading knowledge of a foreign language, if that. And they want their children to learn how to *speak,* so that they may travel, for business, pleasure, or even war, and make themselves understood wherever they go.

Who will win out, the scholars who say: "No languages till college," or the parents who say: "Languages in the kindergartens"?

Curiously, it is the latter, not the former, who have the backing of linguistic science, experience, and experimentation. There are a few (very few) schools in the United States today where six-year-olds are taught foreign languages—not out of grammars and dictionaries, as a classroom exercise, for three hours a week, but by exactly the same method by which they learn English—speaking it and hearing it spoken, reading it out of little six-year-old readers with plenty of pictures of doggies and cats and dollies, and writing it in easy one-syllable words. The results are astounding. The children in these schools grow up to be perfectly bilingual. Far from suffering, their English is much improved because they have, from the very outset, a point of comparison and a language sense.

There is a public school in Mott Street, in the heart of New York's Chinatown, where the American-born tots of Chinese ancestry learn their Chinese along with their English. Recently they gave a performance which I attended. Their Chinese was beautiful, tones and all. They sang quaint little Chinese songs, put on a Chinese sketch, and delivered Chinese elocution pieces just as well as it could have been done in Tai-pei. Later I spoke to some of them, lapsing into English by reason of the insufficiency of my spoken Chinese. There was not the slightest trace of a "No tickee no shirtee" accent, intonation, or grammar in their remarkably correct Americanese.

In another progressive school of my acquaintance, run by Sisters, French is used in the kindergarten and elementary classes, with children of pure Anglo-Saxon stock. But they talk like the tots of the Champs-Elysées—or like the tots of Central Park, according as you start them off in French or in English.

In Europe, language classes for the very young children have long been commonplace. Hedged in as they are on every side by nations speaking different tongues, the Europeans believe in starting their language training early—at six or before. I had a smattering of French and a few words of English before I arrived in America at the age of seven.

What they can do, we can do. The beauty of it is that it need take absolutely no time from any other kindergarten or elementary school subject, for the language is not *taught* as such; it is merely spoken in conducting certain classes. Geography in French, history in Spanish, arithmetic in English, which is much better than beginning Spanish in college, three hours a week, with a grammar, ten or twelve years later.

Even in America this system has been tried and found satisfactory. It used to be the system employed in the Cincinnati public schools before the First World War. Half of the day's classes were taught in German, the other half in English, and the children grew up bilingual. It is the system followed today in several parochial schools conducted by Polish and Italian nuns in communities where Poles and Italians are numerous. Norwegian is learned that way in many Minnesota communities, and some Midwestern kindergartens attempt to teach "manners" in French.

But these are exceptional cases, because so far there has been no widespread community demand for foreign languages at an early age —the right age. If half the time and money that go into teaching music to children who are constitutionally not musicians were devoted to languages, there would be far better results, because all children of kindergarten age are constitutionally linguists. But the 50 per cent of parents who believe in languages before high school must organize and demand them from the local school authorities.

Language aids, both in and out of school, are there for the asking. All we need to do is mobilize them—the foreign language films, which proved so effective in the army language courses and would be hailed with delight by the children; foreign language phonograph records, providing mechanical as well as linguistic interest; and, above all, the radio.

New York has several stations that "speak your language" and give excellent foreign programs. Many universities teach languages over the radio; Ohio State University, to cite only one instance, has its French and Spanish "School of the Air." But while young children have occasionally been known to listen to these programs, a new radio technique will have to be devised for them—some sort of "Superman" type program in very simple French, Spanish, German, and Russian, to supplement school instruction and continue kindergarten training in the mental surroundings natural to the young. Here again, the problem is one for community groups to solve. The demand must be there, and it must be organized. When, as, and if this demand crystallizes, we shall see America turning, by highly natural processes, into a nation of linguists.*

---

* The FLES (Foreign Languages in Elementary School) program has become quite popular in recent years. In 1948, however, it was a distinct innovation even to mention its possibility.

CHAPTER 24

Fashions in Language

To use the words of a popular newspaper columnist, "Fashions in languages, as in women's skirts, have their stylish ups and downs." The languages that enjoy widespread popularity at one period do not necessarily hold their lead forever. This seems to hold true for all countries and all eras, but, of course, it is superlatively true of our own land, which by reason of its relative youth and zest for life, goes in for fads to a greater degree than do the more sedate nations of Europe.

As we peruse the educational history of America, we discover that in the American colonies of the British Crown only dead languages were deemed worthy of the academic accolade. Latin, Greek, and Hebrew were the early languages of the curriculum in prerevolutionary America. When Harvard was founded, in 1636, the admission rules required that students be capable of understanding the Latin classics on sight and of speaking or reading Latin in prose or verse. A favorite translation exercise in the early days of Harvard was from Hebrew into Greek, and an early president of Yale delivered his commencement speech in Hebrew.

The modern foreign languages began to make very modest headway in the seventeenth century. In 1608 French was taught by missionaries in Maine, but the beneficiaries of such instruction were for the most part French Canadians or half-breeds, so it is doubtful if we can use the term "foreign language instruction" in this connection. In Florida and the Southwest, at about the same time, Spanish was imparted under very similar circumstances. German was likewise taught in Pennsylvania before 1700, but here again we must recall that the original population of Pennsylvania was over one third

German. Benjamin Franklin at one time expressed his fear that the German-speaking element might make German instead of English the official language of the commonwealth. So here again we are left in doubt as to whether it is legitimate for us to use the term "foreign language study."

The study of modern foreign languages in America may be said to have made its first official bow at Harvard in 1735, when students were permitted to substitute French for Hebrew (but not for Greek or Latin). Around the middle of the eighteenth century, a Philadelphia academy tried the novel experiment of offering French and German, while in 1779 the College of William and Mary established the first American professorship of modern languages.

It is indicative of the nature and growth of our American civilization that during the early part of the nineteenth century the only two modern languages that succeeded in gaining a firm foothold were German and French, with the former beginning to outstrip the latter around 1850, at the time of the great influx of German immigrants, and holding a position of predominance in our high schools and colleges until the First World War, when French took the lead and Spanish began to be taught on a wide scale by reason of our new trade relations with Latin America.

I do not have at my disposal the very latest official figures for high school and college registration in the various languages. Without going into unnecessary detail, the main facts nevertheless are sufficiently well known. For the country as a whole, Latin has now yielded first place to Spanish, with French a close runner-up. German is a somewhat distant fourth. Then, strung out over the field, come Italian, Russian, Portuguese, Greek, Hebrew, and the many newcomers to the American language-teaching scene—Norwegian, Swedish, Polish, Czech, modern Greek, Esperanto. It is hardly necessary to mention the exotic languages that are imparted to handfuls of specialists in the great universities—Japanese, Chinese, Arabic, Turkish, Persian, Hindustani, Burmese, Thai.

The point that particularly interests us in this discussion is the relative position of the various languages in the favor of the American public, along with the reasons, real and alleged, for that favor. Permit me to reminisce from my own experience.

I first came to this land as an immigrant boy in 1908. At that time, it seemed to me that insofar as New York could be said to be under any foreign influence, that influence was German. The German language was currently spoken in the streets and satirized on the vaudeville stage. Store signs were frequently written in German. German songs were current. I do not recollect that German was taught in any of the elementary schools that I attended, though I learned later that such elementary instruction was current in other cities, notably Cincinnati and Milwaukee, but the over-all impression that was gained by a youngster of seven to thirteen in the years immediately preceding the First World War was that in this metropolis German was a very important language indeed.

The Jesuit high school I began to attend in 1914 prescribed four years of Latin, three and a half of Greek, and three of a modern foreign language. There was no choice about the Latin and the Greek—everybody had to take them, and I have not yet ceased to utter daily thanks to God that this was so.

The choice came with our second high school year, in 1915, when the First World War had been in progress for almost a year. It was at this point that I first came in contact with fashions in languages. Down to the year of our choice, Xavier High School had offered only two modern languages, French and German. In 1915, the United States had not yet entered the war and American thinking was still very much divided as to the merits of the two sides. The choice between French and German began to take on something of a political coloring. Those among us who were pro-Ally tended to gravitate toward French, while the students who had leanings toward the Central Powers favored German. But at the very last minute, a third contender entered the arena.

That section of public opinion that might be described as isolationistic advocated the proposition that in view of Europe's internal squabbles, of which we wanted no part, the thing for us to do was to cultivate intensive economic, political, and cultural relations with our Western Hemisphere neighbors south of the Rio Grande, whom we had up to that time almost completely neglected. Spanish, we were told, was the great language of the future, because our coming trade would be with Latin America. Spanish, accordingly, must be taught in all our schools and colleges to the total or partial exclusion of the languages representative of the countries that had played leading roles in getting the Old World into the sorry mess it was in—German and French.

It may be noted in passing that in those days it did not occur to the apostles of the South American trade that half of South America was Portuguese, not Spanish-speaking. That realization was not achieved until the days of the Second World War. In many quarters, it has not been achieved yet.

Xavier High School was a very conservative institution. The impact of the propaganda for the Latin-American trade may be gauged from the fact that even this Jesuit stronghold of conservatism was swayed into adding Spanish to the linguistic curricular offering. But it was suddenly discovered, after the addition had been made, that there was no one on the faculty who was qualified to teach Spanish. There was a hurried conference among the good Jesuits, and a quick solution of the problem. The man who ordinarily taught physics volunteered (or perhaps was drafted) to steer the first Spanish class in Xavier's history past the shoals of *ser* and *estar, tener* and *haber* and radical-changing verbs. I myself, being a traditionalist, did not select Spanish, but the following story was relayed to me by a classmate who did. The volunteer Spanish instructor, on entering the class, addressed the students in these words: "Boys, Spanish is new to you. It's new to me too. We're all starting from scratch. But this I will guarantee you. I will always keep one lesson ahead of you. We'll all learn it together."

He kept his word, too, duplicating in reverse the exploit of the great physicist Millikan, who having started his academic career as a professor of Greek was given one summer vacation in which to prepare himself for teaching physics, and did such a good job that he became one of the world's foremost scientists. Had our Spanish instructor had a whole summer's handicap instead of one lesson, he, too, might have turned into a leading Hispanicist.

When all the votes were in, it was found that the sophomore class had divided itself about evenly among the three languages, Spanish, German, and French. This ratio held, to the best of my recollection, for the class that followed ours and made its choice in 1916.

Then came 1917 and America's entry into the war on the side of the Allies. And here is where an extraordinary change took place. Among the sophomores of that year, no more than five or six selected German. The rest went to swell the ranks of French and Spanish, particularly the latter. It did not seem to occur to anyone that the enemy's language might be worth while knowing for military purposes, if nothing else. The line of reasoning appeared to be: "We are at war with the Germans. We don't like them. Hence, we don't like their language. In fact, we refuse to recognize its existence."

It is a matter of common knowledge that in many schools and colleges throughout the country the teaching of German was altogether discontinued partly by reason of the drop in student demand, partly by decision of the administrations. This strange phenomenon of linguistic intolerance was paralleled by the discontinuance of German music in some artistic milieus and other examples of rampant and unreasonable prejudice. The depth of absurdity was reached with the attempted replacement of certain time-honored expressions, like *sauerkraut* and *hamburger,* by *liberty cabbage* and *Salisbury steak.*

With the close of the war came a partial return to a common-sense point of view. Some of the extravagant claims made for Spanish were exposed when the great South American trade failed to materialize. It was fortunate in this respect, however, that the bottom did not fall out of the Spanish-learning market, as one might perhaps have anticipated. The true merits of Spanish, cultural as well as economic, were recognized, and Spanish, while losing some of the abnormal gains it had made during the war years, took its legitimate place by the side of French and German as one of the great modern languages of general interest to American students.

For the period between the two wars, one or two added details call for mention. The classical high school and college curriculum had generally called for both Latin and Greek. While Latin managed to hold its own, Greek unfortunately sank into the background before the determined onslaught of the physical and social sciences clamoring for increased time in the curriculum. Among the modern languages, a fourth, Italian, came to the fore. Italian had behind it a great cultural tradition that placed it on a par with French, German, and Spanish. Its economic importance in the twentieth century world was relatively low, but this was compensated by the large number of students of Italian ancestry in some of our most populous states and cities. Italian accordingly became one of the four general high school and college modern tongues, though it has never attained the vogue of French and Spanish.

Other languages of the American high school curriculum are local phenomena, due to the presence in the locality where they are taught of large nuclei of immigrant speakers. Polish, Czech, Swedish, Norwegian, modern Greek, modern Hebrew are to be found in communities where the elements to which these languages are native are numerous.

The onset of the Second World War proved again that we are, as a nation, subject to fads and prejudices. Before its outbreak, the relative position of the four major languages was: French, Spanish, German, Italian, in the order mentioned. As the events of 1939 and 1940 unfolded before our eyes, German, somehow associated in the American mind with Nazism and Hitler, and Italian, similarly linked with Fascism and Mussolini, sank to all-time lows. French this time did not escape, because, after the French surrender, it became the language of Vichy and Pétain. Spanish, despite Franco, managed to hold its ground by reason of its Latin-American connections.

Due credit must be given at this point to the ASTP and other military language programs for injecting a certain amount of hard realism into our national language outlook. The men of the ASTP knew that in the course of their African and European campaigns our soldiers would come in contact with German, French, and Italian, and they accordingly restored those languages to their rightful place of importance.

But they did so only as a matter of immediate necessity, and not at all with any view to the cultural future. To the directors of the ASTP there was no such thing as a cultural hierarchy in languages. It merely happened that the tongues which American educators had long ago selected as of greatest cultural importance were also of greatest strategic importance.

It was at this point that exaggerated claims began to appear for certain hitherto neglected languages. *Coronet* extolled Pidgin Eng-

lish as the vehicle of communication of the future. No less a magazine than the *National Geographic* allowed itself to be hoodwinked
into presenting a map of the world showing the "great language
empires"—English, Spanish, Russian, Chinese, and Arabic, with no
mention made of French, or German, or Italian. A very well-known
writer stated in a leading article that in the postwar world French
and German would be nothing more than drawing-room accomplish-
ments, like playing the harp, and that if we wanted to be realistic
about foreign languages, we would have to teach our children to
speak fluent Russian and Chinese. It so happens that I knew this
writer well, and when I discovered that his own children, far from
learning Russian and Chinese, were still striving for perfection in
Spanish, French, and German, I took him to task for not practicing
what he preached. "You have to be sensational to earn a living in my
field," he frankly avowed. "If I urged people to study what they have
always studied, there would be no salable article."

Nevertheless, many people took him seriously to the extent of
wondering why, in a rapidly changing world, we did not replace
French and German with Russian and Chinese.

Actually, registration in Russian and Chinese courses, particularly,
the former, grew by leaps and bounds between 1941 and 1947. Then
the Soviets turned out to be foes instead of friends, the Chinese
turned from Chiang Kai-shek to Mao Tze-tung, and our interest in
Russian and Chinese collapsed. At that same time, France, Italy, and
western Germany, becoming our partners in the Marshall Plan and
the Atlantic Alliance, regained favor in our eyes. Today the study
of French, German, and Italian is on the upgrade once more. Portuguese, for which there was a wave of enthusiasm when it was discovered that Brazil spoke it, has sunk once more to a very secondary
position. Ten years ago the head of the Hispanic department of a
great university assured m; that i ten years the teaching of Portuguese would be on a par with that of Spanish. He evidently read his
omens wrong.

What conclusions are to be drawn from the very sketchy and in-
complete survey we have just made?

The first and most obvious would seem to be that we, as a nation,
are far too easily swayed in our choice of languages by our political

leanings of the moment. When we like the Germans, we study their language. When we dislike them, we stop studying it. That this is not a situation peculiar to German alone is proved by the varying fortunes of French, Italian, and Russian during and after the Second World War.

Do fashions in language appear elsewhere than with us? They do indeed, but as a rule with highly logical and practical motivations, quite unmixed with emotional reflexes, and they have nothing to do with how the learners feel about the speakers of the language they are studying.

In Czarist Russia, practically all high school and college students learned French and German; learners of English were few. Today, over 50 per cent of all Soviet students take English. This is merely a reflection of the relative practical importance of the three languages in changing times. The general increase in the study of English noticeable in most foreign countries is not at all due to popularity of Americans or American policies. It is merely a recognition of our growing importance in science, technology, business, and international affairs.

Above all, nowhere save in the United States is the attitude to be found that leads to the boycotting of a language because we are at war, hot or cold, with its speakers. The practical bent of Europeans is perceptible in the statement made by a French officer to his son at the close of the First World War: "You must study German, because we shall be at war with Germany again within twenty years, and it is highly important that we know what the enemy is saying."

The not so obvious corollary to this initial conclusion is that we are rather poor judges of permanent cultural values, as well as of the political, historical, and geographical factors that should influence our linguistic choice. If languages are to be studied for immediate practical use, then there is no absolute standard by which to judge them. Each individual case rests on its own merits. The man going on an assignment to Brazil obviously needs Portuguese more than he does French, German, or Russian; if the assignment is to China, then Spanish and Italian won't do him any good. The only advice that can be given in these cases is to choose and study the language of the country with which you, as an individual, are going to have dealings.

But cases like those described above constitute a very minor fraction of the nation's total language study. In fact, our entire academic language-learning machinery has been set up on the presupposition of general, broad, cultural values rather than of the utilitarian principle, which is far better taken care of by specialized language methods, such as Berlitz and Linguaphone.

If we are going to retain languages in our general high school and college curriculum on the basis of cultural values, and as a part of a broad preparation for life, then it behooves us to set up our cultural standards and not let ourselves be swayed by temporary political or even economic factors.

There is a balanced unity to our Western culture which cannot be upset by such infinitesimally minute factors in the history of the world as Kaiser Wilhelm, Hitler, Mussolini, Franco, Laval, or Stalin. Historically speaking, to say we should not study German on account of Hitler and Goebbels is as much arrant nonsense as to say we should not study Latin on account of Nero and Caligula. Political episodes and political regimes are fleeting instants in the lives of nations. Long after they have passed, culture endures. Just as Virgil and Horace outweigh Domitian and Galba, just as Homer and Plato outlive Dionysius and Alcibiades, so Goethe and Schiller, Dante and Boccaccio, Villon and Racine, Cervantes and Lope de Vega will long outlive all the dictators of our times and their obnoxious regimes.

Our Western civilization is built squarely upon three great languages of antiquity, Hebrew, Greek, and Latin, and upon the five great languages of modern western Europe, English, French, German, Italian, and Spanish. A true understanding of our type of world can be based only upon those tongues. If the shape of things to come calls for an admixture of other cultures and other languages, or, worse yet, for what a German philosopher has described as *der Untergang des Abendlandes,* then we may as well face the fact that Western culture, as we know it, is doomed, and if this is the case, it will be far more than language programs that will have to be revised.

But as yet, there is no conclusive proof of this. Western culture has weathered the storms of Persian might and Carthaginian supremacy, of Saracen invasions and Turkish conquests. It turned back the Huns at Châlons, the Arabs at Tours, the Turks at Vienna and Lepanto. The great nations of the West have undergone, each in turn, the most tremendous of vicissitudes, yet have triumphantly emerged. Spain turned back the Moorish tide at Covadonga and marched on to the glories of the Reconquista. France repulsed in turn the Huns, the Arabs, and the Northmen. Italy survived Goths, Longobards, and Saracens. Germany picked itself up out of the ruins of the Thirty Years War just as it later rose from the ashes of the Second World War. A military disaster does not unmake a great nation, nor does a military victory create one.

The four great foreign modern languages of the American curriculum were not chosen by accident. They represent, along with English and the classical tongues, what is greatest and noblest in the culture in which we are steeped. They are the vehicles of our religion, literature, and philosophy, our music, art, and science, our customs and outlook, our political and juridical tradition. By all means let us add other languages to them, and welcome the newcomers. But let us do so with the clear understanding that they are fundamental in our civilization.

CHAPTER 25

The Beautiful Americans

There is a place in Monterey, California, which I love to think of as a factory for the production of Beautiful Americans—men and women who will move around the world not merely speaking many tongues, but carrying in these tongues America's message of genuine friendship and helpful interest to the nations that speak them.

The place is the U. S. Army's Language School of Monterey's Presidio. Here about four thousand army men, ranging all the way from buck privates to ranking colonels, study over thirty foreign languages under the guidance of about four hundred instructors, practically all of whom are natives of the countries whose languages they impart. Over-all direction and supervision were supplied, when I was there in 1960, by an army colonel, James L. Collins, who was both a military man and a language expert.

There are several navy men and officers, too, at the Army Language School, and a few civilian government employes, all busily and happily studying, for periods ranging from six months to a year, such critical and exotic tongues as Korean, Vietnamese, Cantonese, Mandarin, Burmese, Thai, Albanian, Lithuanian, Ukrainian, as well as the more conventional languages of the American college curriculum —Spanish, French, German, Italian, Portuguese, Russian.

As civilian linguistic consultant for the school, I spent ten full weeks in Monterey, watching, observing, studying. When I say studying, I mean that literally, because in order to acquire a full line on the methods of instruction I turned myself into a guinea pig and became a member of a beginners' course in Mandarin Chinese two days after my arrival. My classmates were six privates and a sergeant. For six hours a day, five days a week, we took instruction together from a corps of highly cultured, highly efficient Chinese instructors, both men and women, who changed every hour and who never addressed us in anything but Chinese. Bewildering at first, of course. But we soon learned to associate the Chinese word, tones and all, with the object held up or the action depicted by the instructor. Translation was completely bypassed. When our smiling Tiger Joe (our pet nickname for a Chinese teacher who went after our wrong tones like a tiger after its prey) held up a pencil and said *bi,* and each of us in turn repeated after him, we never thought of the English word "pencil"—only of the object and its Chinese name. When he offered one of us a pencil, intoning *"wo gei ni bi,"* we instinctively knew he was saying "I am giving you a pencil," and repeated after him. After a while, and with a little patience on his part, we were even able to make the appropriate response: *"Ni gei wo bi,"* "You are giving me a pencil."

This sort of thing goes on week after week, in Turkish, Persian, Slovenian, Serbo-Croatian, Bulgarian, Rumanian, Arabic, Hungarian, Czech, Polish, and a score of other languages. At the end of their respective courses, the soldiers and officers speak fluently and understand readily the language to which they are assigned. They can read and write it too, for written-language instruction begins a few weeks after the spoken tongue has gotten off to a flying start.

After three weeks I had to relinquish my Chinese course, save for an occasional private lesson. The pressure of my other duties was too great. I had to lecture to the staff, give a course in linguistics, and examine each of twenty-seven other departments, including those with whose languages I was somewhat familiar. Here it was that I came across the most fascinating variations on a now familiar theme. One Bulgarian group was carrying out a process of prisoner interrogation, with one class member acting the role of a prisoner just taken in front-line action, another questioning him in his own language, a third relaying a translation of the information sweated out of the captive to the officer in charge. In a Rumanian class, an airplane specialist was detailed to draw a plane model on the board, then lecture to the other class members, in almost flawless Rumanian, on the parts of the plane and how they function. An advanced Japanese class was discussing an intricate engineering problem involving water levels in different tanks.

One of the most absorbing proceedings was that of a Spanish group subdivided into two different rooms, with telephone communications. Both rooms had small-scale models of a battlefield terrain. One was complete, with enemy forces, weapons, and lines of defense; the other was empty. In the first room, the students were peering through peepholes at the field, then relaying their observations on the phone to their partners in the other room, who filled in their model in accordance with the information received. "Northeast sector, to the right of the clump of trees," came the observer's voice in crisp Spanish. "Enemy pillbox with what looks like five machine guns. One medium tank skulking in the hollow behind the pillbox." In the other room, the man on the phone reported in Spanish to the officer in charge, who quickly arranged the toy pieces in position. "Ask him are there any mortars in sight," the officer queried. "No, he says he doesn't see any," came the reply. In less than fifteen minutes, the second model battlefield was an exact duplicate of the first.

Do they have fun while they learn? Listen to this. In a Rusisan class about to graduate I found a WAC captain and four male officers. The instructor was leaning back and taking it easy. He had assigned roles to the lady captain and one of her masculine comrades. She was a waitress in a Russian restaurant, he an American tourist. "Carry on from there," said the instructor. "In Russian. Unrehearsed. You're on your own."

"Comrade," said the WAC, "how do you like our city?"

"Huh!" with a shrug.

"Don't you like it?"

"Yeh—so-so!"

"You know, we have lots of places of attraction here."

"Such as what?"

"We have a beautiful museum."

"I never go near museums."

"We have a fine old cathedral, from the days of Ivan the Terrible."

"I never go near churches. I'm an atheist."

"We have a splendid library."

"I've been allergic to libraries ever since my college days."

"Well, comrade, what *do* you like?"

"Girls!"

"We have a night club with a girls' orchestra."

"Yes, but can you take the girls out after the show?"

"Sir!" The WAC captain became very prim. "Is your wife here with you?"

"Oh, no! I left her back in the States!"

The instructor, the rest of the class, and the civilian consultant were in stitches. The Army knows how to play even while it works.

But in the midst of all this hard work and fun, I soon began to notice an undercurrent of something else—something infinitely desirable, even though unplanned.

The Army's purpose in running its school is to create linguists—people who will be able to speak and understand, in peace or war, the language of the country to which they are assigned. The higher ranking officers are usually scheduled to occupy posts as military attachés or liaison men in specific countries, occasionally to join the ranks of Military Intelligence. The non-coms and privates, all volunteers, with an aptitude for languages, carefully screened and given a stiff entrance exam, go to join a pool of trained army linguists ready for any emergency in any area of the earth.

What the Army does not reckon with is a by-product of its activities which may well turn out, in the long run, to be far more important than the avowed purpose of the school.

Student soldiers and officers are superior, intelligent, educated, but still fairly normal Americans, endowed with the customary American background. The instructional staff is composed of about four hundred natives of many foreign lands, men and women who are gifted, efficient, often highly cultured (there are many M.A.s and Ph.D.s among them), but still fairly representative of their respective countries. These two groups are brought into intimate, daily contact, not only in the classroom, but also on picnics, excursions, field trips, fiestas, and celebrations of all kinds. I, for example, accompanied Bulgarians, Hungarians, and Italians on picnics where nothing but the foreign language was spoken, nothing but the foreign foods were eaten, nothing but the foreign songs were sung. I was also an active member of the Chinese Mandarin choir, which twice gave public performances during my stay, one of them at the Chinese Feast of Lanterns celebrated by the Chinese community in nearby Pacific Grove.

It is also quite customary for the instructors to invite the soldier students and their wives to their homes, where they meet the instructors' families on the most friendly social basis imaginable. Fast friendships are formed between the American students and their foreign teachers, and between their respective families. In the Officers' Club, the student officers and the instructors share meals, drink together, bring in their wives for the Happy Hour dancing that takes place every Friday night. Instructors' wives and officers' wives join the same women's club, share recipes, plan social events together. By the time a student leaves the post to go to his assignment, he has formed a circle of intimate friends among the foreigners who have taught him. When he goes to the country to which he is assigned, it is impossible for him, his wife, or his children to look upon the people of that country as anything but duplicates of the men and women they have grown to know and love. The American speaks their language fluently; he knows their customs; he has partaken of their hospitality. How can that American soldier or officer ever set himself apart from the people of that country, form himself or his family into an inner circle that refuses to deal with the natives save on terms of assumed superiority, refrain from mingling with a people that he already knows, esteems, and appreciates? How can his wife, who in many cases has taken the foreign language by her husband's side, and who in any case has the most pleasant recollections of her foreign friends of the Women's Club, restrain her activities to the PX and the American colony?

So the graduates of the Monterey Army Language School go off throughout the world, carrying the message of common humanity and American good will to the lands to which they are assigned— lands to which they are not foreigners, but practically natives by adoption. Their attitude, their friendliness, their readiness to speak the language, participate in the country's social activities, respect the country's customs are quickly sensed, quickly appreciated. "These," say the natives of the nations to which our Army Language School graduates are assigned, "are not Ugly Americans, concerned only with impressing us with their money, their higher standards of living, their vaunted superiority. These are Beautiful, Lovely Americans, Americans who know us, understand us, appreciate us, love us. They want to be our friends. They are ready to prove it by the fact that they do not require us to speak English or supply interpreters, but come to us speaking our language. They prove it by their readiness to join us in our festivities, to share our food, to discuss things with us on a basis of perfect equality. They want to help us, not rule us or exploit us. They are our friends, our good friends. They love us and our country. We love them and their country in return!"

I cannot prove it with statistics, but it is my guess that one Beautiful American from Monterey's Army Language School is worth thousands, perhaps millions of dollars in foreign aid in terms of international good will.

PART FOUR

The International Language

The International Language

If language is here to stay, then what is the world's language picture? A brief examination reveals that it is a highly complex one.

There are many languages—far too many for comfort or adequate coverage. The need for communication is becoming ever more urgent. Can we achieve a single linguistic communication medium, and end the language traffic jam? What solutions have been offered over the centuries? Can we take one of the existing languages and use it internationally? Or is an artificial, constructed language better for the purpose? What languages, natural or constructed, are available? Which have the best chances of adoption? What would the adoption process consist of and entail? What must be done after adoption to prevent the language from breaking up into new, mutually incomprehensible dialects? What will a universal language do for us? What will it not do for us? What will it do to us?

Granted that the question of an international language is still viewed in many circles as largely academic, and that decision may be staved off for a time, are the "academic" features not somewhat on a par with those of air, water, and noise pollution? The time for a compulsory solution approaches rapidly—perhaps far more rapidly than many think. Ought we not to think about it in leisurely fashion while there is still leisure, rather than try to work out a solution on a crash basis at the last possible moment?

CHAPTER 26

Man Talks
in Three Thousand Tongues

From the time the Lord punished the children of man for trying to reach Heaven by way of the Tower of Babel, the world has been sundered by communication troubles.

Ever since, mankind has spoken different languages, and for years scholars have been trying to sort them out. It was established by the French Academy nearly forty years ago, and confirmed by an independent American survey, that the precise number of languages in the world, including extinct languages known once to have existed, but excluding hosts of minor dialects, is 2796. An effort to bring the count up to date was made more recently by the late Prof. Siegfried Muller of Adelphi University, with a grant from the Office of Education. A still more recent classification and count was made by Prof. C. F. Voegelin of Indiana University, and the results published; but a planned revision is in progress. These new surveys, including languages recently discovered, give slightly different totals, but the ultimate figure still hovers in the vicinity of three thousand.

Well over two thousand of the world's languages are spoken by small groups of a few thousand or even a few hundred persons. This is true of a good many of the 132 Papuan tongues, spoken in the interior of New Guinea; of more than a hundred native Australian languages; of some five hundred African Negro tongues; and of more than twelve hundred Western Hemisphere Indian languages.

This does not mean that all African and American Indian languages have small bodies of speakers. In the heart of South America, for example, Quichua, the ancient language of the Incas, is still spoken by more than six million people. In Africa, the Hausa of Nigeria is estimated to have at least ten million speakers, and the Swahili of East Africa, the language of safari, more than ten million.

But there are many American Indian groups, particularly in North America, which are close to extinction, and here it is a race between time and linguistic scientists to get them recorded and classified before they die out. In one Brooklyn block, for example, there is a small community of Mohawks, who, by reason of their extraordinary sense of balance, work for the most part as steeplejacks. These Mohawks speak their language, and even have a church in which services are conducted in it. But while the Mohawks themselves may not be dying out, their language is, for their Brooklyn-born children tend to speak nothing but English. A Columbia University graduate student is busy recording their language before it disappears.

There is an instance of a European language dying in very recent times. As late as the end of the nineteenth century, a few old-timers on the island of Veglia, at the head of the Adriatic, spoke a language which was a remnant of the ancient Dalmatian, a variety of Romance. Their descendants spoke nothing but Italian and Serbo-Croatian. An Italian linguist, M. G. Bartoli, went to Veglia around 1900, found three speakers of the traditional Vegliote, and recorded their speech. They all died a few years later, and Vegliote became extinct.

Despite the impressive total of 3,000 languages, there are only slightly more than a hundred that boast a million or more speakers. The languages that have over 50 million speakers (the giants of the language world) are only thirteen in number. They are Chinese, with all its dialects (over 700 million speakers; but even if we restrict Chinese to the official Kuo-yü, or North Mandarin, dialect, its 450 million and more speakers suffice to place it at the head of the list); English, with at least 300 million, and a leader among the world's languages by reason of its widespread distribution and the scientific, industrial, and cultural achievements of its speakers; Hindustani, which includes the Hindi of India and the Urdu of Pakistan, and now comes close to the 200 million mark; Russian, native to well over half of the Soviet Union's population of 230 million, but spoken as a second language by practically all the inhabitants; Spanish, with about 160 million, mostly in the Western Hemisphere; German, Japanese, and Indonesian, with perhaps 100 million each; French, Arabic, Bengali, and Portuguese, with more than 75 million each; Italian with over 55 million. Approaching the 50 million mark are the Ukrainian of southern Russia, the Bihari and Telugu of India. Other languages trail.

The most widely spoken language of Europe is German (Russian has more speakers, but they straddle two continents); Chinese is the most widely spoken tongue of Asia; Arabic, though it originated in Asia, holds the palm for Africa; English leads in North America and Oceania; Spanish in Central and South America.

The areas where English is either native, or the official language, or the tongue of common intercourse, cover roughly one fifth of the earth's land surface. Russian has one sixth. India, where perhaps 25 million out of a total population of nearly 500 million speak English, prides itself on being the third largest English-speaking country in the world, following only the United States and the United Kingdom.

How are the world's three thousand languages classified? At one time people thought that all languages came from a single source, the biblical Hebrew. This idea was abandoned in the course of the period of discovery and exploration, when more and more languages became known, and it was seen that they could not possibly be related. Lately it has become a vogue among some linguists to uphold once more the theory of monogenesis (single origin), but the evidence is still insufficient.

More than half of the world's people, roughly 1½ billion out of 3 billion, speak languages that are definitely related. The group is called Indo-European because it extends from northern India to western Europe. Among Indo-European languages are such diverse ones as English, Russian, Irish, French, Greek, Albanian, Armenian, and Hindustani.

It is possible to prove Indo-European unity by three tests: (1) grammatical structure, which is similar in all the languages, and becomes more similar the farther back we go in history; (2) vocabulary, which shows striking similarities in key words, such as numerals and nouns of family relationships, like *father, mother, sister, brother;* (3) consistent sound shifts, as when Germanic languages invariably show *f* in words where other languages show *p* (Latin *pater, pes,* English *father, foot*).

Within the Indo-European group we find eight modern subbranches: Germanic or Teutonic (this includes English, Dutch, German, Scandinavian); Latin-Romance (Latin and its descendants: French, Spanish, Portuguese, Italian, Rumanian); Balto-Slavic (Lithuanian and Latvian on the one hand, Russian, Ukrainian, Polish, Czech, Slovak, Serbo-Croatian, Slovenian, Bulgarian on the other); Celtic (Irish, Welsh, Breton, ancient Gaulish); Indo-Iranian (the languages of northern India, like Hindustani and Bengali, and those of Iran and Afghanistan); Greek; Albanian; Armenian.

But this classification leaves out half of the world's population. Other large and apparently unrelated families are: 1. Semitic-Hamitic (Hebrew, Aramaic, Arabic, the Akkadian of ancient Babylon and Assyria, the Phoenician and Punic of ancient Tyre, Sidon, and Carthage on the one hand; ancient Egyptian and modern Coptic and Berber on the other); 2. Ural-Altaic (this includes European languages like Finnish, Estonian, Lapp, Hungarian, on the Uralic side; Turkish and most tongues of the Soviet Union in Asia, as well as Mongol and Manchu, on the other); 3. Sino-Tibetan (Chinese, Thai, Burmese, Tibetan); 4. Japanese-Korean; 5. Malayo-Polynesian (the big language in this group is Malay or Indonesian, but to it belong most of the languages of the Philippines, like Tagalog and Bisaya, as well as Hawaiian, Tahitian, Samoan, the Maori of New Zealand, the Malagasy of Madagascar); 6. Dravidian (here we have the tongues of southern India, Tamil, Telugu, etc.); 7. three separate groups of African tongues, the Bantu, the Sudanese-Guinean, and the Hottentot-Bushman; 8. the twelve hundred or more American Indian languages; but among these there is such diversity that a precise classification would show over fifty separate groups, as different from one another as Chinese is from English. Other, smaller, unaffiliated families include the Eskimo-Aleut, the Caucasian, the Papuan and Australian, the Ainu of northern Japan, the Basque of the Pyrenees.

The oldest language on record is the Sumerian of Mesopotamia, spoken in that region before the coming of Semitic speakers of Akkadian. Sumerian records, written in cuneiform characters, go back to at least 3500 B.C. The ancient Egyptian of the hieroglyphic inscriptions is almost as old, and ancient Chinese records go back to about 2000 B.C., as do also those of Sanskrit, oldest of the Indo-European tongues to be recorded. Greek, first appearing in the Homeric poems (*Iliad* and *Odyssey*), goes back to about 800 B.C. (but the Minoan so-called "Linear B" inscriptions, claimed to be Greek, go back to about 1400 B.C.); Latin to about 500 B.C.

The first Latin inscription is the Praenestine fibula or belt buckle, on which are inscribed the words *Manios med fhefhaked Numasioi.* In later classical Latin this would read *Manius me fecit Nummerio,* "Manius made me for Nummerius." This is also the oldest commercial on record, bearing the name of both manufacturer and customer.

The "newest" language is undoubtedly to be sought among artificial, constructed tongues devised for international use, like Esperanto or Interlingua. But since more of these new artificial languages are constructed and submitted all the time, it would be difficult to say which is most recent. Among national, official tongues, on the other hand, it is possible to point to Indonesian as one of the newest. Although Indonesian is constructed along the lines of the old Malay that used to serve all the Dutch East Indies and British Malaya as a trade language, there are enough innovations in it to permit us to differentiate between it and Malay.

Curios abound in the field of language. In the matter of sounds, we have languages like the Hottentot-Bushman, in which some consonants are produced by sucking in air instead of letting it out. The clucking sound you use to a horse or a chicken, or the smack of your lips when you kiss, is a regular consonant sound in these tongues. In the matter of grammatical structure, some languages of the Caucasus find it impossible to say "I see him"; you have to rephrase it "He is seen by me." There are languages, like Basque and some American Indian tongues, in which the verb often includes subject, object, and all modifiers, so that the entire sentence comes out as a single word. Some languages are extremely specific; in the tongue of the

Kwakiutl Indians, it would not be possible to express such a concept as "The man is ill." One must phrase it somewhat like this: "This-visible-man-near-me, I-know, lies-ill-on-his-side-on-the-skins in-the-present-house-near-us." In some Eskimo languages a noun can have more than a thousand different forms, each with its own precise meaning.

Concepts which in Indo-European are basic, like gender and number, are not at all observed in many languages. Hungarian uses the same word for "he," "she," and "it." The plural is seldom expressed in Japanese. This, however strange it may seem, parallels what happens exceptionally in English, where we distinguish gender in "he," "she," "it," but not in "they," and where we distinguish number in "house-houses," "foot-feet," but not in "sheep" or "deer."

Where Indo-European languages use prepositions, many other groups use post-positions. Hungarian says "the house-in," "the houses-from." In Japanese the verb is completely impersonal; it expresses not "I go," "he goes," but "there is a going." In Chinese, time can only be expressed by means of modifiers; you do not say "I go," "I went," "I shall go," but "I now go," "I past day go," "I bright day go."

What seems to be basic to all languages is the transfer of meaning from one human mind to another. This is effected in different ways, just as transportation in various parts of the world may be by train, automobile, elephant, or camel back. If there is no transfer of meaning, there is no true language.

CHAPTER 27

A Universal Language
Can *Be Achieved*

It is unkind, unjust, even unright to laugh at the earnest and well-meaning efforts of others, particularly when these efforts represent a vast total of hard work and real scholarship. Yet the practical linguist, faced with the labor and bickering of the interlinguists who are so laboriously trying to evolve a language for international use, has no choice but to laugh. For he knows that both the labor and the bickerings are predicated upon two fundamental errors, one of which follows logically from the other.

Interlinguists (this includes advocates of natural languages; apostles of modified modern tongues, like Basic English, and modified dead tongues, like Peano's *Interlingua* or *Latino Sine Flexione;* and constructors of purely artificial tongues for international use) lose sight of the fundamental fact that every language, however intricate it may seem to those who try to learn it as adults, is simple to its own native speakers, who have learned it from childhood by natural speaking processes. Worse yet, as a result of this oversight, they proceed to plan, not, as they should, for the future generations, but for existing adult speakers who will die out, for the most part, within the next fifty years. They ignore the fact that the people now alive will be completely replaced, within less than a century, by other people whose habits, linguistic and otherwise, are not yet formed because they are not yet born, and so can be given, with proper planning, any set of linguistic or other habits that it pleases their enlightened elders to impart to them.

This means that there is no rhyme or reason to the controversies now bitterly raging as to whether it would be better to use a natural, a modified, or a constructed language as an international medium of communication. Esperanto, Interlingua, Basic English, natural English, French, or Russian—what difference does it make which one is selected, provided all people now living agree to use it—not for themselves, but for their children and descendants? What is needed for the solution of the world's language problems is simply *a* language—any one of the world's three thousand or so natural languages, or of the thousand or so constructed ones which have at various times been proposed. With just two limitations, however: the language selected must have absolute correspondence of written symbols for spoken sounds; and it must be adopted, by international agreement, in all countries at the same time, not in the high schools or colleges or universities, but in the kindergartens and lowest grades of the elementary schools, side by side with the national tongue, so that it may be learned easily, naturally, and painlessly.

Let us consider the logic of these propositions. There is no linguistic scholar on earth who will deny that all *spoken* tongues are essentially "easy" to their own speakers. Chinese, Russian, American, and Zulu children speak their own tongues with approximately the same ease and fluency up to the time their schooling begins. It is when the speaking process becomes a conscious learning of grammatical rules, and, worse yet, when it becomes a conscious tie-up of spoken with written forms, that the difficulties begin; and these are greater (sometimes tremendously greater) in one language than in another. If this is granted, then it follows that any *spoken* tongue, natural, constructed, or modified, may be adopted with equal chance of success to be imparted by *natural speaking* processes to all the world's children as soon as they become old enough to go to school. We need not worry about their having previously learned, in part, their own national tongues. The experience of multilingual countries like Belgium, Switzerland, Canada, and South Africa shows that one language can be started at birth, another at six, and both come out equally well. And it does not matter what the languages are: "easy" or "difficult," inflected, isolating, agglutinative, or polysynthetic. All these terms represent *conscious* processes of language acquisition *after* linguistic habits are fully formed: that is, when we try to learn languages at the rate of three hours a week in high school or college, by the grammar method, which is simply comparing the language we are learning with the one we already possess.

On the other hand, the *written* form of the language we are acquiring has a great deal to do with true "ease" and "difficulty." In languages like Spanish and Italian, or even more, Finnish or Turkish, where there are few or no exceptions to the sound-for-symbol correspondence, the process of learning to read and write and spell is quick and simple. In the case of English or French, where there is a strong divergence between spoken sounds and written letters, with sounds assuming all sorts of written appearances and letters of the alphabet representing all sorts of sounds, learning to read and write is far more complicated. In Chinese and Japanese, where complete spoken words are represented by arbitrary symbols, the process is still more complicated. Therefore, the language selected for international purposes must be written absolutely phonetically.

Beyond this, the problem rests with the world's governments. Do they want an international language, for full and complete international (and even national) use? If they do, the remedy is in their hands.

In round numbers, some one thousand constructed languages, modified natural languages, blends of languages for international use, have been proposed since the seventeenth century. In all of them, one outstanding preoccupation is in evidence: to make things as "easy" or as "logical" as possible for the greatest possible number of learners of the *existing* generation. Since the existing generation speaks a vast number of widely diverging languages, this preoccupation is doomed to sterility in advance. The Spanish, Portuguese, or Italian speaker who likes the largely Romance vocabulary of Esperanto or Interlingua is still stumped by features that run counter to his habits and therefore confuse him. The French speaker who tries to use Basic English must give up words which to him are perfectly accessible and meaningful, like "to abandon," and learn combinations which are idiomatic, like "to give up"; while the native English speaker finds himself beset at every turn by galling restrictions and prohibitions in the use of words which to him are perfectly natural.

Meanwhile, the real point is lost sight of. That is, the interlanguage of the future is for *future*, not for present, generations; and it does not have to be made "easy" or "logical" for anybody in particular, provided it is imparted in the right way and at the right age.

Either the world's governments are interested in giving the world's future generations the means of mutual understanding, or they are not. If they are not, nothing more need be said, save that governments, even in totalitarian countries, are usually responsive to popular pressure if it is strong enough.

If the governments are or can be made to be interested, the solution is relatively simple. A commission of international linguists can be set up for the purpose of selecting one of the world's many natural or artificial languages to serve as an interlanguage. Which one they select is of comparatively little moment provided they do select it. Once it is selected, it goes into all the elementary schools in the world to be imparted (not "taught" as a foreign language) by natural speaking methods, from kindergarten on, side by side with the national tongue and on an absolute parity with it. Within ten years, a new generation of interlinguists will crop up all over the world; within twenty, it will have grown to maturity; within thirty or forty, it will be ready to take its place at the helm of the world's affairs; within fifty or sixty, at least in civilized countries, the person that is not equipped with the interlanguage will be rare.

The present adult generation? Let it do what it wants. It will be gone within a century anyway. Those who want to keep up with the times can take up the new interlanguage in special classes and acquire it painfully, the hard way, as they acquire foreign tongues today. Those who are too lazy, or haven't the time, or don't believe in the idea can be left completely undisturbed. The use of the national language in their own country will continue to be universal, and will certainly last as long as they do. Is it callous to treat the present adult generation with so little regard? Certainly no more so than when we ask it to sacrifice life, liberty, and comfort in order that future generations may be assured of certain advantages, economic or political, which those same future generations may not look upon as advantages at all.

Is this too simple to be true? Perhaps so. To begin with, the will to international understanding must be there, just as the will to peace must be there in the matter of disarmament and peace. This means *international* government action—a concerted move on the part of all governments to make possible what is desirable. One government may initiate the movement (why not our own?). Then we shall see whether the others are willing to cooperate in the interests of those "children and children's children" concerning whom so many fine words flow, but for whom so little of a truly constructive nature is ever done.

Secondly, there is the problem of the linguistic commission. Were all the governments to agree in advance to abide by its decision, the commission would have to be carefully picked and even more carefully watched. The number of delegates from each country would have to be determined in advance, and not necessarily by a "one man one vote" system. Other factors (productivity, industry, general advancement, literacy) might well play a part in weighting the representation from each country, Literacy would be particularly important, since the immediate results of the commission's decision would in practice apply only to that portion of a country's population which has the possibility of schooling. The principle of using literate population as the basis for representation might even have the beneficial side effect of encouraging national governments to develop literacy within their borders.

Thirdly, the selection of representatives by the individual governments is of importance. Known advocates of one or another of the systems now vying for supremacy should *a priori* be excluded. The qualifications of every delegate should be passed upon.

But even more important is the question of time and procedure. Left to their own devices, linguists might bicker forever. Since what language they select is not one tenth so important as their selecting it, a definite time limit should be placed on their labors. While all languages could be presented for candidacy at the outset, the procedure should involve a series of compulsory run-off votes, with stragglers weeded out until an absolute majority for one tongue is reached. Lastly, it should be understood that the language selected, if a natural tongue, would be given a phonetic spelling for international purposes. The charge of cultural imperialism against any national tongue that might be selected would be done away with by two factors: (1) The choice would have been made by a fully international commission, in which all nations would have had full representation on a proportional basis; (2) Its system of writing would be changed to conform with phonetic requirements, thereby differentiating it, at least in written form, from the national tongue.

The process of training teachers in the international language would take considerable time; but with educational facilities, teachers' colleges, and normal schools what they are today, it might be hoped that the actual process of starting to impart the international tongue in the kindergartens could begin within four or five years of the commission's decision.

Will the rise of an interlanguage ultimately do away with existing national languages? All who are at present engaged in trying to sell us a particular interlanguage scheme assure us that it will not, that it is meant "only" for international communication, with the existing languages surviving and flourishing. My answer is that in the long run the universal language will obliterate existing languages. But the "long run" will probably turn out to be a few centuries. The language that is good at all times and in all places will eventually supplant languages whose currency is limited to their own territory. The transition will of course be gradual, but we may expect that the present spoken languages will, in the course of time, tend to become cultural relics, like Latin or ancient Greek, until they are ultimately studied solely for their literary and cultural values. It may be added that our present national languages will, in the course of the next five hundred years, so evolve and change as to be foreign tongues to their present speakers, as Middle English and Old French are foreign tongues to modern English and French speakers, so that the ultimate result will be the same, whether or not we have an international language.

What are the chances that the new interlanguage will dialectalize, just as the Latin of the Roman Empire broke up into the various Romance languages? Under present conditions of communications (widespread literacy, radio, TV, Telstar) those chances are very slim. The Roman Empire's means of communication and education (roads, trade, military service, books, schools) were rudimentary as compared with those of today. Yet while those rudimentary means endured, the language remained substantially one. It was only when communications failed after the Empire's downfall, and each community became a semi-isolated, self-sufficient unit, that incomprehensibility arose. Under modern conditions, our comparison should be with the Anglo-American of the English-speaking world rather than with the Latin of the Empire. The King's English and the American language, which had been diverging more and more down to the turn of the century, began to grow together again with the advent of radio and spoken films, to which international TV is now added. These inventions, by bringing the pronunciation, intonation, and vocabulary of one set of speakers to the other, caused each one insensibly to modify its own habits of speech in the direction of the other's. Today, a thoroughly British program like "The Avengers" can appear on the American TV screen and never cause a ripple, while our "Dragnet" can similarly appear on British "telly." In the world of tomorrow there will be far more travel than in the past, but even the obdurate stay-at-homes will get standardized radio, movie, and TV programs.

One more question: In what language or languages would the commission carry on its proceedings? The answer is that if a body of international linguists could not solve that problem for itself, we would have *prima-facie* evidence that an international language cannot be established, and that the Tower of Babel must stand. But of that, fortunately, there is little chance.

CHAPTER 28

Ending the Language
Traffic Jam

In 1950 a Gallup Poll was conducted in the United States, Canada, Norway, Holland, and Finland. The first question asked was: "It has been suggested that every school child in every country should be required to learn one other language beside his own, which would be understood in all countries. Do you think this is a good idea or a poor idea?" The response was about 76 per cent "good idea" in all five countries, with 15 per cent opposed and 9 per cent undecided.

The poll, repeated in 1961 in the United States alone, indicated that the majority in favor of the proposal had grown by eight percentage points to 84 per cent, while both the opposition and the group that could not make up its mind had correspondingly dwindled.

A while back the inquiring photographer of the New York *Mirror* asked four people in the New York streets: "Think a universal language is needed?" Three said yes, one said no.

These are clear indications of how people feel about the issue. They don't go out and agitate for an international language in the same way they would agitate for national independence or lower taxes, because the issue has not been, in the past, a burning one, or one that seemed to call for direct and violent action. It is more like the traffic problem in a big modern city, which everyone agrees someone should do something about at some time or other, before we are tied up in a knot.

Language is basically a communications tool. When we share a common language with the person with whom we wish to communicate, we have no trouble. When we do not, we hire a translator or an interpreter, use sign language, or do without the thing we want.

So long as only a few high-placed or wealthy persons find themselves in need of communicating with people who do not speak their language, the problem is rather easily solved, though the solution may be expensive. President Johnson and Chairman Kosygin have their interpreters, and the room clerks and head waiters of the Hilton Hotels scattered throughout the globe speak English for the benefit of our dollar-laden tourists. The problem is no more acute than was the traffic problem in New York City in the days when one person out of fifty owned a car.

The traffic snarl begins when one person out of three owns a car and wishes to drive and park it on city streets. The communications problem grows acute when travel to other lands becomes widespread. Fifty years ago, your chances of either going abroad or having to deal with non-English-speaking persons on your own soil were roughly one out of fifty. Today they are one out of ten. Before long, they will be one out of two or three.

Lack of linguistic understanding is certain to become a more and more critical problem, not just for the diplomat and pleasure traveler, but for the soldier, airman, technician, mechanic, or secretary stationed abroad; for the physician or scientist who needs to keep abreast of his field's latest developments in a large number of countries that publish periodicals in their own languages; for the student or intellectual whose activities call for foreign contacts; for the businessman who wants to take advantage of the vastly improved possibilities for foreign trade that modern means of transportation now afford. The days when your children, unless you happened to be a member of a very small privileged minority, were doomed for life to remain farmers behind the plow or manual workers toiling at a lathe are gone, never to return. Today, both farmer and manual worker dream of sending their children to college and turning them into intellectuals, professional people, or, at the very least, white collar workers. People in these categories cannot very well escape international contacts, and to take full advantage of their opportunities they need a language in common with their fellow intellectual, professional, or semi-professional workers throughout the world.

That all this is true seems to be felt, perhaps in a hazy, confused way, by over three fourths of the people who are asked: "Is an international tongue desirable?" I seriously doubt that the majority of them are influenced to any great extent by the argument that such a language will lead to greater international understanding, and thus promote the cause of peace. Too many of us remember such bloody episodes as the Civil War in Spain and our own War Between the States, where a common language did nothing to prevent hostility. The real argument on behalf of an international language is that in a modern world it is a communications tool that we can no longer do without.

What substitute is most commonly offered for an international language? "We should have more study of foreign languages," people say. No issue can be taken with this proposition as matters stand today. Short of having an international tongue at our disposal, we, and everybody else, should certainly study and learn more foreign languages. But how many languages can you study and really learn? One, and learn it thoroughly, so that it becomes second nature to you? Two, three, or four, not so thoroughly, but so that you will have a working knowledge of each? Become a language specialist, like the present writer, so that you can speak four with absolute fluency, be able to stumble your way around in a dozen others, and know something about perhaps a hundred more? If you do that, you won't have time to do anything else. And even if you do it, you will always run the risk of coming up against the language you haven't studied; when this happens, you are just as helpless as the man who has studied no foreign language at all.

Very few people can determine in advance which language or languages they are likely to need at some time. Choosing a language when you enter high school is pretty much like taking a shot in the dark. You select French and then find out, ten years later, that you should have taken Spanish, or German, or Russian, or Italian, or Indonesian.

An international language is rapidly becoming an immediate necessity. And if we are wise, we shall anticipate the acute need of the future and provide for it, just as wise city planners make provision for the expansion of their growing city and the traffic problems the growth will involve.

The big obstacle in the way of the adoption of an international tongue as envisaged in the Gallup Poll lies not in the principle, but in the choice.

If the movement for the international language were one, it would have a fair chance of success. Fractioned among a hundred living systems, natural and constructed, each with its own followers, however small the group, it can hardly hope to gain acceptance.

We can either insist on the candidate of our choice and hold out until hell freezes over (and this means that we shall have to wait until human nature changes, or until one nation, by force of arms, imposes its language upon the rest of the world); or we can agree, in advance, to abide by majority rule and promise our loyal support to the language that shall emerge from a thoroughly democratic representative process, regretfully discarding the tongue we would have preferred.

If we follow the latter course, we may indeed hope for a world language in our time.

The second question on the same Gallup Poll may give us an indication of what languages would have the best chance of being selected. It was: "Which language (other than your native tongue) would you choose for this second language?"

In the United States, where people could not vote for English, 27 per cent of the votes were for French, 25 per cent for Spanish, 14 per cent for German; the other languages trailed. In Canada, where the question was apparently misunderstood, since French and English are both official tongues, 55 per cent of those polled voted for French. In both Norway and Holland, where a vote for English was allowed, about 60 per cent of the votes were for English, with Esperanto, not French, German, or Russian, as the runner-up. To what extent this picture would change if some Communist countries were included in the poll is a matter of conjecture.

A much more recent poll, conducted in Japan in 1959 by the International Language Institute of Tokyo, a Japanese society interested in promoting a world language for international use, produced some significant answers to the question "What do you recommend as the world language?" Answers given by 190 foreign tourists to Japan, including Britishers, Americans, and other native speakers of English, revealed that twenty-five favored English and eighty-four favored simplified English. When the same question was asked of 200 native Japanese students, eighteen favored English and ninety-six favored simplified English. The rest of the votes were scattered among several other choices.

Of particular interest in this poll is the fact that English, in its present or in a simplified form, won something like 60 per cent of the votes in both groups. Esperanto, not too well favored among the foreign tourists (only about 3 per cent), had 21 per cent of the votes among the Japanese themselves.

English, in natural or simplified form, seems to be the choice of well over half the voters in those countries where it is not native. The Japanese poll does not explain what was understood by English in simplified form. Probably a phonetic form of spelling was meant, since that is the greatest stumbling block to the assimilation of English, both by foreign and native speakers.

The question is often asked whether, if a constructed language such as Esperanto or Interlingua were adopted, the language should not be made truly international by granting proportional representation to all the major languages, particularly the big oriental ones that were altogether neglected by Zamenhof, constructor of Esperanto, and by the linguistic experts who constructed Interlingua. A partial reply was given by Albert Guérard, who pointed out in 1922 that it would be hard to imagine a language fair to East and West alike, and that there would probably be no real objection on the part of the East to accepting a Pan-Western tongue, to which the East could make future contributions. This seems to be borne out by the Japanese poll, which indicates, in an Eastern country, a decided preference for Western-style tongues.

Dr. Alexander Gode of Interlingua goes on to point out that the major oriental languages (Chinese, Japanese, Indonesian, Arabic,

Hindustani) are mutually incomprehensible. A speaker of Hindu-stani will be as much at a loss before a Chinese word as before a Latin one. Hence, if we try to broaden our international base, we run the risk of making our constructed language incomprehensible to both Westerners and Orientals.

Of this he gives a striking demonstration by offering a passage, first in Interlingua as it is, next in Interlingua as it would be with the insertion of Oriental words:

"Le sol dice: 'Io me appella sol. Io es multo brillante. Io me leva al est, e quando io me leva, il es die. Io reguardo per tu fenestra con mi oculo brillante como le auro, e io te dice quando il es tempore a levar te. E io te dice: "Pigro, leva te. Io non brilla a fin que tu resta al lecto a dormir, sed que tu te leva e labora, que tu lege e que tu te promena."'"

This should be readily understood by any speaker of a Western language, including English. But just in case, the translation goes: "The sun says, 'My name is sun. I am very brilliant. I rise in the east, and when I rise, it is day. I look through your window with my eye as bright as gold, and I tell you when it is time to get up. And I say to you: "Lazy one, get up. I don't shine so that you may stay in bed sleeping, but that you may get up and work, that you may read and go walking."'"

Note now the transition to an intercontinental version:

"Mata-hari yu: 'Wo-ti nama mata-hari. Wo taihen brillante. Wo leva wo a est, dan toki wo leva wo, ada hari. Wo miru per ni-ti fenestra sama wo-ti mata brillante como kin, dan wo yu ni toki ada tempo a levar ni. Dan wo yu ni: "Sust, leva ni. Wo non brilla sam-rap ni tomaru a toko a nemuru, sed wo brilla sam-rap ni leva ni, dan que ni suru kam, ni yomu, dan ni aruku."'"

The first point is that no Westerner will even begin to understand this without very special study. The second and perhaps even more important point is that the Indonesian speaker, who supplied *mata-hari* and *sam-rap,* will not understand the Chinese *wo-ti, ni,* and *yu,* or the Japanese *taihen* and *nemuru;* nor will his words be under-stood by the speakers of the latter languages.

But this proves only that there are difficulties—not that the diffi-culties are incapable of being solved. For I am convinced that they can and must be solved. In a world in which every man is swiftly coming to be every other man's next-door neighbor, the inability to communicate is certain to become a more and more serious handicap. An international language is no longer a luxury that can be put off until someone else decides to do something about it. The time for ending the linguistic traffic jam is now.

CHAPTER 29

One Language for the World?

Universality was implicit in the ancient world of the Romans and in the medieval world that followed it. The language of Rome, which had served the universal Roman Empire and the universal Christian Church, continued to be the common language of Western scholarship until the dawn of the Renaissance.

But modern progress, the invention of printing, and the spreading of literacy to upper and middle classes that had been largely illiterate in the past, coupled with the beginnings of the modern national states, brought the spoken vernaculars of the masses to the fore. The fifteenth century witnessed the final triumph of the national languages over the Latin that had dominated the thousand-year period since the fall of the Roman Empire of the West, and Europe assumed its modern linguistic aspect, with an array of national tongues, both literary and official.

It is therefore not to be wondered at that many minds began to turn to the problem of a single language that would serve for the new and numerous cultural exchanges that were being established. Latin no longer sufficed. In the thirteenth century, the traveling scholar would care to communicate only with his peers, and they all knew Latin. In the seventeenth, his desire was for oral communication with all sorts of people: merchants and sailors and soldiers and nobles and perhaps even peasants, and they knew no Latin. The vernaculars were not merely too numerous; they were too much broken up into local dialects.

Yet Comenius, a seventeenth-century educator with an international background, came out with the startling proposal that the leading languages of eastern and western Europe be used in international fashion, with Russian serving the east and French and English the west.

These proposals have been repeated, in one fashion or another, from that day to the present. The *Monde Bilingue* movement, the zonal languages of Stalin, the advocacy of English in normal, Basic, or revised-spelling form, are only three of the many suggestions that existing, natural, national languages be used, singly or in combination, in straight or modified form, for international purposes.

But the proposal advanced in 1629 by the French philosopher Descartes was of a radically different nature. Answering a letter written him by a Father Mersenne, who had enclosed in his missive an anonymous Latin prospectus concerning the desirability of an international language, the great philosopher presented his own views on the subject.

Beginning with an attack on the difficulties of national grammars, which prevent people from seizing the meaning of a passage by referring to the dictionary alone, Descartes goes on to advocate the creation of a tongue whose grammar will be so simple that it can be learned without effort by anyone, by reason of its absolute regularity and logic.

Along with this, he proposes a word-coining system whereby there will be, among the ideas of the human mind, the same order that prevails among numbers in mathematics, so that just as there is in mathematics a logical progression from the known to the unknown, the same process may be possible with words. If this is done, he concludes, peasants will be able to determine truth in better fashion than do philosophers at present.

What Descartes advocates, though he gives no example of it, is a constructed language of the *a priori* or philosophical type, whose grammar will depart from known grammars to the extent that it will be regular and without exceptions, and whose word-stock will not be haphazard, but logically connected. Such a language is perfectly possible, but does not coincide with the structure of any known tongue.

Descartes supplied no sample of his ideal international language, but such samples were immediately forthcoming from several of his contemporaries, Dalgarno, Urquhart, Wilkins, Leibniz. Cave Beck, in 1657, offered an ingenious system based on combinations of letters and numbers to be used in writing, while the numbers would be replaced by sounds in actual speech.

"Honor thy father and thy mother" would appear in Beck's written system as "leb2314 p2477 pf2477," which would be read *leb-toreonfo peetofosensen piftofosensen* (each numeral stands for a spoken syllable). It is perhaps obvious why this system did not take hold. The strain imposed on the memory is tremendous.

Since the days of Descartes, Leibniz, and Beck, it is estimated that close to a thousand different proposals have been advanced for the solution of the world's linguistic troubles. Their chronological sequence has interesting features. Once we are past the seventeenth century, popular interest seems to flag. Between 1800 and 1850, only four important projects appear, but one of them is Sudre's famous Solresol, based on the notes of the scale. This attracted enormous attention, was later sponsored by such people as Victor Hugo, Lamartine, Humboldt, and Napoleon III, and had at one point a considerable body of speakers, with die-hard followers as late as 1900.

Statistically, combinations of the syllables *do, re, mi, fa, sol, la, si* yield seven words of one syllable, 49 of two, 336 of three, 2268 of four, 9072 of five. Shifts of accent from one syllable to another then yield the possibility of changing the function of a word from noun to verb or adjective or adverb. The language could be sung or played or hummed instead of spoken; it could be written as music; knocks, or even colors, could be substituted for the syllables for distant communication. A phrase like "I don't love" is *dore do milasi*.

That the constructed language of the *a priori* type, having no connection with existing languages, has not fully died out is proved by two interesting twentieth-century samples, both of American origin. One is Foster's Ro of 1912, in which the first part of the Lord's Prayer runs: *Abze radap av el in suda, ace rokab eco sugem; ace rajda ec kep; ace va eco uz in suda asi in buba.* The other is Russell's Suma of 1957, in which the beginning of the First Book of Genesis runs: *Talo moti sima baki boto e beto e beto te peka e ena gide e ena doba.*

Far more numerous and varied are the languages of the *a posteriori*

type, based on one or more existing natural languages. Here a distinction must be made between modifications of single existing tongues
and language blends of various kinds.

Typical of the modified natural language is Basic English, which
is ordinary English restricted as to vocabulary, so that "participate"
has to be rendered as "take part," and "selfish" paraphrased into
"without thought of others." The claim (not altogether substanti-
ated) is that with 850 English words at our disposal we can cover the
entire vast range of human language needs.

Basic English does not interfere with normal English sounds or
grammar; but other modified languages prefer to leave the vocabulary
alone and change the grammatical structure. In 1903, Peano presented a system called Latino Sine Flexione (Flexionless Latin), in
which the endings of Latin are dropped or merged: *Studio theorico
proba que es necessario nullo regula de grammatica, nullo suffixo de
derivatione* (A theoretical study proves that no grammatical rule, no
derivational suffix, is necessary).

Language blends run all the way from barely disguised modifications of Latin and Romance to systems that propose to give what
amounts to proportional representation to all of the world's great language families. The original idea, which arose in the middle of the
eighteenth century and replaced the earlier striving for "logic" in
language, was that of "the greatest ease for the greatest number."
But since, at the time when this principle was enunciated, "the
greatest number" referred only to speakers of Western-type languages, many of these blends, even today, resolve themselves into
combinations of Latin, Greek, Romance, occasionally Germanic, still
more seldom Slavic, with little or no attention paid to the vast numbers of speakers of other types of tongues.

The first *a posteriori* language to meet with favor was Schleyer's
Volapük of 1885, a tongue which blends Latin-Romance, English,
and German elements. "I don't want the book, but a book" is in
Volapük *No vilob eli buki, sod uni buki.*

By 1890, the vogue of Volapük had come to a standstill, and
Zamenhof's Esperanto assumed international importance. Here, too,
we have a predominance of classical, Romance, and Germanic ele-

ments, with other languages, including the Slavic, largely left out of the running (this is surprising, since Zamenhof was a Pole).

The popularity of Esperanto continues to the present day, and it is estimated that eight million people throughout the world speak it in one fashion or another. But the popularity of Esperanto seems to have had the effect of encouraging rather than discouraging further attempts. In the course of the present century, well over 500 constructed languages have been offered to the world.

Most of them are of the same basic type as Esperanto, with a grammar that is more or less arbitrary and a vocabulary drawn from the Western languages. This is true even of languages constructed by some of the world's great linguists (de Saussure and Jespersen, to cite only two names).

On the other hand, some very ingenious schemes have been advanced to give some measure of representation to other major language groups. Cheshikhin's Nepo of 1910, for instance, adds Slavic to the Latin-Romance-Germanic combination (*Vatero nia, kotoryja estas in la njeboo, heiliga estu nomo via* is the beginning of the Lord's Prayer in Nepo). Hogben's Interglossa of 1943 presents a Graeco-Latin vocabulary, but with a Chinese word order (*Na Parenta in Urani; Na dicte volo; tu Nomino gene revero*).

Steiner's Pasilingua of 1885 makes provision for synonyms from Latin-Romance and Germanic: "good" may be either *bono* or *guto;* "God" is *Deo* or *Gotto;* "often" is *saepe* or *oftis.* Fred Mill's Anti-Volapük of 1893 goes even further, combining international connecting words, taken largely from Latin-Romance, with nouns and verbs of the speaker's own language, with the proviso, presumably, that each speaker will learn enough of the other speaker's nouns and verbs to be at least able to understand them.

Thus, the sentence "I think he is in the street," would come out in the following English, French, Italian, Spanish and Russian versions:

> "Io think ke le es in le street."
> "Io croire ke le es in le rue."
> "Io credere ke le es in le strada."
> "Io creer ke le es in le calle."
> "Io dumat' ke le es in le ulitsa."

Most comprehensive among proposals designed to give representation to all major language groups is the recent one of Leidenfrost that a Universal Grammar and Vocabulary be constructed by a commission of language specialists on the basis of a blend of ten representative languages: Iraqi Arabic, Mandarin Chinese, English, Hindustani, Hungarian, Indonesian, the Kpelle of Liberia, Russian, Spanish, and Swahili. This still leaves out two major language groups, the Japanese-Korean and the Dravidian of southern India, both of which have well over a hundred million speakers.

One final word may be added, in connection with the desirability (or lack thereof) of a constructed tongue vis-à-vis a national language adopted for international use. One of the great advantages postulated by the proponents of constructed languages is their internationality or neutrality, the fact that no nation need object to them on the ground that they are vehicles and standard-bearers of alien cultures.

This is quite true of the *a priori* languages, which are based on no known tongue. It is far from true of the majority of *a posteriori* languages, which definitely reflect a western European blend to the exclusion of other language groups, which in the modern world are acquiring an ever-growing importance.

The corresponding disadvantage, to which many linguists object, is that the constructed language, not having grown from the soil, is not the bearer of cultural values. For a language that is meant to be, at the outset, a vehicle of material communication rather than an instrument of cultural imperialism, this is not a disadvantage, but the opposite.

In addition, I see no incompatibility whatsoever between the terms constructed languages and culture. Every great cultural language once started out as a rough-hewn tongue fit only for material communication, and then proceeded to polish and refine itself to the point of becoming a vehicle for abstract, cultural thought. In the case of Sanskrit, Greek, Latin, even of Anglo-Saxon, Old High German, and the Romance tongues, this was a long and painful process.

At the present time there is no need for such a process, since any constructed language has the possibility of borrowing and coining a thoroughly cultural vocabulary. What has been accomplished so far by Esperanto and Interlingua, to mention only two constructed tongues, is impressive. Can anyone seriously argue that you cannot express cultural thought in either of these constructed languages? They have the vocabularies of all the cultural tongues in the world to draw from, plus a process for coining new words and expressions as they are needed. The only argument that can be raised against them (and it is, to my mind, a purely negative one) is that they are not the vehicle of any specific culture, but rather of a world culture which, whether our linguistic nationalists like it or not, is on its way, and within the next hundred years will overspread the entire globe.

Two other considerations of a highly practical nature offer themselves. National languages, big or small, seldom have a system of perfect phonetic notation. This is particularly true of languages of century-old civilizations, such as French and English, where the time lag between the normal evolution of speech and the bringing up to date of the spelling has worked to deepen the separation between speech and writing.

Constructed languages, on the other hand, are normally completely phonetized, with absolute sound-for-symbol correspondence (Esperanto is a good example). This means that any national language selected for international use would have to go through a process of spelling reform, at least for international purposes, before it could be properly put into operation, while a constructed language could go into operation at once, without further study or change.

Even more important is the fact that national languages normally show deep dialectal divisions, with frequent uncertainty as to a standard form. This is particularly true of English and Spanish, somewhat less true of French and Russian, where a "correct" standard exists, whether or not it is followed by all the speakers. But the constructed language is normally fully standardized, and the only problem is to keep it that way once it goes into operation.

These two characteristics of constructed languages, phonetization and standardization, are perhaps of greater importance than a "neutrality" which seldom appears and which can in no case be made altogether perfect. They are, in my opinion, of sufficient importance to warrant serious consideration of a constructed language for international use along with the numerous national tongues, old and new, that are offered for candidacy.

CHAPTER 30

The Case for Esperanto

While it is easy to discuss the individual merits of Esperanto, or Interlingua, or both, it is difficult to hold a debate over their relative merits, in view of their avowed difference of purpose. Dr. Alexander Gode never tires of repeating that Interlingua is not meant to be an international language of common intercourse for the world's people, but only a tongue to be used by scientists, preferably in written form, in their journals and at their meetings. Esperantists just as frankly avow their aim to set up Esperanto as a fully spoken language of common, everyday usage for everybody. It is therefore as illogical to debate their relative merits as it would be to debate the qualifications of two candidates for such different offices as President of the United States of America and mayor of Peoria, Illinois.

Dr. Gode is frankly skeptical about the possibility of having a language of common intercourse for all the people of the world, or at least for that portion, fortunately ever-growing, which can be reached by formal education. On this point I have always differed with him, and continue to do so. I not only believe that "One Language for the World" is practical and feasible, but I venture to prophesy that such a language will be in operation, though perhaps not functioning with perfect smoothness, by A.D. 2000. It is badly needed now. It will be more and more needed as the years roll by. Eventually, that need will impinge itself upon the consciousness of the world's governments, and they will act. The rest will be relatively easy, though it may take years and decades to get the world language to function naturally and smoothly.

What the procedure of choice and implementation may be we can only guess at right now. I have suggested a possible mode of pro-

233

cedure in my book *One Language for the World*,* but I am the first
to admit that many other modes of procedure are possible.

While I do not consider it possible to debate the relative merits of
Interlingua and Esperanto because of their difference of purpose, it
is quite possible to exercise critical judgment on them individually
and in turn, always keeping in mind what they are supposed to be
and do.

Interlingua may be of limited value in facilitating the work of
international scientific congresses and summarizing scientific papers,
articles, and books. I use the word "limited" because the true scientist
(as apart from the technician) who is not equipped with one or
more languages beside his own is rare. It is a little difficult to conceive of an Italian, or Japanese, or Iraqi, or even Russian scientist
who has not studied English, French, or German, or all three, at
least to the point of being able to read them. It is quite true that
Interlingua contains all the scientific terminology, based on Latin
and Greek roots, that is common to our Western civilization. But so
do the major Western languages, particularly English and French.
Interlingua, therefore, seems to serve a partly redundant purpose.
Since Interlingua has no ambition to serve as the world language of
the masses, it seems to me that we may safely leave it to fulfill its
limited function. Let its users pass judgment on it. If the world's
scientists decide that it is worth while to have, among themselves, a
language of limited use, they will adopt it. But they may find it
easier and more practical to adopt one of the existing scientific languages, notably English, which is widespread, combines Latin, Greek,
and Germanic elements, presents few basic structural difficulties, particularly in written form for scientific statement, while its tremendous difficulties of spelling vs. pronunciation will be covered up by
the fact that it will be used primarily in writing.

As has been the case all through history, scholars, scientists, and
people of high education are the ones who need an international language the least, because they have all sorts of resources and replace-
ments at their disposal. My own interest lies in a language of common intercourse for the people of the world as a whole, and here, by

* Devin-Adair, N.Y., 1958.

the terms of the debate, Esperanto is left in sole control of the field. Yet the merits of Esperanto can perfectly well be weighed, not against those of Interlingua, which is not a candidate for the same post, but against those of languages, natural and constructed, that are avowed candidates.

Here we can proceed either by linguistic theory or by linguistic practice. Linguistic theory informs us that for the purpose we have in mind one language is as good as another. All languages are on the same plane, because all languages are equally easy and natural to their native speakers, those who have acquired them and used them from early childhood. There is no evidence that any language, in purely spoken form, is more easily assimilated by its own speakers than any other language. Therefore, by linguistic theory, all we have to do is to select, blindly if we wish, any one of the nearly three thousand natural languages of the world, or of the thousand or more constructed languages that have been offered since the seventeenth century, and put it into operation. Any one of them will do the job.

Linguistic practice is something else. In modern civilization, languages must have a written as well as a spoken form. Ease of language-learning is definitely not on a plane of equality so far as the written counterparts of the spoken languages are concerned. Inherent, objective ease and difficulty are in evidence here, and the objective standard by which such ease or difficulty is gauged is the extent to which there is sound-for-symbol correspondence between the spoken and the written form.

Here the constructed language holds a tremendous advantage over the natural language. In the course of their histories, natural languages have developed discrepancies in correspondence. Some have greater discrepancies than others, but there are few natural languages where you can, after an hour's instruction in the correlation between speech sounds and written symbols, pronounce or spell the language creditably, let alone perfectly (English and French, two of the leading contenders among the natural languages for the international post, are unfortunately among the worst sinners in this respect.) On the other hand, constructed languages, by virtue of the very fact that they are constructed, are generally equipped with sound-for-symbol correspondence.

It can, of course, be replied that one can phonetize a natural language. But here another disadvantage of the natural language rises up to plague us. These languages are normally heavily dialectalized. In some, like French, there is an ideal standard, or preferred dialect form, which could be taken as the norm for phonetization and international use. In others, like English, there is no such standard or norm. This means that enforced standardization must be added to (in fact, must precede) phonetization. These twin hurdles, standardization and phonetization, are not insurmountable, but they are grave and time-consuming.

Constructed languages, by virtue of the fact that they are constructed, are normally fully standardized. Add to this that the constructed language, though it may not be quite as neutral or fully as international or intercontinental as some would like, is nevertheless neutral enough to escape the charge of cultural imperialism that may be leveled at any natural language. Among adult learners, everyone would have to make some effort to learn the constructed language, though this effort might be greater or smaller to the extent that the language leans more or less in the direction of the learner's native tongue.

One might say that the reaction of the adult generation of learners is irrelevant, since the international language is meant primarily, almost exclusively, for the unborn generations of the future. Unfortunately, the choice will have to be made by an existing adult generation, and it is very hard to exclude from the consciousness of the adult speaker the purely subjective factor of what is easy or difficult "for me."

The frequently voiced objection that constructed languages are not natural, that they do not issue from the soil, that they do not carry a cultural content and tradition leaves me altogether cold. We are dealing with a twentieth-century civilization, in which the artificial is often infinitely preferable to the natural. For purposes of present-day transportation, I would much prefer to have an artificial automobile, tailored to my needs, rather than a "natural" horse. Cultural contents and traditions, history shows us, can very easily be created, acquired, and borrowed, particularly for that part which is worth while having, and which does not represent an exaggerated sense of nationalism or even imperialism. There is no good reason why the truly cultural content of the world's great cultures cannot be transferred to a constructed language, as it is right now in the process of being transferred from one natural language to another.

All of the foregoing considerations would lead me, if I were a member of a linguistic commission created to select a language for world use, to cast my initial ballot in favor of a constructed rather than a natural language. The constructed language, in my opinion, would materially reduce the very real difficulties and problems of the great innovation that a world language would constitute.

This narrows down my choice to the constructed languages. Here again, practical linguistics comes to the fore. It is as vain to seek perfection in a constructed language as in a natural one, for the very simple reason that in the field of language there is no such thing as perfection. It may be perfectly true that Ido or Novial may express a certain concept more clearly and tersely than Esperanto or Volapük; but Esperanto or Volapük may have certain other areas of superiority. Also, there is nothing to prevent a given constructed language, once it is adopted for world use, from being modified or improved upon by the Language Academy that will under all circumstances have to be created and function, far more effectively than the French or Italian or Spanish Academies, to keep the language from being dialectalized, and to prescribe, in no uncertain terms, what is and what is not correct, standard usage.

In my examination of the numerous constructed languages that have been offered since the days of Descartes, I have come across many praiseworthy features that could eventually be incorporated into a fully functioning world tongue, just as new elements of vocabulary will have to be. But if we undertake to solve now, before the adoption of a world language, the numerous problems of how to improve upon existing candidates, we can easily go on doing this for another thousand years. The thing to do is to adopt the language, put it into operation, and modify it later, as it will have to be modified under all circumstances.

There is one constructed language that has more followers and is more widely recognized than any other. This is a *de facto* situation, and not necessarily predicated upon inherent merits. Whatever its merits or demerits may be, that language has proved: (1) that it can draw to itself a fairly large and highly enthusiastic body of followers; (2) that it can satisfactorily serve all the purposes of a spoken and written language, even to the point of producing its own body of original literature and poetry; (3) that it can draw the interest and attention of governments; (4) that it can draw the interest and attention of outsiders to the point where there are few who have not heard of it, and don't equate its name with the concept of "international language." That language is Esperanto.

Without being in the least fanatical; without at all saying that it must be Esperanto or nothing; without excluding the possibility of another choice, and my own graceful acceptance of that choice; with the full realization that, although based on long years of study of the problem, mine is only a personal reaction, and one that I would not at all care to force down anybody else's throat; I must nevertheless come to the conclusion that Esperanto seems to me the most logical, though by no means the only possible, candidate for the post of international tongue.

THE LORD'S PRAYER IN ESPERANTO

Patro nia, kiu estas en la ĉielo, sankta estu via nomo; venu regeco via; estu volo via, kiel en la ĉielo, tiel ankaŭ sur la tero. Panon nian ĉiutagan donu al ni hodiaŭ; kaj pardonu al ni ŝuldojn niajn, kiel ni ankaŭ pardonas al niaj ŝuldantoj; kaj ne konduku nin en tenton, sed liberigu nin de la malbono.